Rik Scarce

ECO-
HEROES

ECO-HEROES

Twelve Tales of Environmental Victory

by Aubrey Wallace

Edited and with an Introduction by
David Gancher

Foreword by Oscar Arias

MERCURY HOUSE
San Francisco

Copyright © 1993 by Aubrey Wallace and David Gancher

Published in the United States by
    Mercury House
    San Francisco, California

United States Constitution, First Amendment: Congress shall make no law respecting an establishment of religion, or prohibiting the free exercise thereof; or abridging the freedom of speech, or of the press; or the right of the people peaceably to assemble, and to petition the Government for a redress of grievances.

Photo Credits
Cover and Wangari Maathai: photo by Bruce Forrester. Sam LaBudde: photo by Jay David Buchsbaum. Michael Werikhe: photo by Evelyn Bloom. Mehda Patkar: photo by Ali Kazimi. All other photos by Paul Latoures.

Cover design by Sharon Smith
Book design by Amaryllis Design
Printed on recycled, acid-free paper
Manufactured in the United States of America

Library of Congress Cataloging-in Publication Data
Wallace, Aubrey.
Eco-heroes : twelve tales of environmental victory/by Aubrey Wallace : edited and with introduction by David Gancher; foreword by Oscar Arias.
    p. cm.
ISBN 1.56279.033.1
    1. Environmental policy–Citizen participation I. Gancher, David. II. Title
HC79E5W27 1993
363.7'057–dc2   92-16756
5 4 3 2 1   CIP

Contents

vii   Foreword by Oscar Arias

ix   Introduction: On Eco-Heroes by David Gancher

1   Sowing Seeds of Hope
     Wangari Maathai, *Kenya*

23   Madame Loire
     Christine Jean, *France*

37   Undercover Agent
     Samuel LaBudde, *United States*

61   Infighting for the Last Frontier
     Catherine Wallace, *New Zealand*

87   Making Waves
     Jeton Anjain, *Marshall Islands*

107   Teaching Children Well
     Eha Kern/Roland Tiensuu, *Sweden*

117   Step by Step
     Michael Werikhe, *Kenya*

135   Standing Up for Trees
     Colleen McCrory, *Canada*

155 Taking the Heat
     Wadja Egnankou, *Ivory Coast*

167 Mrs. Gibbs Goes to Washington
     Lois Gibbs, *United States*

193 Hell or High Water
     Medha Patkar, *India*

209 Harmonies in the Forest
     Beto (Carlos Alberto) Ricardo, *Brazil*

227 About Sources

229 Bibliography

233 Acknowledgments

Foreword

OSCAR ARIAS

 EVERY TIME A PERSON DECIDES to desecrate nature, he or she inflicts a mortal wound onto the earth's future. No individual or nation nation can single-handedly reverse our penchant for ecological destruction. Therefore, individuals, as well as nations, must work in solidarity to build a sustainable and ecologically conscious world. To lead us in this quest we need the determination and vision of an extraordinary conglomerate of people whose efforts are rooted in the best traditions of our civilization.

Unfortunately, these builders of a better world are often forgotten or lost in the confusion and self-preoccupation that our modern societies produce. For the same reasons we, as humans, often lose our connection with our natural surroundings. How many of us can say if the stars were out last night? How many of us ponder the ecological and environmental history of our neighborhoods? In our hectic lives we need not think of the environment because we are insulated from it.

There are, however, people who strive to help us remember and enjoy our relationship with nature. These individuals look beyond their immediate surroundings and toward the real and pressing needs of people and the earth. It is to them that this book is dedicated.

Through the Goldman Environmental Prize, ecological heroes are discovered in a world that often misconstrues what is important. These heroes do not head countries or multinational corporations—they are people who recognize that the environment, our habitat, is in danger. As true leaders, they have responded and taken action in the name of humankind.

The recipients of the Goldman Environmental Prize have taken important steps to make our world a more secure place to live. They understand that security is not measured by weapons, soldiers, or replete arsenals. From them we learn that true security lies in our environment and our ability to develop sustainably. We must all remember that no amount of missiles can feed a hungry child, but that a solid environmental base and the rational use of the dividends of peace will ensure that no one ever goes hungry. In trying to protect our earth, these visionaries have created an opportunity for us to be secure through a healthy environment and sustainable development; they have pointed us toward lasting security.

The Goldman Environmental Prize and the people represented in this book are for all of us to look to for inspiration. Let us follow them with an enlightened consciousness of our surroundings and our responsibilities, and let us strive to live up to the ideals that the Goldman Environmental Prize and its winners embody.

Introduction:
On Eco-Heroes

DAVID GANCHER

 To raise our consciousness to the level which moves us to do the right things for the environment because our hearts have been touched and our minds convinced. To do the right thing because it is the only logical thing to do, popular opinion not withstanding.

—WANGARI MAATHAI

ECO-HEROES ARE NOT THE HEROES of movies or novels. These twelve tales of boldness and daring have no car chases or terrorist hijackings, no personal violence or glamorous riches. Eco-heroes win victories on a much less dramatic timetable than a ninety-minute movie. Keeping a species alive or a forest intact takes years and sometimes decades of effort. In Western tradition, the hero is a man set apart, different from others, above others. He is defined by his struggles and by the forces to which he is opposed. He is a warrior who may rally large forces behind him but whose ultimate victory stems from individual strength and daring. But the eco-hero is a new kind of hero—and certainly not necessarily male. In fact, much of the environmental movement is driven by women. Eco-heroes are not solitary figures who battle alone.

On the contrary, even an eco-spy (such as Samuel LaBudde) who darts alone through enemy lines to gather information would have no effect without other environmentalists to help disseminate the information. Eco-heroes depend on their fellow environmentalists for support, for power, for sustenance, and for context. But it is the eco-hero who brings the light of vision, inspiration, and belief to the group. The eco-hero does not expect quick victories; quick victories require simple enemies. But the opposition in most environmental battles is not a single enemy or a single industry. In fact, the enemy is rarely even an enemy, but usually only a bureaucracy or an entrenched system, a way of doing things. Wadja Engankou says that in the effort to save the mangroves, opposition comes from ignorance. When Colleen McCrory takes on the timber industry in Canada, she has to fight a set of traditions that are bound to self-destruct. Timber companies are putting themselves out of business, and the environmentalists trying to save the forests are actually also preventing the collapse of the industry. But changing the face of an industry does not happen overnight. This kind of massive change requires constant effort over a period of years. Sheer persistence—especially in the face of overwhelming odds—is what creates environmental victories.

Often, eco-heroes work partly toward spiritual goals. Inner growth is an essential part of the process of becoming an eco-hero. Lois Gibbs, as a high school student, cut class rather than face her stage fright to stand up, and give a book report; a few years later, as the president of the Homeowners' Association of Love Canal, she stood up in front of hundreds of people to confront President Carter and persuade him to send more help. This kind of personal transformation is often the personal dimension of the victories of eco-heroes. After such a transformation, there is no turning back; eco-heroes act for the environment because it is the right thing to do and because they believe in a transcendent value—of wilderness or wildlife—that does not have to be proven.

Eco-heroes appear to be ordinary people, particularly when they first start out on their path. They may not be especially glamorous or talented, but they are dedicated and authentic; they grow stronger as they fight harder; and they sometimes come to display striking bravery, as Wangari Maathai has.

Eco-heroes are peaceful; their tactics are nonviolent. They rely on grass-roots support, and most of their efforts are educational. As Catherine Wallace says, "I do have quite strong faith in the general populace. When things are explained to them, they really do make the hard decisions."

∾

WITH THE GOAL OF DIVERSITY—of species, ecosystems, thought, and people—eco-heroes are heirs of two historical traditions: the scientist/adventurer and the activist/humanitarian. The environmental movement grew out of the efforts of scientific naturalists—the great nineteenth-century European and American explorers and adventurers who set off to study nature in the wild. Their exploits engaged the popular imagination of the newly industrialized society that had the leisure and literacy to imagine adventure without war. The gentleman adventurers created a new fashion—wilderness adventure for its own sake. Darwin set off to study wildlife, but he started a trend that may have begun with science but soon became adventure. Darwin showed the way for John Muir and even for Clyde Beattie, the circus impresario who popularized African wildlife by "bringing it back alive." Today, such writers as Peter Matthiessen, Barry Lopez, Diane Ackerman, and Galen Rowell are the chroniclers and the heroes of eco-adventure.

Early environmental groups functioned as travel agencies, promoting excursions into wild areas for recreation and for "scientific" study. But even as early as the 1890s, such groups as the Sierra Club combined outdoor activities with overtly political lobbying. The two were related: The outdoor activities created the cadres of political activists.

The second tradition of the eco-hero is activism and humanitarianism, as personified by Thomas Jefferson, Albert Schweitzer, Mother Teresa, John Kennedy, and Martin Luther King, Jr. In fact, some environmental activists came straight from the Peace Corps and the civil rights movement to groups such as Friends of the Earth and Greenpeace. The political goals of liberal causes and environmentalism have much in common. The issue of ecology has always been associated with issues of social justice—if only because environmentalists could see oppressed nature and oppressed peoples were both victims of an exploitative form of capitalism. Poverty and pollution, racism and clear-cutting are different aspects of the same social and natural dysfunctions. Eco-heroes are amalgams of warriors, adventurers, poets, and priests. They are warriors because they oppose evil forces—the forces of destruction and death. They are adventurers because they move toward paradise, toward an ecstatic joining with nature. They are poets because their songs and their actions inspire us. They express in their words and actions the unspoken aspirations of all those who are aware of suffering. And they are priests because they represent transcendence—redemption, the healing power of nature, the ecstatic transformation of humanity, the experience of Oneness.

In many ways, eco-heroes are brave because they continue to fight even knowing that in the world of environmental issues, there is no final victory: Even the greatest triumphs are only partial and momentary. Some land is set aside as wilderness. Some species are granted habitat. But despite occasional victories, the global environment seems to be sliding from bad to worse; entropy increases. Yesterday's vast herd is today's endangered species; yesterday's impenetrable rain forest is today's eroded hillside. Environmental victory at best often consists of slowing the slide, with the hope of changing attitudes later. A victory is only another chance to survive.

∾

WE ARE BORN INTO CHAOS, and much of our lives is spent trying simply to make sense of what goes on: We learn language, we learn to behave, and we learn to get along. As we find out more about the world, the chaos does not diminish. We never fully understand the world; we learn only to cope with grander themes of chaos. It is out of this ground, this primal need for order, that each era fashions its own kinds of heroes. Greece demanded warriors; medieval Europe demanded brave courtiers; the Renaissance demanded masters of art. If we have dragons, we need knights. If we have demons within, we need saints. Our heroes typify a successful response to the exact challenges of a particular time and place. They might think globally, but they must act locally, whether they are heroes of war or peace.

All over the world there is an urgent battle against environmental degradation. An eco-hero is someone who can challenge, defeat, or even stave off the particular dangers of environmental collapse.

Eco-heroes enable us to understand the world. They create a story—with us as its protagonists—that ends in victory. This is the essence of the eco-hero: to name and define the dangers and the challenges of the day, and thus to control them. Eco-heroes also serve as models: "Here's how to behave," they say. If we are wondering how to be a man in war, how to kill people and stay alive and human, then we may find Rambo heroic. But if we are wondering how we can be humans on this planet—more or less permanently—eco-heroes show us the way.

∾

THE TWELVE ECO-HEROES profiled in this book have all received the Goldman Environmental Prize, unofficially called the Nobel Prize for environmentalists. The mission of the prize is political: to enhance the efforts of environmentalists by giving them publicity, stature, and money. The Goldman Environmental Foundation selects an outstanding activist from each of six regions—Europe, North America, Central and South America, Africa, Asia, and Australia and Oceania. Candidates are nominated by an international group of activists. The six winners each year are officially treated as heroes, often for the first time in their lives. They are brought together in San Francisco, given prizes of $60,000 each, and ritually honored in a prestigious ceremony attended by some of the city's strongest environmental leaders and most influential citizens. Then they are flown to New York, where they meet with the press and with the secretary general of the United Nations. Next, they travel to Washington, D.C., where they attend another series of meetings, including one with the president of the United States.

The Goldman Environmental Foundation has selected well; since the foundation first awarded prizes in 1990, the reaction from the public, the press, and the environmental community has been enthusiastic. The political influence of the Goldman prize winners has grown—and with it, the prestige of the prize. The rest of the world has begun to see these activists as the heroes they are.

What they do is often pedestrian: write letters, articles, and comments; tally figures; make proposals; conduct interviews; and attend countless meetings. Often they have been literally voices in the wilderness for years, and their individual efforts might go unnoticed were it not for the strength of the numbers of people they gather around them. In honoring these individuals, the Goldman Environmental Prize is implicitly celebrating the groups and alliances behind their victories.

But whereas the strength of their campaigns may lie in the intensity and numbers of activists, the vitality lies within each eco-hero. They are willing to fight as long as necessary—even forever. As Colleen McCrory says, "I would rather die trying than not try at all. One thing I've always found is that the door will open somewhere."

Wangari Maathai

Sowing Seeds of Hope

WANGARI MAATHAI

Kenya

 THE POWER, THE MYSTERY, THE GENIUS OF AFRICA—from the earliest humans climbing out of the Great Rift valley to the great civilizations of the Nile—has always been in the continent's ability to bring forth new life. Africa is still bringing forth new life. From a certain perspective, Africa's prospects look more hopeful than they have in twenty-five years.

A second revolution is happening on the continent, with free elections and democratic reforms now taking place in most nations; they are loosening the grip of the despotic rulers who seized control after independence from the Europeans in the 1960s. A new economy is emerging, one that looks "new" only in this century. In fact, it represents a return to indigenous African values. Today, at least ten million of the twenty-six million people in Kenya make a living from small cash crops, carpentry, metalworking, sewing, brewing, and operating private transport—rather than from World Bank loans or from the Cold War economics of aid-for-alliances. Although parts of the continent pour forth apocalyptic pictures that swamp our emotions and quite rightly beg urgent charity, the Kenya of Wangari Maathai evokes compelling images of survival, renewal, and hope.

When optimism grew wild in Kenya and other newly independent countries with valuable resources, Wangari Maathai went out into her backyard and planted seven trees on World Environment Day, June 5, 1977; from that act has grown an organization called the Green Belt Movement.

"I got interested in environmental degradation and the causes of the problem," says Maathai, "and the more I thought about it, the more I realized that when you talk about the problems, you tend to disempower people. You tend to make people feel that there is nothing they can do, that they are doomed, that there is no hope. I realized that to break the cycle, one has to start with a positive step, and I thought that planting a tree is very simple, very easy—something positive that anybody can do." She was speaking on the U.S. television broadcast "African Connections."

"That's what the Green Belt Movement is really all about. It is a movement to empower people, to raise their consciousness, to give them hope, to give them a feeling that they can do something for themselves that does not require much money, does not require much technology or information. The power to change their environment is within them and within their own capacities."

Of the original seven trees, "two are still standing. They are beautiful *nandi* flame trees." The Green Belt Movement has since planted more than ten million trees. "Many people thought that we were joking because we were just a bunch of women. But many years later, we are talking about millions of trees, and some people have started taking women seriously after all."

∾

WITH HER HAIR TIGHTLY BRAIDED IN CORNROWS, and wearing her native Kenyan dress (with black Reeboks peeking out underneath), Maathai's face radiates light that shines even on film and video. The light is not figurative; it is quite real and not supplied by artistic studio effects. It comes from within. Fifty-two years old and amply built, Wangari makes you want to step into her arms and stay there, to be held like a beloved child. She is Mother Africa.

Environmentalist Samuel LaBudde once spent several days working with Wangari Maathai, and he was overcome with admiration. He asked her what the honorific title was for a woman in Kenya. "Madam, or Mamma," she replied. From then on, LaBudde called her Mamma Wangari.

At the offices of The Goldman Environmental Foundation, which awarded her a Goldman Environmental Prize in 1991, I came across a videotaped interview with her and stepped into the conference room to view my first moving color pictures of her. It was an unusual experience. As soon as she appeared on the screen and began speaking in her compelling way, strong and unfamiliar emotions began to ripple inside me. My heart fluttered the way it does just before I am about to cry. Because of the office setting, I automatically stifled the emotion, though I was uncertain what I was stifling. I snapped off the machine and sat for a moment in the dark, stuffy room. I pulled the tape out of the machine and took it home with me.

Watching the tape in my own living room, I felt the same strong pull, but it was not tears fluttering to the surface; it was something like love and compassion. Within just a few moments, Maathai made me feel connected to her, and through her, to Kenya and to the cause of reforestation. Today, many months later, I think that what I was feeling, what was bubbling up, was my first physical sense of the presence of an eco-hero.

At her age, Mamma Wangari could be taking grandchildren into her arms, rather than taking environmentalists and reporters into her fold. But instead, her tree-planting project has grown with a force that has thrust her into politics—and into direct confrontation with Kenya's ruling group. Yet even baton-wielding police cannot stop her. After one recent conflict, she woke up in a hospital bed, from which she promptly called a press conference.

༄

HALF OF AFRICA'S FORESTS have been felled in this century. Some of the forests were cleared for cash-crop plantations, some because the rapidly increasing population needed firewood. Ninety percent of the people of Africa depend on firewood for fuel. Kenya has no other fossil fuel; coal, oil, and electricity have to be imported. The World Bank says fifty-five million Africans face acute wood shortages. Where there is too little fuel, there is malnutrition. Even though people may have traditional roots and vegetables, they cannot cook them. Maathai says that even in relatively prosperous Kenya, mothers are increasingly feeding families on processed white bread, margarine, and sweetened tea to save on cooking fuel. But the diet produces unhealthy children. "To say that we don't have famine, that's true at the collective level. But we have real hunger at the individual level," Maathai says. "The answer isn't to give these people food, but to plant trees for firewood."

Without trees, overcultivated fields lead to soil erosion because tree roots are needed to bind fertile soil to the ground. In addition, the loss of cover from the trees exposes the soil to the searing African sun and heavy rains that erode the arable land into wasteland. Only about one-third of the total area of Kenya receives sufficient rainfall to support viable agriculture, and Maathai estimates that the forest cover has been reduced to only 2.9 percent of what it once was.

"Poverty and need have a very close relationship with a degraded environment," says Maathai. "It's a vicious circle." The soils of Africa are not particularly rich; and if food production is to be maintained, this rather thin asset must be carefully protected. "Land is one of the most important resources of Kenya and all of Africa," writes Maathai in *The Green Belt Movement*. "Its fertile topsoil ought to be considered a valuable resource—especially since it is so difficult to create. However, . . . thousands of tons of topsoil leave Kenya's countryside every year. During the rainy seasons, it flows in red streams down the slopes, into muddy rivers and finally to the Indian Ocean—where it can never be retrieved. Yet we seem unconcerned.

"Losing topsoil should be compared to losing territories to an invading enemy. And indeed, if African countries were so threatened, they would mobilize their armies, the police, the reserves—even citizens would be called in to fight."

As a member of the National Council of Women of Kenya, Maathai began exhorting farmers—seventy percent of whom are women in

Africa—to plant protective "green belts" of trees. "We made simple and practical presentations and emphasized one activity that everyone could understand—planting trees." In 1977, Maathai persuaded the Kenyan subsidiary of Mobil Oil, along with several international philanthropies, to fund the establishment of tree nurseries. Today, more than ninety percent of the funding for the tree-planting program comes from abroad; most of it is in the form of small checks from women all over the world. The implementation of the program rests with local, barefoot foresters.

To initiate the campaign, Maathai went into the schools. "The children were involved directly: They dug holes, walked to the tree nursery to collect trees, planted them, and took care of them for as long as they were in school," writes Maathai. "It was the children who took the message home to their parents and eventually got women's groups interested."

Today, "there are altogether about three thousand schools which have responded to the Green Belt campaign. With an average of five hundred children per school, this means that over one million children are involved."

They planted indigenous trees: baobabs, croton trees, acacias, cedars, and thorn trees, which are all good for firewood; and fruit trees such as citrus, papaws, bananas, and figs. Most took three to five years to mature. Imported species such as eucalyptus and evergreens had been considered attractive in the past because they quickly produce fuelwood, timber, and fencing. But this "demonstrates shortsightedness and a certain amount of greed and selfishness," writes Maathai. "Many African wild fruits and berries, root crops, and traditional grains have almost disappeared from our midst as we adopt imported crops. By doing this, we have made ourselves more willing victims of disasters like drought."

Most of the organization's one thousand tree nurseries are located in rural areas, where local staffs supervise them, distributing tools and training people to collect and plant seeds. "Hundreds of people—including handicapped and poor people and unemployed youth—have found jobs with the Green Belt Movement in both urban and rural areas," writes Maathai. "They have become advisers, nursery attendants, and promoter/follow-ups. They receive small monthly allowances for their work."

The seedlings are distributed free of charge to groups and individuals who want to plant "green belts" of trees. For every tree that survives more than three months outside the nursery, the person who planted it receives fifty Kenya cents (about four U.S. cents). In 1988, forty thousand people collected trees from the nurseries and established plantings around their homes and farms and on the grounds of factories, hospitals, churches, and schools. Meanwhile, in one of Nairobi's most congested slums, six thousand seedlings are flourishing within sight of single-room shanties and mounds of garbage.

In all, since the reforestation movement was started, fifty thousand Kenyan women have been employed and have planted ten million seedlings, of which almost eighty percent have grown to maturity. Seeing this example, the Kenyan government has increased its spending twenty times over on tree planting in the last four years. In addition, the movement has taken hold in more than thirty other African countries.

Much of the movement's appeal lies in the obvious short-term gains people get from tree planting: money, firewood, and fencing. But in addition, Maathai says, "People can feel the comforts of trees. They will give them a lot of care when it's a case of their personal interests being affected. We have transformed the countryside of many of the communities where they now see a beautiful environment. The birds have come back. People now breathe fresh air because the wind is controlled, and there isn't so much dust. It's really wonderful to see people come back and say, 'You should come and see our village.' That's an accomplishment."

Maathai writes, "We tend to think that protecting our forests is the responsibility of the government and the foresters. It is not. The responsibility is ours individually." In fact, the project found that when seedlings were left in the care of bureaucrats, the plants died.

Maathai's Green Belt Movement now has a half-million-dollar budget, principally from foreign donors, including Scandinavian groups, U.S. organizations such as the Windstar Foundation and the African Development Foundation, as well as from the United Nation's Voluntary Fund for the Decade of the Woman.

The Green Belt cooperatives are not without their problems. Some have fallen apart as members bickered over money; others have folded over land disputes. Communicating with Kenya's communities, where more than forty languages and dialects are spoken and in which most people are illiterate, is a constant problem. In addition, the poorest women tend to drop out of the movement when they do not see immediate returns.

Nonetheless, despite the problems, poor women now harvest fuelwood and fruit from their own trees, and springs have returned to dry land. Having reached so many poor and illiterate women and won their trust, the movement began teaching good nutrition with traditional foods and promoting family planning.

ॐ

FROM THE START, one of Maathai's objectives was try to "empower people, to let them identify their mistakes, to show they can build or destroy the environment." The movement seeks to give the poor, the illiterate, and the disadvantaged the means and confidence to improve their lives. Maathai reasons that if people are able to help change the environment, they will develop the capacity to challenge other social conditions.

"At four percent and rising," writes Maathai, "Kenya's population growth is among the highest in the world." Kenyan women have an average of eight children. The current population is about fifteen million. At the present rate of increase, it will double in about twenty years.

"Suppressed, poverty-stricken, and hungry people do not plan their families, and they are not concerned with environmental conservation, even though they are the first victims of environmental degradation. They do not take their destiny into their own hands. . . . Africans have survived for millions of years. Isn't it ironic that this 'primitive,' technologically backward group survived all these years, only to be threatened after they were discovered by 'civilized' groups? There must be some old wisdom which needs rediscovering.

"Before foreigners arrived on our continent, we knew something. What was it? What did we know of sustainable agriculture, of balanced diets to avoid malnutrition, of child rearing, of commerce, of politics?

What was our attitude toward work, family, society, interpersonal relationships?

"Africans need to go back to their roots with a new awareness and confidence and rediscover our old wisdom. We need to draw from our past experience and build on it. But we can only do this if we have the courage to rediscover ourselves and to liberate our minds from centuries of indoctrination.

"Instead, they place all their hope in God. . . . They are asking God to be a magician, a miracle worker. Many Africans have abandoned their traditional concept of God and embraced a new and foreign concept. [More than fifty percent of Kenya is Christian.] And it is from this power that they expect magic. For if calamities like poverty, hunger, and drought are perceived as natural and, therefore, acts of God, Africans have very little reason to doubt the power of their traditional God and expect miracles from a God who seems to protect foreigners from such calamities.

"But there is growing evidence that these calamities are not acts of God but of humans. If that is so, Africans have to examine where they, rather than God, went wrong."

∞

THE GREAT RIFT VALLEY, with its steep-walled floor dropping as much as three thousand feet from the surrounding countryside, is more breathtakingly dramatic in Kenya than anywhere else in Africa. The valley was created by movement of the earth's surface thousands of years ago, in a time when *Homo sapiens sapiens* had just emerged from the forests of central Africa to walk the still steaming, volcanic earth with primitive humans and many other apes or man-apes. *Homo sapiens sapiens* quickly managed to walk out into all parts of the world. However, when Europeans and Arabs began arriving as explorers or traders centuries later, they settled in chains of trading posts along the coast where they dealt in ivory and slaves. The interior of Kenya remained isolated until the late nineteenth century.

In 1895, Kenya became a British protectorate, and white farmers started plantations to produce crops for export. Along with tea and coffee, the other main industry quickly became travel, particularly as understood by the Swahili word for it: "safari." (Swahili and English are the official languages of Kenya.) Theodore Roosevelt, Ernest Hemingway, and Karen Blixen (Isak Dinesen) soon filled the imaginations of the Western world with images of the magnificent Kenyan interior where millions of wild animals—wildebeest, zebra, elephant, rhino, lion, hippo, cheetah, and giraffe—roamed across golden plains at the foot of blue-green mountains.

During World War II, Africans served in the armed forces, and when they returned they spread a greatly expanded political consciousness throughout Africa. In 1952, Kenyan guerrilla groups who tried to expel white settlers became such a threat that British troops were flown in to crush what was called the Mau Mau Rebellion. By the time it was over in 1956, one hundred thousand Africans had been killed and another twenty-four thousand interned.

After soundly quashing the rebellion, the British administrators began to loosen restrictions on Kenyans, particularly on their rights to cultivate cash crops. An effort was made to encourage the development of a stable middle class. Perhaps eager to be rid of a persistent political nightmare, the British agreed to grant Kenya its independence. In 1963, Jomo Kenyatta became the country's first president and served until his death in 1978. He was succeed by Daniel Arap Moi, who is president to this day.

Today, Kenya is one of the most popular tourist spots in the world, with more than eight hundred thousand visitors per year. Nairobi National Park sits practically at the city gates. Rare game including black rhino, lion, cheetah, hippo, and several species of antelope roam sporadically within sight of the city's modern skyline.

The park is very near the spot where Karen Blixen settled after her arrival in 1914 and about which she wrote in *Out of Africa*: "I had a farm in Africa, at the foot of the Ngong Hills.... The geographical position and the height of the land combined to create a landscape that had not its like in all the world. There was no fat on it and no luxuriance anywhere; it was Africa distilled up through six thousand feet, like the strong and refined essence of a continent.... The views were immensely wide. Everything that you saw made for greatness and freedom, and

unequalled nobility. . . . In the highlands you woke up to the morning
and thought: Here I am, where I ought to be."

ॐ

"I GREW UP IN A VERY BEAUTIFUL PART OF THE COUNTRY, very
green, very productive," says Maathai, born in the highlands Blixen
wrote about. Maathai's hometown of Nyeri lies forty miles north of
Blixen's beloved Ngong Hills. Near the Great Rift valley, Nyeri sits in
the rain shadow of Mount Kenya. Volcanic and snow-capped, Mount
Kenya is the country's highest peak (17,058 feet). It is located near the
Aberdare National Park, site of the famed Treetops Lodge from which
thousands of visitors have enjoyed wildlife scenes. Though within a few
degrees of the equator, much of the region consists of mountains and
high plateaus with a mild, comfortable climate that averages about
65°F.

As a child, Maathai loved a huge wild fig tree that her mother for-
bid to be cut: She wouldn't even let Wangari gather its dead twigs. Fig
trees easily take on an aura of godliness in Kenya. Peter Matthiessen
reported seeing a "giant fig which looks like a small grove in the distance, [and] is at least as old as man's recorded history on this plain.
Its spread is not less than 150 feet, the size of six ordinary figs, and it
is the tree of life. . . . There were no other trees for miles around." To
many Africans, fig trees symbolize the sacred mountains, nature, and
God.

Maathai remembers drawing water as a child from a spring near
the fig tree. She was "fascinated by the way the clean, cool water
pushed its way through the soft, red clay, so gently that even the individual grains of the soil were left undisturbed." In her region, she
says, "I did not see hunger. I did not see starving children. I did not see
slums."

In 1960, the talented young Maathai became one of about three
hundred Kenyan students eligible for what she calls the "Kennedy
Lift"—U.S. college scholarships granted to help prepare Kenya for
its imminent independence. Maathai entered a small college in Kansas,
where she received her bachelor of science degree; she then entered the
University of Pittsburg, where she received a master of science degree

in 1966. She returned to her native Kenya and became the first woman in East and Central Africa to receive a doctorate from the University of Nairobi. She also became the university's first woman senior lecturer, associate professor, and eventually department chair. She married a young member of Parliament, and they had three children. She was the epitome of the stable, professionally trained middle class that the British had envisioned as the foundation of Kenyan society.

But the Kenya she had returned to, however, had changed while she was gone—politically, economically, and ecologically.

"It was very disappointing when, after six years of life in the United States, I went back and saw things that I had not left." The fig tree and those around it had been cut to make way for tea plantations. The spring and stream had dried up. "When I visit this little valley of my childhood dreams, I feel the tragedy under my feet. Gullies stare at me, telling the story of soil erosion which was unknown before: The land appears exhausted. Hunger is on the faces of the local people. Firewood is scarce because every tree has been cut."

As she looked more closely, she saw that "people had converted the land to tea growing and suddenly changed from people who produced their own food, to producing a cash crop to sell so that they could get money," she reported on "African Connections." "I thought, well, money is good, so maybe this is a good idea. But then I noticed that with that money, sometimes they are not able to buy food because there is no food."

∾

WHEN MAATHAI'S HUSBAND WAS FIRST ELECTED to represent one of Nairobi's poorest neighborhoods, she was an ambitious and rising member of the academic community. "I came from the Kikuyu community in Kenya," she said on "African Connections," "a background that did not have discrimination against its women, in the sense that they were allowed to share their opinions, and they played a very important role in all aspects of society. I came from a community that would have agreed with the statement that 'the sky is the limit,' and I actually grew up believing that. It was only after I went to work at the university and held positions there that I suddenly discovered that human beings can be the limit. They can stop you pursuing your objectives, your visions, your aspirations, just because you are a woman; and that to me was a discovery."

Maathai also discovered that her husband was one of the human beings who set limits. "In our society, people have almost idolized education, and the typical African woman is supposed to be dependent, submissive, not better than her husband," Maathai told the *Washington Post*. "Having a Ph.D. was definitely a credit that should have gone to my husband rather than to myself." Her husband had only a bachelor's degree. "It was very difficult for him that the one who had the one credit everyone wishes they had was the woman."

Though it was her husband who was elected in 1974, it was Maathai who respected the voters. "I was trying to see what I could do for the people who were helping us during our campaign, people who came from poor communities," Maathai wrote in *Ms. Magazine*. "I decided to create jobs for them—cleaning their constituency, planting trees and shrubs, cleaning homes of the richer people in the communities, and getting paid for those services. That never worked because poor people wanted support right away, and I didn't have money to pay them before the people we were working for had paid me. So I dropped the project but stayed with the idea." At the time, "in my marriage, unfortunately, I was not aware that if I had an idea I was not supposed to express it," Maathai said in another publication.

Her husband sought divorce, accusing her publicly of adultery with another member of Parliament. Maathai opposed the divorce; she fought for her marriage and lost. "I told the judges that if they could reach that decision based on what they'd heard, they must be either incompetent or corrupt." The swift arm of justice sentenced the uppity woman to six months in jail for contempt of court. She served three days before her lawyers secured her release on the promise that she would apologize. The divorce went through.

"Looking back," Maathai said when accepting the 1990 *Condé Nast Traveler* Environmental Award in New York, "sometimes it seems a blessing in disguise. Because I know I couldn't have done what I had to do if I'd had a husband, or at least the husband that I had. I needed a man who was ahead of me—in thought, in accomplishment—in order to provide me with the support I needed."

She decided to run for Parliament herself and resigned as chair of the anatomy department to do so. But she found she was disqualified from becoming a candidate on a technicality, and then the school refused to take her back. She had tried to work within the system and lost. She began planting seeds. "When we first started, everybody was thinking that we were wasting our time, especially a person like me who has a university degree, a Ph.D. It looked ridiculous, to go out into the field and work with virtually illiterate populations." But Maathai has a commitment that she says "comes out of a feeling that when you are educated, when you have gone to the university and you have been exposed to knowledge, experience, and information, one of the things you should do—certainly when going back to a continent like Africa—is to be a useful person, to be a stimulant, a catalyst in your own society."

A reporter who knew her at the time told me recently that he is certain she had no idea how much of a stimulant she would prove to be.

∾

UHURU PARK IS ONE OF THE FEW GREEN AREAS left in Nairobi, which bills itself as The Green City in the Sun. The park is where "most of the lower-income-group people come to rest on Saturdays and Sundays because they live in very crowded housing estates and slums, and that is a very valuable park for them," says Maathai. In 1989, the ruling political party, the Kenya African National Union, decided to build a sixty-story skyscraper within the park. "To use their own words, 'for prestige reasons.' I felt that is absolutely the last reason we should have it. There are many other ways in which we can create prestige, like running efficient government, managing our resources—especially our cash crops, our product industry—more efficiently so that we can make money."

A sixty-story building is a tower by any standard, but especially in Nairobi, where the average building manages to scrape the sky at twenty-seven stories tall. The proposed building would have been the tallest on the entire continent of Africa. Actually a complex, the high-rise office building was to be flanked by two smaller towers, fronted by a four-story statue of President Moi, and was to include hotels, theaters, and shopping malls. In addition to obliterating the park, the building would increase automobile and foot traffic dramatically in an already hectic city center.

"They were not able to produce an environmental impact report; they had not sought public opinion, even though Uhuru was a public park. They were going to borrow a huge sum even though the country has great debt already," said Maathai to *Traveler*. In fact, the estimated construction cost of $197 million would almost double the country's international debt. In addition, Nairobi is an earthquake area, and architects and engineers say the ground under Uhuru Park is not very solid.

The government claimed that the building would provide employment and proudly pointed out it would bring Kenya its first twenty-four-hour television channel. "Buildings don't make employment," Maathai says, "not in the long run. And the fact is, only one percent of the people own television sets. We need water, food, and medical supplies, not a twenty-four-hour television channel. But this is the ruling party's conception of progress."

Maathai's Green Belters, seasoned activists after more than a dozen years of organizing barefoot farmers, wrote to the ministers; politicians denounced the activists in Parliament. One member of Parliament, taking a swipe at Maathai, said, "I don't see the sense at all in a bunch of divorcées coming out to criticize such a complex."

Maathai filed suit against construction. Members of Parliament called her actions "ugly and ominous" and "a shame of unprecedented monstrosity." They greeted news of her lawsuit with boos and catcalls and demanded that the Green Belt Movement be banned for seeking to destabilize the government. Not a single politician publicly questioned the complex. A judge dismissed Maathai's suit as a "non-starter."

Maathai applied for a license to stage a public demonstration; the license was denied. The Green Belters wrote to the attorney general; he replied through the press that they should mind their own business. Then the government ordered her and the Green Belters to vacate their ten-year-old office on government property within twenty-four hours, and threatened to deregister the group, which would make it illegal.

Africa Watch, a London-based human rights group, stated that there was "a general climate of fear" induced by a government that has become "increasingly intolerant of freedom of expression." The *Toronto Globe and Mail* reported, "Under President Moi, Kenya has outlawed opposition parties, eliminated the secret ballot from some elections, arrested and released scores of political detainees, and banned three journals, two of which were clearly embarrassing to the authorities."

Maathai began to engender a "vilification unusual even in the highly personalized politics of Kenya," according to the *New York Times*. One lawyer said the campaign against Maathai was "sounding the death knell on the freedoms of thought, conscience, and expression in this country." Another citizen said, "We have a democracy, as long as you are silent."

President Moi said Maathai and her fellow activists "have insects in their heads." Maathai replied, "Perhaps there is an insect in my head because I don't know why I am so motivated and committed to what I do. I really strongly believe. So if there is something in my head, it is a positive, strong force that encourages me to continue and to pay no attention to any destructiveness. If that means there is something wrong with my head, then I'm very grateful."

Maathai thinks that she has "been in the forefront probably because I am ordinarily a vocal person, and I have been associated with the environmental movement for a long time, so the press listened and gave headlines to what I was saying.... I gave my opinions, the politicians gave me their insults. But if I didn't react to their interference with this central park, I might as well have not planted another tree."

Her first foray into heavily mined political territory set off fireworks. But that did not worry her. What did worry her was that the political attacks were aimed not only at discouraging her from speaking out, but at weakening the Green Belt Movement. "The majority of the people in the movement are poor," she told the *New York Times*. "They are not reading the newspapers. They hear this secondhand, that the movement is subversive. They are scared. They don't want to be seen as against the government, which can lead you into a lot of trouble. And a lot of politicians know that is the way the people feel."

However, in January 1991, the government announced it would scale down the plan to a thirty-story tower. That smaller version never

got off the drawing board. A year later, quietly, the fencing came
down around the site. Ironically, the protest had succeeded. "What
stopped them, really," says Maathai "was that the foreign donors
they'd lined up—Japanese investors, Danish investors, British investors
including Robert Maxwell—could see the people didn't want the
building and backed off."

It was a costly victory. The Green Belt Movement was left office-
less, with ten years' worth of files and equipment, and seventy staff members. Maathai looked for another space downtown; not one of the jittery
real estate agents would rent to her. So she set up shop in her home,
to which carpenters added an extension. While it was under construction, filing cabinets lined the driveway; Maathai conducted business in the yard, surrounded by flowers and shrubs. Visitors reached
her office by stepping through an opening in a thick, high hedge. But
nothing really changed in the Green Belt Movement. "Thank God,"
she says.

She writes, "I tell people that if they know how to read and write,
it is an advantage. But that all we really need is a desire to work and
common sense. These are usually the last two things people are asked
for. They are usually asked to use imposed knowledge they do not relate
to, so they become followers rather than leaders."

∾

PERHAPS IT WAS INEVITABLE that the tree-planting movement
sprouted political branches. Maathai began to place more emphasis on
public education to teach people that rehabilitating the environment
would take more than planting trees. "We are still dealing with basic
human rights issues," says Maathai, "basic democracy, basic willingness to accommodate dissent. We are still trying to get away from
authoritarian rule, which we have had since colonial times."

As a result, Maathai says, "We have raised the environmental
agenda from one that concerns women and children and unemployed
men in the countryside to a national political issue. This is very, very
important because if we are going to change, everybody has to be
involved: politicians, academicians, industrialists, investors, developers—everybody."

The atmosphere of roiling dissent turned violent. A minister of foreign affairs was killed and his body burned. Maathai stopped going out at night or going out alone.

Maathai's political supporters around the world began to apply counterpressure to the Kenyan government's repression. In October 1991, the United States stepped in to encourage political and economic reform in Kenya. The United States was instrumental in persuading the World Bank and others to delay financial aid to Kenya until some changes were made. Under this pressure, in December 1991, President Moi announced that Kenya would allow more than one political party. The legal opposition party was called Forum for the Restoration of Democracy (FORD), and Maathai lent it her support. A mere seedling of democracy, it nonetheless cracked the foundation of the dictatorship, and the whole house of Kenyan government began to shake.

FORD soon learned of an impending plot by Moi to turn over his government to a military junta in order to preserve his own authority and forestall elections. Maathai and three other key FORD leaders held a press conference to thwart the coup, which they said was to take place the next morning. They also contended that the government had drawn up a list of 144 opposition figures who were to be "liquidated" after the takeover. According to the Los Angeles Times, the press conference was interrupted by a police squad that tried to arrest all the participants but was held at bay by the crowd.

Maathai barricaded herself in her home surrounded by supporters; 150 policemen converged on the scene. After a three-day siege, the police began cutting through windows and breaking down doors to get to her. "When they took me out," Maathai says, "I found this massive throng of policemen all around the house. I felt as a rabbit must feel when the dogs catch up with it." She was jailed on charges of "spreading malicious rumours." Despite her history of arthritis and heart trouble, her requests to see a doctor were refused, and she was forced to stay in a cold, damp concrete cell without a mattress or blanket. By the time of her hearing the next day, she could not move and had to be carried into court on a stretcher. In November 1992, the charges were dropped. After her hearing, she was released and required hospitalization for several days.

According to Gitobu Imanyara, editor of the *Nairobi Law Monthly*, in the thirteen years that Moi "has misgoverned Kenya, the public has learned Moi will go to any length to maintain his rule. . . . Many of us have been in and out of jail so often under President Moi that we have lost count."

But neither the government nor the opposition seemed to have been prepared for the events that took place next. At "Freedom Corner," in Uhuru Park—the crucial inner-city park that came to symbolize opposition to the Moi regime and support for Maathai—a group of mothers, sisters, and other female relatives of some of Kenya's political prisoners began a hunger strike, on behalf of all those who had been jailed or were awaiting trial on political charges.

"Out of desperation," Imanyara wrote in the *Vancouver Sun* during a subsequent trip to Canada to appeal for international support, "a dozen aged mothers of political prisoners went on a hunger strike and peacefully camped in a city park to publicize their sons' plight. This attracted remarkable public support and sympathy. It is unprecedented in Kenya for poor rural women to take such a leading role, given the risks."

These were, in fact, the very sort of women Maathai had been working to help empower. When they turned to her for solidarity, she could hardly refuse. "The mothers are rural women," Maathai said to the *Washington Post*. "Some of them cannot even write their names. They asked me to help. Their sons have been in jail for almost two years. They have not yet been tried, and they were afraid that if they were tried they would be killed. So for a mother, what wouldn't you do?"

On the "MacNeil-Lehrer Newshour" in May 1992, she said, "At this time in the process of democratization of our country, we still have a lot of political prisoners in jail. We feel that these prisoners are prisoners of conscience, men who spoke against the dictatorial regime that we have had in Kenya at a time when it was very dangerous to do so. It is no different from what we have been campaigning for in South Africa. You really cannot keep those men in jail without being grossly unjust. So we joined the mothers of those men in appealing to the Kenyan government to release them."

The government at first tolerated the hunger strikers. But soon the numbers of sympathizers grew to hundreds, and opposition leaders began to use the event to deliver speeches to the ever-increasing crowd. Several times, according to the *Weekly Review*, "there was panic among the crowd at the sight of riot police or army trucks, but calm was soon restored with a simple appeal by one of the strikers." As the crowd grew, so did the number of policemen. "When the police did charge, some groups of youths retaliated, hurling stones and other missiles at them, causing the police to throw canisters of tear gas at the crowd and fire salvos of live ammunition into the air. The battle went on the whole morning.... At 3 P.M., having received truckloads of reinforcements, they stormed the tent housing the hunger strikers, wielding tear-gas canisters and batons and clearing the 'Freedom Corner' of people within less than fifteen minutes."

Maathai, clubbed unconscious, was taken to the hospital where she was listed in critical condition. She has since recovered, although at this writing, months later, she still seems weak. The day before the battle, Imanyara had been injured in a police attack and rushed to the hospital for treatment. He wrote, "It is a measure of the depravity of the regime that the women and their sympathizers were gassed and beaten by the police and the personal presidential paramilitary unit. In the meanwhile, hundreds were trampled or crushed: among them the renowned environmentalist Dr. Wangari Maathai. The silver lining? Women have been recruited into the opposition and are participating in political leadership to an extent that they will never again, I hope, be ignored." In that sense, the event was another victory for Maathai.

∾

I WAS ON AN AIRPLANE over the Pacific Northwest, with a perfect perspective on the sad scars left from clear-cutting the great forests, when a colleague told me about the beating of Maathai and handed me a faxed news report of the details. Maathai was in intensive care, listed in critical condition. Sitting in my narrow chair thirty thousand feet in the air, traveling at 375 miles per hour, my ears roaring with jet engines, ventilation fans and public announcements, surrounded by 150 people, I felt desolate. Though I still had not met this woman, she had come to occupy a place in my heart. That place felt invaded. Again, I felt something in my chest, which this time did mean I was about to cry. The brutal beating of Maathai was a symbol of the state of the planet, all too visible outside my window. Too often, the good guys are losing. And with that, I realized that the good guys were going to keep losing if all I did was cry about it. I told myself that if Maathai could keep fighting, so could I. And that was when I had my second physical sense of the presence of an eco-hero, this time closer to the gut than the heart.

ᗄ

WHILE MAATHAI HAS BEEN GENERATING heat in Kenya, she has been attracting light internationally. Recent honors include The Right Livelihood award (1984); United Nations Environmental Program Global 500 award for protection of the environment (1987); "Woman of the World" citation from the Princess of Wales (1989); an Honorary Doctor of Law from Williams College, Massachusetts (1990); the Goldman Environmental Prize (1991), among others.

"I would love to go back into an academic institution. . . . I earn maybe a tenth of what I could earn on the international market if I sold my expertise and energy, and I'm sure many people would probably consider me a fool," she wrote in *Ms. Magazine.*

"It has been very difficult. I have paid a very heavy price at the personal level, at the family level, in my pursuit of what I believed in," she said on "African Connections." "But I have also felt very free and like I was being useful, so I have no regrets. It is tough, but it is tough anywhere. It is tough for men who want to climb, who want to challenge other men, who want to make their contributions.

"Sometimes I feel very discouraged. Sometimes I feel very angry when people try to put those kind of obstacles in front of me. But because I realize what is going on, I just try to draw a lot of strength from within myself and also from within my friends, a very extended circle of friends and supporters and family members. They continue to give me courage and the strength I need to keep on, but it is not easy. But who said anybody ever succeeded easily?"

Maathai wrote early on that "the main objective of the Green Belt Movement is to raise our consciousness to the level which moves us to do the right things for the environment because our hearts have been touched and our minds convinced. To do the right thing because it is the only logical thing to do, popular opinion notwithstanding."

Since the beating, her speeches have become more and more political, as she attempts to help steer Kenya toward a true democracy. She has become larger than an individual; more than a stimulant, she is a leader. She is a respected player in international events.

Sometimes a symbolic act signals the end of an era, such as when Rosa Parks refused to give up her seat to a white man on a bus in Montgomery, Alabama, or when Gandhi marched to the sea to gather his own salt rather than pay British taxes. Other times, though, the symbolic act signals the beginning of an era, such as when Wangari Maathai planted trees in her backyard. Two of the trees, beautiful flame trees, are still alive.

༽

WANGARI MAATHAI SAYS that most of the support of the Green Belt Movement comes from women all over the world, who send small checks. She recommends that requests for more information or donations to the Green Belt Movement be sent care of Resource Renewal Institute, Building A, Fort Mason Center, San Francisco, California 94123.

Christine Jean

Madame Loire

CHRISTINE JEAN

France

 THE LOIRE RIVER begins simply enough, with a drip-drop out of a pipe over a stone trough, surrounded by a cow-shed, high in the Rhône Alps. An inscription has been nailed to the stone wall above the dripping pipe, with thanks from the people on the great hill of Sancerre, the source of some of the finest white wine in France: "To the Loire, Queen and Mother of its vineyards." No river god, but Bacchus.

The cow-shed sits among sheep walks, farm sheds, and peaks of about five thousand feet. Thirty-four miles down a winding, narrow road that crosses slopes doused with daffodils in spring and with rose-bay willow-herb in late summer, in the little town of Le Puy, you can sit on the terrace of the small chalet hotel eating bilberry tarts and bilberry ice cream till your mouth and lips turn blue. From stalls along the road, you can buy Cévennes hams, sausages, and goat cheese. Good food is at the source of the Loire.

Here, too, in Le Puy, is the source of the fight to save the Loire. A small group of people have camped in the valley since February 1989, to protest proposed damming and to prevent engineers from beginning work. Local citizens as well as men, women, and children from other parts of France, Switzerland, and Germany camp in the gorge full time. On most Sundays, an additional one thousand or so people come to the campsite, some to show support, some to get information. The parcel of land was purchased by a committee called Loire Vivante (Living Loire), formed in 1988 to raise national and international awareness about the dam project. Undoubtedly, it is the most popular environmental issue in France in the last twenty years.

By the time the Loire reaches Le Puy, the drip-drop has collected water from hidden valleys into a trout stream. From here, it wanders north through mountain gorges, past ruined castles and Romanesque churches, hits a stretch of plains, takes shape as a meadow river, merges with the Allier River as it widens at Sancerre, which is where the Loire's controversy begins. At this point the flow of the Loire can become floods. Such floods actually benefit the ecological stability of the entire watershed by depositing silt and other organic material on the flooded soil, thus restoring soil fertility and replenishing underground water supplies; but they can also do tremendous damage. The Châteauneuf-sur-Loire museum contains prints, photos, and newspaper clippings that show children clinging to chimneys while trees, houses, corpses, dead cows, and pigs sweep past, and rescue boats toss in the turmoil. The city of Tours suffered 153 floods in 148 years, from 1820 to 1968. However, the worst flood, raising the river by twenty-three feet, occurred more than a century ago. Flash floods have happened in recent history; a storm high above Le Puy once raised the river thirty feet in an hour, after which it rapidly dropped again.

The Loire flows on from Sancerre, past nuclear power stations, past Orleans to the valley of the famous châteaus—now tarted up for the tourist trade—past another nuclear power station, downstream to Tours, where she is joined by the Cher River, past another nuclear power station, to Nantes, with its willow-covered islands and channels, to the Atlantic. More flood plains here—islands have been washed away overnight. And here is where Loire Vivante has its headquarters, with Christine Jean at its helm.

Vivacious and passionate about the Loire River, Jean wins you to her cause with her enthusiasm. Her personality is like a river: rushing and tumbling one minute, slowly lazing along the next; silent and deep for a moment, then bubbling and swift. In 1987, Jean began bringing together all the local, regional, and national groups concerned about proposed development of the river and formed the Loire Vivante. Trained in agronomy, with a master's degree in ecology, she uses her scientific expertise to lobby officials, counter the arguments of pro-dam engineers, and educate the public. No stuffy academic, Jean is intense and emotional, and quite equal to the task of rallying thousands of people to demonstrations.

Like the river, Jean's work crosses boundaries, swirls into eddies, and spins off into tributaries, or, as she says, "You have to be everywhere. And it's very difficult. But it's very interesting, too, because of different peoples' way of campaigning." She has so completely been everywhere in the fight to save the Loire for the past five or six years that she has come to be called Madame Loire.

∾

THE LOIRE IS THE LONGEST RIVER IN FRANCE, draining about one-third of France. It is also the last wild river in Europe. The Loire has been extensively diked but remains pristine enough to be called "wild" because of its capricious nature; the water flow varies significantly from a torrent to a trickle. It is precisely these water-level variations, seasonally flooding and ebbing, that create the ecological wealth of the river valley and its tributaries.

On the rich wetlands flanking the river, millions of birds stop over on their migratory routes. Many species live there all year; wading birds populate the floodplains, and terns nest in the steep banks along the river's edge. The little and common terns and the little ringed plover lay their eggs directly on the beaches and banks. Otter and beaver thrive in the river, along with eel, trout, and Atlantic salmon. The salmon, in the longest migratory route in western Europe, still swim upstream to where the Loire meets the Allier River. Because of the dikes, the migration that used to take three months now takes twelve. All of these animals, as well as the local people who depend on them for their livelihood, would be seriously affected by the proposed damming of the Loire.

In cities like Tours along the course of the Loire, the river winds through the parks and streets with grace and beauty. Beside its banks, people jog, sail, picnic, and gather with their families and friends on holidays. The river valley is a popular rural vacation spot of unspoiled natural beauty. The French call the Loire River Valley "the garden of France" because it produces a bounty of beef, poultry, game, fish, butter, cream, wine, fruit, and vegetables.

In 1982, a group with local interests launched a project to "domesticate" the Loire, to prevent flooding, to increase farm irrigation, and to ensure minimum flow during dry years. They formed a syndicate called EPALA, which stands for Établissement Public d'Aménagement de la Loire et de ses Affluents (Public Committee for the Improvement of the Loire and Its Tributaries). EPALA's grand design involves controlling and developing the Loire River Valley and its tributaries with a series of dams. Two dams would be on the Loire itself and two more on tributaries, the Allier and the Cher. Five additional dam sites have been proposed for study. The proposal also calls for raising and strengthening dikes and deepening the lower Loire's riverbed. In the end, the proposed "improvements" would be the death of the Loire; they would drastically alter the natural landscape of the entire river system. The dams would radically suppress the exchange between the river and its flood plains, destroying the very river dynamics that create diversity and maintain the ecological balance. The dams would also drown the sandbanks of the Loire and vast areas of surrounding pastureland; the increase in erosion and sedimentation would create serious problems for irrigation. Thousands of the Loire's islands would disappear and, with them, valuable habitat for many resident and migratory wildlife species.

EPALA unifies six regions, fourteen departments, and seventeen cities under Jean Royer, the mayor of Tours. Environmentalists have accused the organization of lying, intimidation, and bribery. They say the huge reservoirs, theoretically intended for irrigating farmlands, will mainly benefit the nuclear power industry, which would use the stored water to cool reactors. "The river Loire is already the most nuclearized river in all the world," Christine Jean says. France does not even need the power. Électricité de France recently announced that it has a surplus in generating capacity equivalent to the output of seven nuclear power plants.

EPALA also claims the project is necessary to control occasional severe floods on the lower Loire. Furthermore, it contends the dams will promote tourism, drawing boaters and sunbathers. Environmentalists argue that drowning beautiful gorges, traditional villages, rare wildlife, and archaeological sites will not attract tourists but drive them away. In addition, the endangered gorges now shelter an estimated ninety-seven protected species of animals, yet EPALA has stated that the dams will "protect and enrich the natural surroundings."

Most environmentalists believe that EPALA's arguments are specious and ridiculous. They also believe the project reflects both the mayor's egotistical obsession to complete what he calls his *oeuvre immense* (great work) and the greed of construction firms that stand to make massive sums of money for themselves and their political parties. "When we studied the technical dossier of EPALA, we saw that they say that they want to protect people against high flooding, but in fact what they want to do is develop again and build again, more and more, in dangerous zones," says Jean.

∾

FROM EARLIEST HUMAN HISTORY, people have been trying to tame rivers. Dams are among the earliest human structures known; a fifty-foot-high dam on the Nile was recorded in about 2900 B.C. The first modern dam, by contemporary scientific standards, was built in France in 1866; it was specifically designed to be strong enough to hold backwater and to withstand ice, silt, uplift pressures, temperature changes, and earthquakes. The pace of dam construction in the world accelerated after World War II, thanks in part to the World Bank, formed in 1945 as the International Bank for Reconstruction and Development, a specialized agency of the United Nations. Headquartered in Washington, D.C., the World Bank controls capital of $24 billion and is self-sustaining and profit-making. It lends money to developing nations for development projects, economic growth, and poverty alleviation. About thirty-eight percent of the money loaned by the World Bank for

agricultural development schemes has funded irrigation projects—
and ninety percent of that lending has occurred in the last ten years.

The world's early dams may have been modest affairs, but today,
there are more than one hundred dams over 490 feet high, of which
almost half were built during the 1980s. But Jean argues that the era
of the dam is over: "In Europe, all the rivers of importance have
already been dammed, and in Holland, for example, or in Germany,
they are now destroying what they've done and are rehabilitating
their rivers. So what we were thinking was, why should we do what
they are undoing?"

Dam proponents typically cite a group of benefits that dams are supposed to provide; the most popular is cheap power. At $1,000 per kilo-
watt of installed capacity, hydroelectricity costs far less than power from
a thermal plant, let alone a nuclear reactor. But there is a very limited number of rivers in the world suitable for damming. The World Energy Conference has estimated that all the feasible damming in the world
could generate about 19,000 terawatt-hours (1 terawatt equals 1 tril-
lion watt-hours) per year. And that is it—that is all the hydroelectricity we might ever hope for. At present, the world produces about
1,300 terawatts per year. So a significant increase is possible, but the
point is that very soon the world is going to have to start conserving
on electricity anyway. Why not conserve now and still have some wild
rivers left, too?

The second great lure of dam projects is irrigation. About fifty
percent of the earth's surface is classified as "arid" or "semiarid,"
and an estimated half million square miles were under irrigation in 1982,
according to the United Nations Food and Agricultural Organization
(FAO). At the current rate of increase of food demand, we will need
to irrigate another 386,000 square miles by the turn of the century. Once
we run out of rivers, only two other sources of fresh water remain: the
polar ice caps and desalinated seawater. Neither of those is currently
practical. Trapping rainwater with dams is the only viable large-scale
irrigation source today, but it presents problems. All soil naturally
contains salt; and if the salt level gets too high, the land becomes ster-
ile. Irrigation development projects disturb the delicate water-salt balance of many areas. Perennial irrigation waterlogs the top layer of

earth, sucking salt up by capillary action, particularly in arid and semiarid regions, where salt has been accumulating in the soil for eons without enough rainwater to flush it out. In hot dry areas, surface water evaporates quickly, leaving salt on the ground. With the insidious combination of waterlogging and evaporation, irrigated areas can soon become covered with a white, saline crust. In many cases, when the land becomes salinized, it is effectively dead forever. Millions of acres of farmland are lost every year because of salinization. The FAO estimates that at least fifty percent of the world's irrigated land now suffers from salinization. According to another recent study, as much irrigated land is now being taken out of production due to waterlogging and salinization as is being brought into production by new irrigation schemes. Meanwhile, water-saving drip irrigation systems such as those pioneered in Israel, and conservation methods that have worked in Texas, can cut agricultural water use by ten to fifty percent.

Another major problem with large dam projects is the social upheaval and poverty they create by displacing large rural populations. (Most of the potential dam sites left in the world today are well-populated valleys.) Unfortunately, relocation and settlement arrangements in the past have failed. In developing countries, where most of the past decade's huge dam projects have been implemented, the local residents—sometimes as many as a million of them (as in India's Narmada Valley)—have been subjected to misery and tragedy. Relocation plans tend to ignore local ethnic rivalries, often creating bitter disputes between new neighbors in resettlement projects. Local customs are also generally ignored, and local economies are considered expendable. Too often, the result is a destroyed society, its means of livelihood drowned and its children starving. The dispirited victims drift to the cities, to overcrowded slums where conditions are even worse; alcoholism, malnutrition, and prostitution prevail. For most people who have had to move to make way for a dam project, the "transition period" has only ended at death.

Dams also cause serious medical problems in both developed and developing countries. Dam projects with large bodies of stagnant water can create hazards even worse than the hundred-year floods that dams are intended to eliminate. The introduction of modern, perennial irrigation schemes has caused widespread malaria, which now kills one million people a year worldwide. Unfortunately, once the conditions for malaria have been established, the disease is virtually impossible to control. Not least among the problems is the remarkable ability of mosquitoes to develop genetic resistance to insecticides deployed against them. As a result, malaria has returned in many countries where it was once practically eliminated. Large dam projects have spread malaria more widely and made it more lethal. Another disease, schistosomiasis, is caused by a fresh-water parasite that finds an ideal habitat in large reservoirs and irrigation projects. The debilitating parasite enters the human body by boring through the skin, invading the bloodstream, and spreading throughout the body. Today, at least two hundred million people are infected—a number nearly equal to the entire population of the United States.

Dam projects cause vast ecological destruction by drowning living, productive rivers and creating, in their place, reservoirs that are biological deserts. Even fish do not like reservoirs; repeated efforts to establish viable fisheries in them have failed. In fact, in terms of fish yields, replacing a river with a reservoir results in a net loss of fish populations.

Flood control, historically one of the most attractive benefits of dams, has become more mythical than actual. There is now an increasing body of evidence that structural controls actually do little or nothing to reduce the ravages of floods. On the contrary, they make the problem worse by increasing the severity of flooding. The flood damage is not eliminated; it is just moved from one area to another. During periods of heavy rain, free-flowing rivers regularly overflow their banks and inundate low-lying regions, in which, until fairly recently, people very sensibly avoided building. Today, however, people have been persuaded that enough money can be spent on structural controls to make it safe to build on the floodplains of even the wildest rivers. As a result, in 1969, the United Nations Conference on Floods singled out the intensified use of floodplains as a major cause of the increased costs of floods in North America and Western Europe.

For dams to effectively keep floods under control, reservoirs must be kept low. But low reservoirs are less efficient for generating electricity and providing water for irrigation. A choice must be made: high reservoirs and bad floods, or low reservoirs and less electricity or irrigation. History has recorded which choice is almost invariably made. For example, in 1983, heavy snowfall in the Rocky Mountains poured more water into the Colorado River than had ever been recorded. At the urging of high-water advocates—the farming lobby and power authorities—reservoirs had been kept filled to the brim. When the water finally had to be released, a disastrous flood resulted, inundating fifty-five thousand acres of farmland and causing an estimated one hundred million dollars' worth of property damage.

Most very large dams have been functioning for fewer than twenty years, so we have little experience of their actual failure rates. However, small dams have not proved particularly reliable; about one percent of them fail every year. Nonetheless, new dams are getting bigger and are being built on questionable sites (because all the good sites have already been used). For example, the Malpasset Dam near Frejus in France failed because it was built in the wrong place, despite engineers' warnings. When it collapsed in 1959, it caused the death of 421 people. Evidence has shown that as the dams become larger and the sites less suitable, dams can cause earthquakes by overloading fragile geological structures with reservoirs. The first hint came as far back as the late 1930s, when increased seismic activity was noted after the Lake Mead reservoir was created by Boulder Dam, in Colorado. However, it still remains difficult to establish the geological conditions under which earthquakes will be induced. "By building dams, man is playing the sorcerer's apprentice," says Jean-Pierre Rothé, a French seismologist. "In trying to control the energy of rivers, he brings about stresses whose energy can be suddenly and disastrously released."

ॐ

CHRISTINE JEAN FLOPS INTO AN EASY CHAIR; she is exhausted. Her English is not very good today, she says, and conversations do not go easily because she is always searching for the next word. She uses body language when words fail, gesturing with her hands, expressing with her face—especially with her large, green eyes. And as she speaks about her cause, she begins to energize. She takes on a kind of glow, and after an hour she radiates. She says, "I think that this issue fits my passion. I need passion."

Organizing around an environmental cause in France has required a mighty effort. For one thing, the French people are noted for being strongly individualistic and difficult to organize around anything. For another, the political climate in France has been a little forbidding. The French government has only recently made tentative steps toward acknowledging environmental consciousness. President Mitterrand canceled plans for a new expressway through the historic forest of St. Germain, west of Paris, and lead-free gasoline has finally become available in the past few years. But as recently as 1985, the French secret police admitted bombing the Greenpeace ship *Rainbow Warrior*, killing one crew member in the process, to prevent further demonstrations against French nuclear testing in the Pacific. Such heavy-handed government actions have made even French activists reluctant to speak out against official policies.

Acting as coordinator of Loire Vivante under a contract with the World Wide Fund for Nature-France, Jean brought together the local, regional, and national groups concerned about the proposed dam. "Even in France we have been told that it was the first time that so many organizations could agree all together. I think what helped us was that we were few, and then suddenly so many, and with hope. So as we could hope, we just worked together to go on." The organization began by focusing on public education, and thirteen thousand people signed an anti-dam petition addressed to President Mitterrand. In addition, Loire Vivante began insisting that a comprehensive environmental impact assessment be carried out before any further dam construction could take place; previous EPALA studies, which had focused only on the immediate area of the dam, were inadequate. Loire Vivante argued that the assessment of the dam's environmental impact had to take into account the general effects of the project on the whole region. In addition to these efforts, Jean says, "You also have to organize a fight. It's not to fight because you want to fight; it's because you need to fight. In fact, you are not against things; you are for things—for rivers to be natural, for water to be of good quality, for sustainable development.

But you also have to fight and prevent construction, to say no, just no."

That was why Loire Vivante bought the small parcel of land at Le Puy, the site of the first dam, Serre-de-la-Fare, and began an occupation in February 1989. Later, in April 1989, Jean and Loire Vivante organized a demonstration in Le Puy that drew ten thousand people, who waved multicolored cardboard fish and assorted banners. "When you are walking, and there are thousands and thousands of people behind you, you feel very impressed," says Jean. "You feel so happy to be together. I think it's very important to feel that." For the same reason, she frequently visits the campsite at Le Puy. "Last year, one of the leading figures in Le Puy got married on the site. It was wonderful in the moonlight and with the music. And a baby was baptized on the site. And you are there, and you feel good. You know it's really living." Jean lives for the intensified level of existence that goes beyond ordinary happiness. "I'm interested in many things, so I could be superficial. But when I become involved in something, I want to go deeply into it, passionately. So this is the Loire."

In her office in seaside Nantes, she usually works alone, without the emotional drama on which she thrives. She keeps herself going by shifting into relentless action, the kind of action that will cut through any obstacle. "One day you are only writing like a secretary, and the day after you have to go and meet the prime minister and media. Also, because I am a scientist, I have to argue on the technical. I think the hardest part is to keep abreast and go everywhere. For the last three years, it was twice a week to Paris" (a four-hour round trip on the new, high-speed train, the TGV; before that, the trip took seven hours).

Jean has two small children, and their father is a busy man, a city planner, who was recently transferred from Nantes to Montpellier in southern France. "I would like to go there, but the Loire is not going there," she says. So for now, he lives in Montpellier and she lives in Nantes, and they see each other only about once a month. "I understand him, and I don't want him to sacrifice himself for my job. But I don't want to leave the Loire. So there is a problem." For now, she is a single woman with two small children. "Taking care of children, I can tell you, it's not easy. Because I get tired, and children ask so much of you, so much much." She feels isolated in this respect because most of her fellow activists are either men who have women in their lives to take care of the children, or women whose children are already grown.

The emotionally intense Jean has trouble with mixing her private and professional lives. "When you are completely, entirely in your job, no problem. Entirely in your family, no problem. But in fact, I am entirely in my family only during vacation. It's difficult because you see them growing up. Sometimes when I am on vacation for maybe four weeks, I am thinking, I could move and not work on this program anymore, and I could be happy. And I am sure it could be. But then, when I come back, I am so happy. Because I also like a challenge."

Jean has come to understand how much she shapes public opinion. The popularity of the Green Party has increased as a result of the Loire campaign. In the dam-site region, the Greens won twenty-two percent of the votes in a recent election. "Democracy is not something forever. It's something you have to gain every day. For me, it's a little bit special because it's my job. Maybe I'm the first woman in France who has been paid to fight like this. I was just a scientist, and I am more and more interested in politics now. I am feeling very strongly that my work, ecology, and democracy have to go on together."

∾

IN AUGUST 1991, the French government finally responded to pressure from environmentalists and canceled plans to build a dam on the Loire River at Serre-de-la-Fare as well as a second controversial dam at Chambonchard, on the Cher. Jean learned of the victory while on vacation in Scotland, on the Isle of Skye, where she was alone in a very wild landscape. Remembering how much work had gone into the victory, she cried with an intensity that still impresses her. It felt like a blow in the face, to see, perhaps for the very first time, all the events that had led to this moment. She saw all the moments she had spent yearning for this moment; and when she reached it, it was not all she had yearned for it to be. Although two dam projects were canceled, two more were still slated to go ahead. Environmentalists fear that the present policy on the Loire may last only as long as the present government. The mayor of Tours has said he expects the next government to be much more receptive to damming the river. Even in the victory, defeat still lurked; Jean had it all, and something was still missing.

This, she supposes, may be "the reason why people are afraid to fight like this. But we can give a lot for our fight and still treasure our own life. You can be a little bit involved and not too much. If you are numerous, but a little bit involved, then you can share the work. The problem is that we are few. There are many sacrifices, but you get as much as you give. And if you don't want to give so much, you are not obliged to do that. But if you want to do something, but you don't want to sacrifice your life, just do whatever you can do, because we need every help. Even if you just write us, even if you just sign petitions, even if you just send money. And when there is a demonstration, even if you are only there one or two times, it's important."

Jean sees now that "we live in a democracy, so a few people can change the law. But you have to have a number of people to change the culture and the point of view. The people, they are citizens, and they don't have to be only a citizen when they are voting; they have to be citizens every time. They have to feel concerned by things. They can become volunteers in organizations. And if it's too much? I think they can join the organization. An organization can do many things, so you can become a member. There have to be members because the bigger your organization, the more powerful she is. You see what I mean? On every level you can act."

❧

You may contact Christine Jean at Loire Vivante, 7, rue Cassini, 44000 Nantes, France.

Sam LaBudde

Undercover Agent

SAM LABUDDE

United States

SOMETIMES ONE PERSON can make an enormous difference. Although most environmental victories result from the effort of many people who research issues, attend hearings, write letters, campaign for public support, raise funds, stage demonstrations, and work in local elections —masses of people trying to convince greater masses—some battles can be catalyzed by one person acting alone.

Samuel LaBudde's first, and quite distinctly solo, flight into the storm of environmental action changed millions of minds almost instantly. Heroic, controversial, and rebellious, his action could not have been accomplished by a group; only an individual, and a rather special individual at that. His actions grew out of a sense of frustration and impatience, more than out of innate nobility.

LaBudde was a brilliant but slightly alienated loner until a decisive moment brought him to the center of the stage where he asked, not What can I do? but, What needs to be done? There's a difference. In the end, the difference stopped the senseless slaughter of dolphins by tuna fishermen.

∾

LABUDDE GREW UP "in the country, sort of, and I spent a lot of time in the woods, wading around in the creek and things like that. . . . I've always found it much more intriguing to be in the woods than to watch television."

As a child in southern Indiana, the heartland of the nation, he displayed strong and uncritical love for America. But his mother was part Cherokee Indian, and as he gradually became more aware of his heritage and what had happened to Native Americans, his patriotism changed profoundly. As he later wrote to me, "America was not founded solely on truth and justice, but also on slavery, genocide, and that opportunism characteristic of colonization. I rebelled against what I perceived were efforts to mold me into just another mindless, unquestioning product of society. And given the fact of the Vietnam War, the civil rights debacle, and Watergate, there was plenty to question. These were efforts to choose my own identity, reject the status quo, and to assert my hope for something better than what was being offered."

LaBudde's hunger for validity, for authenticity, for identity, for justice, and for belonging, led him from school to a series of outdoor jobs. Disillusioned by society and its disappointments, he instinctively sought a closer union with unspoiled nature. Perhaps he was really seeking a purer life, a set of ideals to which he could devote his considerable intelligence and energies.

"I went to Alaska in 1980," he says, "because I wanted to see what America looked like before suffering the heavy hand of European influence. I spent years in the Rockies and Cascades planting trees and doing such things. Everywhere I went, the land had been compromised. I wanted to see the land as it was. And so I went to Alaska. While I was up there, back in 1982 and 1983, I started hearing about the rain forest and the Amazon." In order to work in the rain forests of the Amazon, he returned to school and crammed the courses for a four-year degree in biology into two years. With the anticlimax of finishing his degree and disenchanted with the prospect of pursuing a graduate degree, he was essentially broke and unclear how to make the transition to the rain forests.

∾

ON THE WAY TO SOUTH AMERICA IN 1987, LaBudde stopped by
Earth Island Institute's San Francisco office to ask for a job working
with saving the rain forests. In the waiting room, he happened to read
a magazine article about dolphins being killed by the tuna industry.
For reasons we don't understand, dolphins and tuna swim together in the eastern tropical Pacific Ocean. Dolphins, although they swim
beautifully, are not fish, but mammals that breathe air. As they come
to the surface to breathe, they show fishermen where yellowfin tuna
might be. In the 1960's a fishing method was developed that includes
using explosives to herd the dolphin and the tuna presumed to be
below them. Then fishermen in speedboats drive the dolphins into a
net, much as cowboys on horses drive cattle into a corral.

The net is called a purse seine because once the animals are surrounded, cables are tightened, gathering the seine, or net, into a ball
like a gigantic purse. Hauling in the purse seine sometimes traps dolphins underwater, where they can drown. The fisherman are supposed to stop at a certain point in order to release the dolphins, a
nicety often ignored. Dragged on board along with the tuna, the dead
dolphins are unceremoniously tossed back in the sea.

The issue of the effects of purse-seine fishing on dolphins was not
new. Environmentalists had championed the cause of dolphin mortality
in the tuna industry since 1970. Since then, the issue had fallen almost
entirely beneath public notice despite the fact that by 1988, over
100,00 dolphins were being killed by U.S. and Latin American tuna
boats. Despite having worked as a fisheries biologist for the U.S. government in the spring of 1987 and believing himself well informed about
conservation issues, LaBudde had never even heard of the problem.
Once he learned about the dolphin slaughter, he could not turn his back
on it. The fact that he appears to be a drifter at times may stem from
his tendency to be "more introspective and critical of my motivations
and impulses than anyone I know." Once he makes up his mind to do
something, he moves quickly and directly into action. At that point, he
does not shy from confrontation, "where a balance needs to be restored
between what is happening and what ought to be happening instead."

He had been "toying with the idea of driving my motorcycle down to Patagonia to trade it to some gaucho for a horse and ride the horse back up to the Andes, which I figured would take me six or seven years, which was fine. I didn't do any of that. I still haven't made it to the rain forest. Because once you learn how bad things are, how can you turn your back on something like the dolphin slaughter or snow leopards going extinct? Then go hang out in the mountains and pretend it's not hapening? I can't do that. In retrospect, I think that sooner or later I would have started fighting for something I believed in, no matter where I ended up.

"The first time someone explained to me how there were fishermen out in the middle of the ocean chasing dolphins with helicopters, speed boats, high-concussion explosives, bombing them into submission, and catching them intentionally in these mile-long nets where they were dying by the thousands, my initial reaction was, get the hell out of here. Dolphins and whales are protected. Nobody would allow it to continue for a moment. And these folks were like, 'Sorry, but you're wrong.'"

ॐ

EARTH ISLAND INSTITUTE'S DOLPHIN PROJECT directors said they needed photographs to stop the practice. Even after an estimated seven million dolphin deaths, no visual evidence existed of the practice.

LaBudde told Earth Island's staff that he had just been offered a job on a tuna boat out of San Diego. "They [the National Marine Fisheries Service] didn't tell me it was to go out and count dead dolphins they were intentionally hunting down and killing. But they offered me a job. You want pictures. I'll take the job. I'll get you all the pictures you want. Then you can show people and make this stop."

"Well, it's very noble of you to take this job in order to get the pictures, but they don't let cameras on U.S. boats of any kind," Earth Island told him. U.S. tuna fishing boats did not allow any cameras on board, even with (or especially with) official government observers.

LaBudde was surprised. "What do you mean? I was just a National Marine Fisheries Observer on a Japanese trawler in the Bering Sea.

I was not only the scientist on the boat, I was a cop on the boat. I could call for the Coast Guard if I wanted to and shut down their whole show. You're telling me that on a U.S. boat as a U.S. scientist and a U.S. citizen there to gather data on the fisheries, I can't even take a camera and get snapshots?'

"No."

"Why?"

"Because the U.S.tuna industry is in bed with the U.S. government."

LaBudde began asking more questions. "What are the alternatives to getting on a U.S. boat? What about going undercover on a foreign boat? Do they have as much sensitivity to the public fallout from images of their fishing operation?"

"Nobody's ever been there," Earth Island told him, "but probably not."

After further discussions with Earth Island Institute, LaBudde spent several days with Stan Minasian of the Marine Mammal Fund, who LaBudde credits with making "everything that followed possible." Afterwards, LaBudde "went down to Ensenada and just made it up as I went along. And I managed to get a job on a boat."

ॐ

AS A CREW MEMBER aboard the *Maria Luisa*, a Panamanian-registered fishing boat, LaBudde saw for himself the harsh reality: The ship's first catch destroyed two hundred eastern spinner dolphins, and the *Maria Luisa* ended up with only one yellowfin tuna.

LaBudde soon managed to change his job from deckhand to cook. As cook, he could hide his camera and tapes in the galley's locked cabinets. In addition, he felt the cook's job provided him with a safer cover story. "On the tuna boat, what I did was cultivate eccentric behavior. . . . Once I became cook that was very easy to do. . . . Before that, I had to be a normal member of the crew, and that was a bit stressful. But once I became the cook, I was basically self-governing. . . . The stranger I acted, the more it expanded my arena for erratic behavior, like my being fascinated with dolphin mortality. Really, when I think back, there were times when I would sit there for fifteen minutes and just film dolphins dying in the net with my little video camera as a gringo amid all the Spanish and Basque and Latin American crew. I'm not sure they ever had a clue as to why I was really there."

For months on end, LaBudde led a life of deception. "In spite of my formal training as a biologist, virtually all my field experience," he says, "has been as an actor. It's all been like representing myself as somebody innocuous in order to get the documentation. You know, I meet all these people in Los Angeles who are actors and actresses. . . . But it's always funny when somebody introduces themselves to me as an actor because I think, Oh yeah, I used to do acting. But mine was different because I didn't get any script, I didn't get any rehearsals. I had one take and it had to be right because if I screwed up, the picture was over. When you're in a situation where you're miserable and you're around people you don't particularly care for and you're saying things you don't believe in, three hours is interminable, three months is brutal, it's masochistic."

∾

LaBudde's experience with dolphins included much that was horrifying. But there is another side to the human/dolphin relationship, an almost mystical tie that has existed for centuries. From Greek art to New Age musings, people have celebrated the mysterious communications between cetaceans (the order that includes whales, dolphins, and porpoises) and humans.

Dolphins and whales are the only wild animals that voluntarily associate with humans without being fed. Dolphins, in fact, not only associate with us, they have frequently acted as our saviors. Numerous instances of dolphins rescuing drowning people have been documented. In addition, through the ages, people who have enjoyed encounters with dolphins in the wild come away thrilled. They report establishing friendships, feeling loved, and even being miraculously cured of rare illnesses.

It may be that people love dolphins because they seem to smile. However, according to Kenneth S. Norris, the grand-old-man of cetacean studies, this feature really is not a gesture of friendship or happiness. Rather, he declares, "the lower jawbone flares outward and serves as an ultrasensitive ear that enables them to hear sounds from fellow dolphins."

I first experienced dolphins in the wild in the eastern tropical Pacific in 1973, aboard a whale-watching ship traveling from San Diego to Baja California. The first night out of port, our boat churned through phosphorescent waters. The prow stirred up tiny luminous creatures and threw bow waves that glowed like fire. Just below the surface, tiny fish streaked by like falling stars, while schools of anchovies swirled by in a galaxy. I lost track of which way was up: above, the dark sky and luminous stars; below, the dark water and luminous fish.

Shortly before midnight, the first dolphin—or rather, the first cometlike flame—headed directly for the glowing bow waves. As it reached the boat, the blaze of light became discernible as a dolphin whipping its body underwater at about twenty-five miles per hour. At the last minute, it leaped into a hairpin turn and rose above the bow waves with a loud squeak. It dove and rose and rode the waves of light like a neon surfer. Soon other flaming comets converged, and a dozen dolphins were leaping and turning, surfing and swimming, squeaking and blowing just five feet below my stand at the bow. They smiled, they squealed, they played with each other—and, it seemed, with me. They were beautiful, graceful, and strong. Their dark, expressive eyes caught mine: I fell in love.

I stayed up most of the night, not wanting to miss a thing, not wanting even to blink my eyes. After collapsing into my bunk for a few hours' nap, I returned to the bow as the sun began to rise over the Mexican mountains in the east, and early dawn light stole the phosphorescence from the water. Dolphins still played on the bow, their sleek lines and smooth skin outlined in gold dawn light and silver luminescence. Over the next week, I stayed up every night the "light show" was on. I wrote pages of feelings in my journal. Gradually, the need to write began to wither away, and the last few days were marked by just a few scribbled lines.

∾

IN THE EARLY 1970s, people were just beginning to learn that dolphins could talk and that whales sing. It was, after all, only in the early 1960s that the American public "discovered" dolphins and whales, largely through Flipper, the dolphin television star. Circus stardom quickly followed. The intelligence of whales and dolphins and their use of language became well known.

One of the more surprising things about dolphins is their attitude toward humans—any humans. They simply will not attack a human, though they certainly have teeth and use them, and they have demonstrated a willingness to defend themselves against sharks. Many of the species greatly outweigh us (the bottle-nosed dolphin averages four hundred to five hundred fifty pounds and runs about nine feet) and could do a lot of damage if they chose. Scientists have performed the most horrifying experiments—driving metal hooks into a dolphin's skull with a hammer—and still the animal does not bite its torturer.

In 1991, I sailed aboard a research vessel in the Bahamas to study spotted dolphins, the species that is the main victim of the tuna fishery in the tropical eastern Pacific. Though spotted dolphins are distributed widely in all tropical and some warm temperate waters, the Atlantic spotted dolphin is a coastal variety found in shallower waters. A resident population of spotted dolphins was discovered in the 1970s by divers working on a wreck off Grand Bahama Island.

The old Spanish galleon had $850 million in treasure aboard, and divers worked long hours for years to recover it. The dolphins visited the site often, and divers swam with them during breaks from work. Their encounters came to the attention of scientists eager to study them, but the treasure hunters refused to let anyone else near their sunken pots of gold. After the treasure hunters sailed off with their millions, the scientists sailed in with their notebooks.

This Bahama dolphin population is unique because individual dolphins stay in the area all year, so their individual histories and relationships can be studied. The site, though twenty-five miles offshore, is shallow—no more than twenty-five feet to the sandy bottom—and the clear waters provide excellent visibility. Good underwater observations can be made without having to use scuba gear, which frightens off most dolphins. Researchers in swim trunks or bikinis (most of them are women), face masks, and snorkels spend weeks at a time swimming with the dolphins in encounters that—by the rules of the research program—happen only if the dolphins initiate them.

The encounters occurred in the open waters, not in pens or tanks. Dolphins came to visit us in their own time and place; we were not allowed to feed, touch, chase, or harass them. Bobbing aboard a small sailboat, we took turns standing "watch" for the thrilling moment when the dolphins decided to come to call. Grabbing our gear and jumping in the water, we swam and observed them, sometimes for an hour or more at a time. We interacted with them on their terms; though we were not allowed to attempt to touch them, they sometimes touched us with their snouts or flanks.

Once, a well-known dolphin, Stubby, stayed with me and swam for twenty minutes. He looked me in the eye and seemed to challenge me to a race, which I was happy to attempt but quickly lost. Another time when I was in the water with him, he suddenly broke loose from our free-form underwater ballet and dove to the bottom where he chased away an approaching sting ray before returning to play again. On another occasion, I watched two dolphins dive to the shallow bottom and pick up a conch shell that they tossed back and forth to each other. Unsettling for the conch inside, perhaps, but amusing to me and the dolphins.

From the ship's deck, I once observed a dolphin playing with one of the woman swimmers. She was trying to keep him in view to determine the vital statistics we were gathering (distinguishing marks, sex, age, and so on), and he had her swimming around in a small circle before suddenly reversing direction. Then he reversed again. Back and forth he kept her going in a comical dance one might act out with a child. From the dolphins' point of view, we may have looked like children: small, awkward, weak, vulnerable, and unable to say anything in their language.

After spending some days in the wild with the dolphins, in their element, most of us entertained the possibility that human beings may not be the superior species. Certainly, dolphins and whales are the more fully evolved species; they were completely developed at a time when human beings were still, theoretically, tree shrews. If, as LaBudde says, three and a half billion years of evolution has been "life struggling to achieve consciousness," maybe the older species has something to tell us. In the Bahamas, a large part of the continuing research attempts to find a common language with which we could further communication and learn what we are capable of being taught.

ॐ

MONTH AFTER MONTH ABOARD SHIP, LaBudde lived a life of sickening sights and disheartening events. To pass the time, he read a lot. But he says, "I remember when the boat would come in sight of shore, my heart would take off. I could see myself walking through the villages and down the mountain roads and not doing anything but enjoying myself. I couldn't do that on the boat really. There were times when I would try and grab moments, like at three in the morning on the back of the boat with my flute. But by and large, there wasn't any place to hide or let it down, really. I couldn't even get in the water; there were sharks following the boat all over the place."

After five months on the *Maria Luisa*, he had all the footage he needed and all the time aboard ship he could stand. He resigned in Panama City and flew out of the country. The *Maria Luisa* put out to sea again—for the last time. Its engine exploded and two crew members were killed.

By then, LaBudde was in San Francisco, editing his videotapes. Once the tape was completed, he, Stan Minasian, and Earth Island Institute's dolphin staff went to Washington, D.C., to meet with the heads of environmental and animal rights organizations. LaBudde, brand-new to the world of environmental activism, "was honored just being in the room with these people—they were from Greenpeace, the Environmental Defense Fund, the Center for Marine Conservation, the World Wildlife Fund. When I sat down, I thought, God, this is great.

"I didn't really know how they worked. I thought I'd brief them about what was going on with the footage, and they'd kick me out of the room to figure out what to do about it. What I heard instead was a lot of bullshit about what their compromise position should be, and they hadn't even fired the first shot yet! They were talking about the impossibility of going anywhere on this issue.

"After half an hour, I was just furious. I had thought I was going to spend five months making this film so that I could provide the environmental community with the tools they needed to win this. And the environmental community in Washington didn't think they could win it, period—with any tools. I was screaming at the director of one of the largest organizations within the space of forty-five minutes. They said, 'We've been here fifteen or twenty years, and we know what we're talking about.'

"And we rejected them. I was with people from the Earth Island Institute's Marine Mammal Fund, and we basically went back to San Francisco and said, 'We'll do this ourselves.' And that's why the dolphin campaign happened out of San Francisco rather than Washington, D.C. In Washington, there is a lot of compromise; it's based on the ethic of compromise, which is no ethic at all. There are a couple of organizations there that are really good at selling out."

The major environmental organizations in Washington represent a formidable force of perhaps fifteen million members in total. They administer budgets totaling about $600 million. The top executives earn six-figure salaries, like their counterparts in government.

Samuel LaBudde's dolphin footage became notorious; it was shown on every network. LaBudde told his story before Congressional committees. No one could deny the shock value. But tuna fishermen and politicians argued that such acts simply did not happen on U.S. ships (which would not allow cameras on board); LaBudde, Earth Island Institute, and the Marine Mammal Fund said they did. There was a standoff. Nothing changed.

∾

IN THE SUMMER OF 1988, Earth Island Institute fired up a national tuna boycott that had been on the back burner for years; the fuel was provided by the videotapes of purse-seine fishing on tuna. "What we did is let people know that if they bought canned tuna, they were just as responsible as the guys throwing the nets," LaBudde says. The boy-

cott and the ensuing changes in policies by the world's major tuna packing companies, at least, "just about dried up the market for this type
of tuna, which left little incentive for the fishermen to go out there and
fish this way."

In addition, Earth Island Institute and the Marine Mammal Fund
filed a lawsuit against the National Marine Fisheries Service for fail-
ing to protect the dolphins as required under the Marine Mammal Protection Act. "We also started putting pressure on key people in
Washington, D.C., to change the law. We started an effort on the
state legislative level to address the issue in California because California
has such a big percentage of the population that if you can change the
ground rules in California, the rest of the commercial industries just
about have to change their whole product line.

"And we started saying nasty things about the companies that
were buying the tuna from the fishermen. Now H. J. Heinz, which owns
Star-Kist, spends tens of millions of dollars a year making Americans
believe they're just a mom-and-pop company that's as wholesome as
apple pie. The last thing they need is for someone to show up and
make them a dolphin-killing company. That costs them a lot more than
tuna fish sales. That costs them the image of their company, which cost
them a lot of years and hundreds of millions of dollars. They don't want
to risk that."

In 1990, Earth Island Institute and the Marine Mammal Fund
intensified the campaign. "The Marine Mammal Fund completed a documentary narrated by actor George C. Scott for national television about
the dolphin slaughter, and some of the larger national animals rights
organizations like Friends of Animals, the ASPCA, and the Humane
Society of the United States joined the boycott. For three months, we
conducted an offensive.

"We wrote a ten-page circular and distributed it to our activists
around the country. It was basically an agenda for 'how to start a
shit storm about the dolphin issue in your community.' We sent them
broadcast-quality tape and photographic slides, sample radio PSAs
[public service announcements], a television PSA, and everything they
would need to become dangerously knowledgeable about the issue. It
was like a seven- or eight-pound pack of information, and people

started getting a lot of local publicity. And we made sure that a couple copies of this thing were leaked to the Heinz people.

"We were directing a three-month offensive that was designed specifically to make Heinz the dolphin-killing company in the eyes of the American people. I met with their director of public relations before we started doing this and said, 'Look, you guys can put on the white hats and be heroes, or you can be the black hats and have everybody know that you are the company that kills dolphins. It's your decision. But the longer you wait, the uglier it's going to get. It's your call because we've told you what we're going to do, and the only thing that's going to get us off your back is for you to do the right thing here.' And less than seventy-two hours before we were ready to kick off National Dolphin Day demonstrations in thirty metropolitan areas across the United States, Heinz called a press conference and went 'dolphin-safe.'"

Heinz announced it would no longer purchase tuna caught in nets that kill dolphins. Heinz was followed by Van Camps Seafood and Bumble Bee Seafoods. Today, according to LaBudde, you can safely eat just about any tuna fish sold in the United States, whether in cans or in sushi bars. "The only thing that might be suspect is this industrial pack stuff, the four-pound cans you get from caterers or restaurants."

To keep the pressure on, Earth Island Institute undertook to police the industry. "If somebody wants to use a 'dolphin-safe' label they have to talk to us, because if they don't and they use it, we'll make life miserable for them. We had to bust Bumble Bee about nine months after this 'dolphin-safe' thing. They were taking drift-net-caught tuna in Thailand, and we found out about it." When Earth Island Institute confronted Bumble Bee, it said, "We're not doing anything wrong," according to LaBudde.

"And we knew they were. They unloaded three thousand tons of drift-net-caught tuna. So we did full-page ads in the *New York Times* and the *Los Angeles Times* saying: 'Bumble Bee Lies/Dolphin Killers.' And they did a really dumb thing. They put their own full-page ad in the papers three days later, attacking us. Very stupid. We love specific targets. When we were fighting the tuna industry, it was difficult, at best, because the 'tuna industry' doesn't really exist. But a specific

company you can point to, name the CEO, name their corporate officers, give out their phone and fax numbers to thousands of activists
around the country, have the activists call and write, and tell the company what they think. We had a very brief campaign with Bumble Bee
that lasted about a week, and then they ran up the white flag and
said, 'Okay, we fucked up. We lied. We were wrong, and we won't do
it again.'

"And as far as we can tell, they haven't," LaBudde wrote to me
recently. "Earth Island Institute has about thirty people employed
worldwide in over a dozen countries working to ensure that dolphin-
safe is just that. More important, though, it has given us tremendous
leverage in closing down global fisheries that are dolphin-unsafe
because dolphin-unsafe tuna is off limits to the majority of the canning
industry, and the price offered for that type of fish is pitiful in comparison to what is paid for tuna that is dolphin-safe.

"Just good old consumer democracy in action, but an incredible
example of what started as a grass-roots campaign quickly evolving into
sweeping international reforms. So this is what I tell people: Pick one
thing, make it your own, and figure out what are the pieces that allow
this to continue, then go after the weak link. Or, if you've got enough
time and energy and personnel, go after every link simultaneously."

ॐ

LABUDDE IS NOT PROUD that he has become one of the environmental movement's most effective leaders. He considers it an indict-
ment of the environmental movement "that a jack-of-all-trades, a soft
scientist from Indiana like myself can join the environmental community and stir so many issues up when there are thousands out there
who ought to be eminently qualified, when there's Greenpeace with millions of dollars. . . . What I've found is that not only are many of the
people who are in the environmental community or the animal rights
community just as consistently fallible as individuals in any other
aspect of American culture, they're often more so.

"And the reason they are is harrowing to me. It's ridiculous. Environmentalists, conservationists, and animal welfare people don't have

to routinely furnish an actual service or a manufactured good. For that reason, you get people in environmental organizations that you wouldn't let polish the hubcaps on your car. If the American public had any idea of how gutless and impotent the mega-environmental groups actually are, they'd stop giving their money to the Audubon Society, the National Wildlife Federation, the World Wildlife Fund, and Greenpeace, and get directly involved, which is what really needs to happen. They've rested their laurels so long they're completely composted."

Thinking further about this, LaBudde later added a note to me, "That's not to say there are not some really good people in different organizations, including Greenpeace. But by and large, the larger these organizations become, the more bureaucratic, more compromising, less cost-effective, and less productive they are. The 'cheerleading' generation of environmentalists with their huge and essentially inactive memberships is over; everyone realizes there are problems, and what needs to happen now is a transition to community-based activism. The groups on the front lines are focused, homegrown, and intimately acquainted with the issues, not sequestered in their D.C. offices and engaged in rampant conjecture about issues of which they have no direct or experiential knowledge."

In addition, LaBudde says, "I think the thing that separates the doers from the wannabes is a specific vision. They have a specific goal of what they want to achieve. Because you have to know what you want or you can't get it. Cosmic serendipity aside, it just generally doesn't happen. That's what makes Earth Island Institute and some of the other people I've worked with very good. They know what they want, and they know how they expect to achieve it. And after that, it's just a matter of engineering. There are no heroes in the environmental movement; only mechanics. They do what is necessary to achieve the goal. They are willing to get obsessive about something and fight for it and be miserable and suffer for it.

"What was much more important to me in terms of preparing for environmental work than anything academic was being a machinist in Alaska. Basically we would take raw or broken pieces of steel; and we would bore, mill, drill, weld, polish, and otherwise torture them into a functioning apparatus. Now that doesn't sound like much in itself, but if you're turning a steel rod into a propeller shaft, the game is to get there as painlessly and as quickly as possible.

"So what you're talking about is a lot of imaging—knowing where you are and what you want to achieve. Getting there is just a matter of engineering or choreography or orchestration. I mean, people think I get up in the morning, go down to the beach, and save some dolphins, then sit down with a bowl of Wheaties. It doesn't happen that way. When you look at environmental activism, it's all about selling ideas. But more important, its about giving people the opportunity to empower themselves and make a difference. An environmentalist without a video camera, these days, is like a soldier without a gun. They might as well stay home and not even get out of bed.

"You've got to go public with these issues. Five years ago if somebody had asked me to assemble a crack team of environmentalists, I would have gone out and gotten all wildlife biologists and people like that. I probably wouldn't even consider biologists now. They would be helpful, sure, but I'd be much more interested in someone with a polisci, paralegal, marketing, and telecommunications background. In the natural world, reality is much more important than perception. But in terms of affecting what happens in the natural world, the perceptions are more important than reality.

"When the guys from Sea Shepherd, Earthtrust, and Greenpeace went out in their boats to save whales, they never saved any whales. The best they ever did was they sent one boat out for a couple of hours on an afternoon and caught one boat out of the huge fleets of whaling ships and hassled it for a few hours. They never really saved any whales—but what they did do was get people to think, a lot of them for the first time, "save the whales." And that was used and twisted and turned to save whales.

"It's the easiest thing in the world to make a splash in the media. But to birth a campaign in the media, to use the media to mainstream an idea, or encourage outrage, or reform something in society—that's extraordinary. That takes a lot of stamina, a lot of relentlessness and cleverness, really. Grass-roots activism is essential, but you have to fight your way up. It's very difficult.

"Democracy relies on informed, involved individuals participating in the process. Very key words: informed, involved, participating. And we have none of those things in this country. Everything that has happened on the environmental issues is mild compared to what ought to be happening, given how desperate circumstances are and how little attention most people pay to their future.

"People are willing to dump hundreds of thousands of dollars a year into insurance policies, but are they willing to actively participate in their future? No, they want to pay somebody else to take care of it. That's what the whole insurance model is about. People feel like that's what they do when they donate to environmental groups: It's insurance. 'Give to Greenpeace and the World Wildlife Fund, let them take care of it.' But it's not taken care of. People think the environment is out there and that the environment is peripheral to human experience. It's not. It's our backyard, and it's central; everything we do is ecology.

"The perception of environment needs to be expanded. And what they are doing instead in the national media, and those clever, corporate-funded public relations firms, is pitting the environment against the economy and talking about the environment like it's some sort of discrete commodity in someone's warehouse. When they talk about compromising the environment to satisfy the economy, that's a contradiction in terms to me. The best insurance of long-term economic viability is a healthy ecosystem, a healthy environment."

LaBudde continued this theme: "They like to talk about us as environmental terrorists, even though the ones talking are the guys with the bulldozers, the chainsaws, the chemical factories—who are destroying entire ecosystems, poisoning the earth and sacrificing long-term viability of the environment for a one-time economic windfall."

∾

LABUDDE CURRENTLY WORKS as a biologist for Earth Island Institute and is finishing up what he hopes will be the end to fishing on dolphins. He lives in a flat on Russian Hill in San Francisco. The little Victorian house is one of the few on the hill that has a front yard. It used to be filled with an overgrown tangle of wild ivy and parsley until LaBudde took it upon himself to turn it into something more beautiful and in a way, slightly wilder.

He cleared the yard and terraced the hilly slope with bricks he scavenged from around the neighborhood. On the terraces, he planted wildflowers and small trees in varieties that require little watering, an important consideration for both the city's precious water supply and LaBudde's pressured schedule. To encourage pollination, he also planted species that attract hummingbirds, and he started a beehive that now bustles with friendly, fuzzy bees that LaBudde sometimes holds in his hands. The yard displays the beauty and charm of Monet's gardens at Giverny. Though he says he has not felt like he had a home since he left high school, this is "an acceptable compromise which will sustain me until I get a farm and, hence, a home."

In addition to his position as director of the Endangered Species Project for Earth Island Institute, he distributes video cameras to scientists, conservationists, and human rights activists around the world and continues to work with mixed success on other marine mammal conservation projects.

A campaign with Earthtrust, modeled on the dolphin-tuna strategy of undercover filming, quickly shut down drift-net fishing that was massacring scores of species. While purse-seine fishing uses dolphins as guides to the good tuna-fishing locations in the ocean, drift nets don't discriminate. Drift-net fishing became widespread during the 1980s. Drift nets may be as much as forty miles long and so thin as to be virtually invisible. They catch everything in their path: fish, dolphins, seals, swimming birds, turtles, trash—everything. LaBudde says that essentially drift-net fishing is strip-mining the sea. One U.S. report estimated that in order to harvest 106 flying squid, more than 41 million other creatures representing more than a hundred species were captured and killed. Most of the world's drift-net fishing was being committed by Japan, Taiwan, and South Korea, although several European nations have engaged in it as well.

"Drift netting is the largest, most destructive fishing industry in the world," LaBudde says. "In the North Pacific alone you are talking about in excess of a thousand boats collectively using 30,000 miles of net every night—enough to go from Los Angeles to Tokyo and back six times. And they put this net out in straight walls about fifty to sixty kilometers long, maybe more, ten to fifteen meters deep. It's a curtain of fine nylon, like gossamer, and everything that runs into it gets caught. They take the fish that's marketable and throw the rest back as compost."

Just six months after LaBudde returned from his sojourn aboard the *Maria Luisa*, he went back to sea with his video camera. "So I spent over half of my first year in the environmental community out at sea. And I don't even like boats that much."

The drift-net exposé involved even more danger than his earlier venture into eco-spying. "We were on a twelve-meter wooden sailboat for two-and-a-half months out in the middle of the Pacific on stormy seas. We had no business being out there with that type of boat and an inexperienced crew. But we wanted this documentation so badly we were willing to take the chance.

"We just showed up and pretended we were an amateur film crew looking for whales. We captured the imagination of the captain and the crew, and we just stayed for a while, watching them routinely kill seabirds, dolphins, turtles, sharks, and everything else, day after day after day. We got the first documentation in history on open-ocean drift neting. It was so dramatic we didn't have to go through the public sector. The footage went right to heads of state and United Nations representatives. It was the catalyst that produced the UN General Assembly resolution that banned open-ocean drift netting at the end of 1992." The major drift-net fishing countries, including Japan, Taiwan, and Korea, have agreed to abide by the resolution.

∾

LABUDDE HAS ALSO WORKED to save various other dolphin species around the world, including rare river dolphins. He recounts, "I went to China and did a project on White River dolphins, the most endangered cetacean species in the world. . . . It's a fresh water species in the Yangtze River that's going to go extinct as a result of 350 million people living in the watershed. Most of China's heavy industry is there. It's the agricultural viaduct for one-fifteenth of the world's people. The Yangtze River valley is their everything: It's their lifeblood, their collective sewer system, highway. . . .

"The miracle was that the dolphins were alive at all. And the only reason that they were able to survive is that the Yangtze is the third-largest river in the world, behind only the Amazon and one other. It's a huge river that just dumps torrents of water out of the Himalayas and Central Asia and purges itself. They are building something now called the Three Gorges Dam, which will be the biggest dam in the world. It's going to back the river up a hundred miles, and that'll be it. The dolphins won't survive. That will be the first dolphin species to go into the tank—to become extinct in human history. These dolphins would probably become extinct with or without the dam. Pollution, over-fishing, boat traffic, and general disruption of their environment, all compromise their ability to survive."

His work on the river dolphins came about because he got a phone call from an "American who had been doing a two- or three-year ongoing project with the Chinese on the White River dolphins. His money hadn't come through for a year. I didn't know anything about the situation, and he explained it to me. I said, 'Well, are you documenting what you're doing?' And he says, 'Sort of. Not really.' And I said, 'You've got to have documentation.' You've got to go public with these issues. Otherwise you can't marshall the wherewithal or the concern. You can't make the wheel squeak unless you get people informed."

The scientists and activists in China "put three years into this [White River dolphin] program, and they don't even have a ten-minute film they could use for fundraisers to get 5 or $10,000 from foundations. That's all it takes. So, I thought, I'll see if I can get some funding and I'll come there and get some documentation for you. So I managed to pull some strings, and I crossed the Chinese border with $12,000 cash in my pocket. . . . I gave $10,000 in hundred dollar bills to a couple of scientists over there to buy stuff for their project. If we had gone through the government, God knows if they'd ever have gotten any of it. We spent a few weeks trying to film the dolphins on the river."

In addition, he began a campaign to stop poaching of Alaskan walruses for their tusks. The campaign is moving ahead after a period when he didn't have time to devote to it—he was spreading himself too thin.

"I am a scientist as well but I haven't done any honest biology in years. I do things I never dreamed or desired to do. I do PR, telecommunications and marketing, a sort of applied political science—not what is in my gut to do, but I do it because it's just what you have to do to make things work. You have to do whatever works."

ꙮ

HE IS TRYING TO FIGURE OUT A WAY to really change society, "at least to the extent of making species extinction a 'sociological impossibility.' I went through this period where I was reading all these books on historical figures like Gandhi, Marco Polo, Madame Curie, and some other people who had really changed society. Like Gandhi— here's a man who had a more profound effect on society and more people in history than anybody, literally hundreds of millions of people. And how did he do that? He was the catalyst for phenomenal changes. What energy did he bring that deflected the course of history, that moved hundreds of millions of people into fundamental change in the way that society, not just thought, but behaved?"

Just before we went to print, LaBudde wrote to me: "I'm really becoming disenchanted with fighting symptoms while the essential causes of ecological ruin remain intact. From a biological standpoint and in the context of viewing the destruction of ecosystems, population growth and the unprecedented disappearance of species, you either recognize that what we're experiencing is something akin to ecological triage, or you bask in a willful form of insular naïveté and indifference.

"I keep searching for a way to precipitate something symbolic or fundamental that is powerful in a truly epic sense. Like what Gandhi did when he marched to the sea to gather his own salt. A little white-haired man in homespun cotton walked to the sea to get his own salt, and the world shook. The world rattled when he did that and is a better place because of it. I'm afraid that humanity needs something like that if we're to have any hope of saving what is left of the natural world from our 'civilizing' influence and ensure the possibility that future generations don't end up characterizing this time in history as a tragic era of retrograde evolution. I'm looking for a situation or dynamic with the kind of potential energy that traps, that kind of falls in on itself and implodes like a collapsing star. We need something like that to precipitate an ecological revolution and restore some of the balance we've mortgaged in running up this staggering environmental deficit."

∾

For more information, contact Earth Island Institute, 300 Broadway, Suite 28, San Francisco, California 94133.

Catherine Wallace

Infighting for the
Last Frontier

CATHERINE WALLACE

New Zealand

SO FEW PEOPLE have ever visited Antarctica that penguins in the wild have no instinctive fear of people. Quite the reverse: They have been known to waddle right up to field biologists and study *them*—untying their shoelaces, slipping a beak up their sleeves, and messing up their hair. Fewer people have ever set foot on the continent of Antarctica in all of history than visit Yosemite National Park in three summer days. As a result, penguins have lived for thousands of years in what is paradise to them. But like all the other paradises on earth, today, people are taking an interest in it, despite the fact that most of us will never go there.

In some ways, Antarctica bears more resemblance to Mars or the moons of the outer planets than to anywhere on earth, even the Arctic. It has been seen as an intensely intellectual landscape. "The more deeply one goes into the interior, the more tenuous become its ties to the Earth and to human understanding, the more self-referential its processes," says Stephen J. Pyne in *The Ice, A Journey to Antarctica.*

Yet other explorers declare it a treasury of the physical. Diane Ackerman, the brilliant poet-scientist, writes in *The Moon by Whale Light*: "Before coming to the Antarctic, I had thought that penguins lived in a world of extreme sensory deprivation. But I had found just the opposite—a landscape of the greatest sensuality. For one thing, there was so much life, great herds of animal life to rival those in East Africa. Many people have compared Antarctica to a wasteland; instead, it is robust with life. For another, the range of colors was breathtaking; though subtle, it had changing depths and illuminations, like flesh tones. The many colors were in the ever-bluing sky, in the cloud formations, the muted light, the midnight sun, the auroras dancing over still waters with icebergs and crash ice, and in areas that dazzled like small hand mirrors through which black-and-white penguins dove."

The life that teems around the penguins includes the largest whales and the smallest wingless flies. Seals, porpoises, and flying birds, as well as penguins, feed in the waters that contain the world's largest storehouse of shrimplike krill. Of course, most of these great herds of animals are migratory and leave as the long winter of darkness approaches. To see Antarctica's permanent land animals—arthropods, mites, metazoa, tardigrades, protozoa, worms, crustaceans—you need a microscope. In the icy water, the most distinguished animal other than the krill is the eerie-looking ice fish, with a transparent body and no red blood (its veins flow with a bloodlike antifreeze that allows it to swim with the icebergs).

The icebergs are always changing and moving, forming ice tunnels, grottoes, sculptures, ice gardens, and mountains. Some of them are tens of thousands of years old. Some icebergs have become so compact they have crushed all the air bubbles out and look blue; others are so full of algae and plankton that they look green.

The last pristine continent on earth, Antarctica holds an ice locker full of environmental issues. Key questions of mining, energy consumption, economics, wildlife, wilderness, national politics, international diplomacy, and grass-roots organizing are shaping its future. You can reach into the ice locker and pull out subjects as vast as the continent, 5.5 million square miles in all (twice the size of Australia), and as contrasting as its landscape, a glittering jewel of ice and fire (a volcano still steams a bit of the landscape).

It is this complexity and vastness that fascinates Catherine Wallace. She comes to the issues globally, abstractly, but with great energy and intensity.

She recently sat in a room of conservationists at an environmental conference in Oregon and heard Dave Brower, the grand old man of the environmental movement, give a speech in which he referred to the problems caused by "those brain-damaged economists." Wallace, who holds two degrees in economics and a position as lecturer in economics at a university in New Zealand, enjoyed the slam against her profession so much she used it to introduce herself before her own talks at the conference. Speaking in a soft New Zealand accent, she says, "I am of that brain-damaged class Dave Brower referred to yesterday. . . ." Of course, the audience loved it. And her.

In the world of environmental activism, Cath Wallace is an exception. She is no less committed than any other activist, but her relationship to her issue—Antarctica—is different, because she has never seen the place. She is passionate on an intellectual level. For ten years, the conservation effort has commanded all of her passion and formidable intellect; it took a toll on her health and her small wealth, and it continues to require her constant attention and fifteen-hour days.

Wallace's personal presentation is professorial. She wears her long, blond hair in a sensible bun on top of her head; she wears no make-up nor does she need it to make her blue eyes sparkle. Though small earrings dangle beside her pale cheeks, the jewelry is neither gold nor silver, both of which she has refused to wear ever since the first time she saw the massive destruction caused by mining those metals. "I think people who wear gold jewelry should also be made to wear the dead fish that result from mining waste in the water," she says. Her clothes are made of natural fibers, sometimes woven in native designs. Sitting in a sidewalk café in Berkeley, California, she fits in so neatly that she disappears in the crowd of the liberal college town.

Wallace came to San Francisco, across the bay from Berkeley, for a few days' vacation after the conference in Oregon, but soon became wrapped up in visiting economists and ecologists. While the warmth of the spring air has enticed other San Francisco tourists into parks or onto the bay, Wallace, instead, got up this morning in her small, economical motel room and rode the subway to Berkeley, where she spent the morning closeted in university rooms discussing environmental economics. She sat with me in a Berkeley café at a table just large enough for two drinks and maybe a plate of pastry, to plead once again for the cause of Antarctica.

As she stirs her glass of iced tea, she says, "We're at a very dangerous point now because people are sick of these negotiations—even among the ranks of the campaigners, certainly among the diplomats, and undoubtedly among the government. It started in 1982, and now lots of people just don't want to know about it. They have other pressing issues. The attitude seems to be: 'Not another word about Antarctica, please.'"

∞

WHAT STARTED IN 1982 felt quite small and lonely to Wallace and four other environmentalists who sat down in a shabby little office of a nonprofit organization in Wellington, New Zealand, and tried to think how to catch the attention of the world. The activists had attended the first Antarctica Treaty minerals negotiating meeting, held in New Zealand, where representatives of various national governments convened to plot the fate of Antarctica.

"According to the diplomats," says Wallace, "this meeting was a timely development of international law to provide control of what might otherwise be an unregulated scramble for minerals. They argued that by imposing rules, they were imposing some environmental protection; and life would be a great deal better, which sounded plausible enough. But it seemed to me that what was really happening was the removal of obstacles to beginning mining. Rather than regulating it, they were actually making it more likely to happen by setting up a legal and political framework of property rights. So while they were sitting down to debate laws that would regulate mining, we developed a counterargument, saying we wanted laws to prohibit mining."

But changing basic assumptions—to mine or not to mine—can only be done before the exploitation starts. Wallace's perspective needed to be heard before it could be heeded, and the minerals meetings at that time were closed to all but the twenty-six Antarctica Treaty nations. Governmentally, the continent of Antarctica is what Wallace refers to as "a bit of a dog's breakfast," or hash. The first flag was raised on aptly named Possession Island in 1884; by 1920, the map of the continent had been divided up like a pie with a multitude of sometimes overlapping claims in wedge shapes with the pointed end at the South Pole. Great Britain, France, Australia, New Zealand, and Norway recognized each other's claims, but Chile and Argentina disputed Britain's claims, as well as each other's. The United States reserved the right to make a claim, and the Soviets seemed to have some undisclosed plans.

For decades, the disputes simmered along harmlessly. No one had much reason to go near the place—or to care if anyone else did. For one thing, it was virtually impossible to get there. For another, the only known resource, a stock of easily accessible seals, had already been slaughtered and their populations virtually extinguished by the end of the nineteenth century. (Once the populations were nearly extinct, laws were passed against hunting, and slowly the population has come back to numbers now thought to be about the same as the original.)

Though whale hunting began about the time seal hunting stopped, it, too, soon put itself nearly out of business; the efficiency of the operation quickly reduced the population of the blue whale—the largest creature ever to have lived on earth—to fewer than one percent of its original numbers. Humpback and fin whale numbers are nearly as low. (In the 1970s, international regulations began to afford some protection to the whales.)

In the second half of this century, the main harvest has been knowledge. There is something in Antarctica for all the sciences: glaciology, geography, geology, volcanology, meteorology, biology, marine biology, and oceanography. By the late 1950s, the world's scientific community had come to value the continent's tremendous importance for research enough to dedicate part of the International Geophysical Year to Antarctica, along with the exploration of outer space—two unknown and inaccessible regions.

The resulting scientific discoveries and spirit of international cooperation brought about the Antarctica Treaty, which the twelve main territorial claimants signed into law in 1961. The treaty articulated significant principles: that the land be used only for peaceful purposes, for scientific cooperation, and for preservation and conservation of living resources. But one of the continent's most fascinating sciences became political science.

"The genius of the treaty," says Wallace, "is that territorial claims are neither recognized nor rejected. What that means is a wonderful phrase the diplomats use, which is that you have a 'constructive ambiguity.' I mean, most people I know try to make things clear. Diplomats try to fudge it. However, if you were one of the countries that laid claims to territories, you could sign this document and not in any way relinquish your claims. If on the other hand, like the United States, you did not recognize claims, you could sign this document and not in any way concede recognition. It's a bit weird, but it does seem to work."

Indeed, the treaty recognizes that the question of territorial sovereignty is insoluble and freezes the status quo. Countries are allowed to become consultative parties to decision-making meetings if they are engaged in "substantial scientific research activity," a mantle that now covers twenty-six countries. In addition, another class of countries, while not engaged in substantial research, are allowed to participate as nonvoting members.

"The countries with scientific expeditions are considered to have sufficient experience to make decisions, which is a bit of a joke," says Wallace, "because the people who go down there and do that work are not the people who make the decisions. It's all the diplomats who make the decisions, and they've never been near the place, a lot of them. So that sort of activities criterion is a bit of a fiction."

∾

"DEPENDING ON ONE'S PERSPECTIVE, this treaty system may be regarded as the last stand of colonialism, an association of the world's largest real-estate operators, a political anachronism whose days are numbered, or an astonishingly successful experiment in international cooperation among antagonistic nations," says Philip W. Quigg in the *Twentieth Century Fund Report, A Pole Apart, The Emerging Issue of Antarctica*.

Whatever the shortcomings of the Antarctica Treaty, it has become an important precedent for treaties governing outer space—particularly the Moon Treaty—and the control of resources there. Whether the moon is made of blue cheese or solid gold, who is going to get it, and how much of it, is being negotiated already.

∽

WHEN BOTH VOTING AND NONVOTING PARTIES WERE INCLUDED, the group of nations negotiating about Antarctica expanded to representatives from thirty-nine countries, with many different interests, which led to cumbersome decisionmaking. This resulted in the formation of a smaller, more powerful group holding special consultative meetings, which are held in the capital of each nation in rotation. The Antarctic governmental system has no executive branch and no bureaucracy, only a legislative branch consisting of the consultative members. Their meetings are closed, and their documents are guarded because they are major, secret international agreements. By 1982, the status of Antarctica had gone from a rather muddy situation to one that was quite clear to a few—but quite obscure to nearly everyone else.

By then, not so coincidentally, a growing interest had developed in Antarctica's resource potential, particularly in its mineral wealth. Substantial deposits of iron and possibly the world's largest reserve of coal had been confirmed. Traces of numerous other minerals including gold, titanium, tin, copper, cobalt, and uranium had been found, although exploitable quantities had not.

Mining hopes ride on the theory of continental drift, which postulates that a supercontinent called Gondwana once comprised what is now known as South America, Africa, Australasia, India, and Antarctica. Over millions of years, subtropical Gondwana broke up like a jigsaw puzzle, and Antarctica, the centerpiece, became isolated and slid down to the South Pole, where it was surrounded by cold, stormy circumpolar currents. Land temperatures dropped dramatically. The forests and animals disappeared, and for the next twenty-five million years, Antarctica lay wrapped in white splendor: a frozen, windswept desert with a climate drier than the Sahara, more than ninety-nine percent of its area covered with ice estimated to average eight thousand feet thick.

Scientific expeditions to Antarctica in the 1980s found fossils and other support for the continental drift theory. At the same time, the fossils heightened interest in mineral deposits because similar geology in once-adjacent South Africa had proved to be among the richest mineral sites in the world. However, Antarctica's ice cap makes exploitation of the minerals too expensive at the present time. The possibilities look a little different for oil and gas, though. The United States discovered offshore oil and gas deposits in 1973, about the time of the sudden rise in price of Middle Eastern oil. Existing technology could be used for exploration, and exploitation would require only a few advances in technology.

The discovery of oil and gas also came at about the time of the first serious suggestion of granting Antarctica and its icy seas the status of a world park. New Zealand announced its support for the world park concept and gained some backing from Chile. However, it was not given much weight within the Antarctica Treaty. Signatories to it were earnestly debating the question of whether mineral exploitation should be allowed and, if so, under what conditions. Gradually, New Zealand's internal political structure changed. The nation backed down on support of the world park idea and became a leading advocate of mining.

This, then, was what Wallace calls the "recipe for almighty conflict and scrap and potshotting at each other." She and her group began to publicize that "recipe" in 1982. The group, Environmental and Conservation Organizations of New Zealand (ECO), is a consortium that runs the gamut from the Royal Society for the Protection of Birds to Greenpeace, and represents a membership that may number as high as half a million—a hefty part of the nation's population of three million.

"We received a message from Friends of the Earth in the United States asking if we would provide logistics for conservationists coming in from the rest of the world to attend the first meeting of the Antarctica Treaty partners on a minerals convention, being held in New Zealand. We agreed to do that, but then most of the conservationists didn't turn up. So we found ourselves becoming having to become involved in this Antarctica debate. The core of the debate is that there are some radical gaps in the Antarctica Treaty, which says nothing about minerals, or really about the environment." The situation intrigued Wallace, in part because she had already dug into local antimining battles.

ᘐ

WALLACE WAS BORN IN HAMILTON, NEW ZEALAND, a busy farming, industrial, and agricultural research center that has been dubbed the "fountain city" because it is rich in parks and gardens. Her parents both held doctorates from Cambridge University, her mother, Charlotte, in marine biology, her father, Lyn, in agricultural science. They had a sheep ranch on the Coromandel Peninsula, near Hamilton. They were only evening and weekend farmers, and home was a huge tent Charlotte had bought at an auction. Charlotte frequently took her five children on rock-pooling expeditions along the coast, where the surf crashed against rocky cliffs and gently lapped sandy crescents. "That's where I got my sense of ecology," says Wallace. "She taught us that you don't pick up a rock and not put it back—because creatures live under it. She taught us that sense of all things being connected."

When Wallace was in her early twenties, she took time out to live on the family farm for five months. She followed that up with nine months as a sheep-shearers' cook in Australia before returning to Victoria University in 1977. Then one day in the summer of 1979, she and her mother were on the farm mustering sheep for the summer shear, when they found red plastic ribbons tied on the plants every ten feet up the creek. Wallace made a few calls and discovered that a mining company was doing some exploration. (The Coromandel Peninsula had been the site of a gold rush in the 1860s.)

Wallace knew nothing about mining or the law, so back in Wellington she began researching her family's rights, as well as the company she would have to confront. She had already cut her activist teeth on civil rights issues and knew that somewhere the company would have a fat flank for her to sink her teeth into. Yet when she asked about the mining company at the New Zealand mines division, they told her these were political questions, and they would not answer them.

One morning while she lay in the bath listening to a BBC news item on a South African gold and diamond king, she learned the local mining company was a subsidiary of the biggest gold mining company in

South Africa. She was incensed that her government not only was dealing with one of the biggest and dirtiest multinational mining companies in the game, but also had refused to divulge that fact to one of its own citizens. She leaped out of the warm bath and into the heat of campaigning.

Tenacious, Wallace earned a victory in the personal fight for her family's farm. But the effort cost her parents more than $25,000; in the process, her doctoral thesis fell by the wayside. "But if you manage to stop one company, it doesn't prevent another trying it afterwards. People will give in rather than face that sort of process. It's entirely unreasonable and unconstitutional to have people put through a palaver like that."

She formed a grass-roots organization of farmers and activists, started a regular newsletter, and campaigned for change. As a result, the Mining Act of 1981 was amended. She was still extending the campaign when the call from Friends of the Earth came into ECO.

ल

The Antarctica Treaty Special Consultative Meetings negotiating the minerals convention were being held in secret. "We had to get a sort of crowbar in a crack in the doors and ram them open." The crowbar that comes most quickly to hand in cracking any secret is, of course, publicity. Environmentalists passed out leaflets, went to the press and the United Nations, staged street theater—did everything they could think of to get the rest of the world to pay attention to the fact that the Antarctica meetings were being held behind closed doors.

The first really big break came in 1983 when Wallace's group, now a dedicated organization called the Antarctic and Southern Ocean Coalition, ASOC, today an international alliance of more than two hundred organizations in thirty-five countries, got its hands on one of the secret negotiating documents, a U.S. position paper, which the activists summarized, critiqued, and published.

To Wallace's amazement, the head of the U.S. delegation denied the contents of the publication. "I mean, I sat in the back of a press conference while he systematically misled the world's press to believe that what we had said was not true." After that, they published the next secret papers they got in full; it was the document the convention's chairman had put together as the basis for negotiation.

In order to protect their source, the conservationists retyped the entire document rather than photocopying it; they had no way of knowing what secret markings on the papers might identify it. "This was before we had computers, and none of us were good typists. But we didn't dare take it out to a proper typist because we didn't want to put anyone else at risk. We suspected this might be considered more than a leak—it might be an international diplomatic incident. So we retyped the entire thing and also analyzed it. We explained it and put a spreadsheet of how it worked in the center, then we published it." To obscure the source even further, they published it simultaneously in Wellington, Sydney, Washington, D.C., and London. "There was a stunned silence for the first twelve hours, and then there were denials. It was indeed an international diplomatic incident. They were furious with us. Absolutely furious."

Sitting in the café in Berkeley, remembering the outrage, Wallace laughs. The incident was the beginning of the end of the environmentalists being shut out, and it was also the beginning of Wallace's rise to international recognition—in certain circles, anyway.

The timing of publication meant the incident hit headlines on the Monday before a major seminar in New Zealand (an Institute of Public Affairs seminar on the minerals regime) that was scheduled to start on Friday. "It did wonders for the seminar participation," Wallace said.

But the environmentalists did not stop there. "Having given it out to the press at the beginning of the week, we then gave it out to the seminar participants. We didn't dare just leave a stack for people to pick up because we knew someone would take them all away. So we had somebody go around the program at the afternoon tea break and distribute one for each seat. I remember standing in the foyer getting my cup of tea and watching the whole tempo of the groups change. It was like sharks going into a feeding frenzy."

New Zealand's top foreign affairs official, Chris Beeby, who chaired the international meetings and was key in negotiating the convention, was scheduled to speak next. "Beeby was white with anger and then red with anger. Giving the papers to the press was one thing. Giving them to a seminar for the public was quite another." Later, Wallace was called before the New Zealand environment commissioner, who "tried to do the schoolmaster-to-naughty-schoolgirl thing." Though Wallace has an inbred courtesy, the kind that might be mistaken for weakness, she stood her ground. "I was too angry, too conscious of what the stakes were, and too aware of what had to be done." In addition to being well bred, she says, "One of the heritages I've got is that sense you can muck around in the political process and get change." Her English forebears campaigned for national parks, fought beside the suffragettes, helped to establish the British Labour Party, and aided the French resistance.

The environmentalists continued campaigning, leaking document after document. "Mostly the papers came to us in the proverbial brown envelopes. Sometimes we didn't even know where they came from; sometimes we did. Sometimes the sources were people connected with the negotiations; sometimes they were officials who were consulted about it back home. And we got quite good at actually picking up documents ourselves along the way, too.

"Then new countries began to come in who didn't have the background about what was going on. You'd find these new people at the meetings would be totally perplexed by these very complex, very hard-to-grasp terms that carried all sorts of negotiating history with them. So some of them—for instance, the Chinese—we were briefing before they got into the negotiating room. The environmentalists were the ones who were supplying other countries, the media, and the public with accounts and analysis of what was happening. We became sort of established as the only people who would talk about what was going on.

"As we took on that role, the new players would turn to us and work with us. And yet the environmentalists weren't allowed in the negotiating rooms. The diplomats would come out of the meeting and ask, 'Hey, what do you think about this?' and we'd sit there and look at the papers, which our government said we were not allowed to see. Sometimes they'd give us copies. And people would leave things lying around. And those got published."

Right before the most recent meetings, the environmentalists received a document sent from Americans who obtained it through the Freedom of Information Act. "Then I received two phone calls, one from Reuters and another from the Malaysian embassy, both saying,

'We want the documents for this meeting, and Chris Beeby said as chairman he can't release them to us because we're outside the negotiation, but he did say that you might have them.' It was quite hilarious. Here we were fighting Beeby tooth and nails. . . . But we've become so established, we're part of the furniture." She laughs. "He's actually a nice guy and quite intelligent, and even though he totally disapproves of what we're doing, he does at least have a sense of humor."

&

IN THE EARLY DAYS, gaining access to the diplomats in person required equal amounts of skill and cunning, as well as a strong dose of brash behavior. The environmentalists followed the meetings from one capital of each participating nation to the next. ASOC would rent an office that looked out over the intersection next to the meeting building, so the environmentalists could lean out the window and see when the coffee and lunch breaks occurred. Then they would run after the delegates. Gradually, the delegates from Germany, Chile, Argentina, and Uruguay, among others, began letting the environmentalists into the meeting building to have morning and afternoon coffee with the officials. "We couldn't get into the negotiating room, but at least when they'd come out fresh from the discussion—there we were."

Wallace says that sort of lobbying was the hardest part of the work for her instinctively gentle nature. "We used to just gate-crash these receptions. We would find out when they were and just turn up. Sometimes they actually turned us away. More often, they could see we were going to create an even bigger fuss if they didn't let us in, so they would. But diplomats really know how to make people feel unwanted. There were horrible, awkward social situations; but we had to impose ourselves. And I'm actually quite shy, and I've got a poor memory for names and faces. I'm not a small-talker at all." Wallace drops her head in her hands as she relives some of those moments. For her, it is easier to work nights, days, and weekends, killer hours of overtime on top of her full-time job. It is easier to detect and expose deception and corruption; it is easier to spend most of her own small income traveling the globe speaking to large groups of strangers in strange lands—anything is easier than walking uninvited into a cocktail party and try to make conversation. She is more adept at defending a whole icy continent than breaking the ice at a reception.

"I remember saying to myself, 'I loathe this. I hate it. It's just horrible.'" She shakes her head and laughs at her own excruciating discomfort.

"But I never thought of giving up. Certainly one has bleak moments, no doubt about it. But it helped to have the solidarity of other people. And there's the sense that this is an irreversible issue. If you don't win this, then the whole continent is at risk, which makes your own personal concerns seem relatively minor. With the Antarctic, there's no domestic constituency of people, no people who are indigenous to the continent. It's something that all of us on this planet have to look after."

Gradually, the environmentalists were allowed to distribute their journal to the delegates at the meetings, then they were given identity tags as lobbyists. Eventually the environmentalists were granted observer status at the standard treaty meetings and at the associated meetings. "Nonetheless, for a long time the treaty nations ignored what we were saying. They wrote us off as being funny socialist greenies, which we're not. They thought we were running a simple-minded anticapitalist line, and they didn't really listen. For years, the diplomats have said how much they would like to be idealists like us, but they have to be realists. What they mean is that they'll take more notice of a few politicians than they do of the actual physical reality—that you can't take oil tankers into an environment like that without an accident. Oil and ice don't mix."

◌

"WHILE SHOWING PROPER RESPECT for conservationists in public, officials involved in Antarctic affairs in the United States and Britain particularly are in a state of more or less perpetual irritation with the environmentalists for what is often seen as their demand for absolutes, their unwillingness or inability to comprehend the reality of international politics and the processes of negotiation among sovereign states. And inevitably, for every well-informed conservationist, there are ten whose ignorance can confound issues. Also inevitably, the sin-glemindedness of conservationists, even when they are knowledge-able, is bound to grate on those who must reconcile varied domestic and foreign interests," wrote Philip W. Quigg in the *Twentieth Century Fund Report, A Pole Apart, The Emerging Issue of Antarctica.*

∿

PRACTICALLY SPEAKING, Antarctica is a continent composed of a sin-gle substance: ice. Antarctica is the coldest (average mean temperatures between -58°F and -76°F), driest (yet it is the world's greatest storehouse of fresh water), windiest (winds have been clocked up to 200 m.p.h., and 80-m.p.h. gales can blow for two days without letup) continent on earth. For six months of the year, the continent lies in darkness. Great cyclonic storms circle Antarctica in perennial procession, mak-ing for the roughest seas in the world, seas strewn with dangerous icebergs.

"However," says Wallace, "it has only been considered inhos-pitable since we arrived there." It is not a hostile place to be if you are a penguin occupying one of the nesting areas that penguins have been using for thousands of years. Everything that lives there naturally—seals, penguins, skuas, scant mosses, lichens, algae, and ice fish—have been equipped by nature to survive. As Wallace says, "The southern ocean is a very sensible place to be if you are a whale or one of the highly spe-cialized creatures that evolved to be there. It is a very silly place to be if you're an oil rigger."

Obviously, the climatic conditions increase the possibility of acci-dents and oil pollution either from offshore wells, or, more likely, from tankers. The icebergs plow along like big ships themselves—but ships driven by unseen, deep currents with enormous momentum. Were one of these bergs on a collision course with an oil tanker, it would be virtually impossible to stop the berg, or for the tanker to change course in time to avoid it. Leaks would be extremely difficult to plug under conditions nearly as harsh as outer space. Blizzards come up fast, swirling ice with the force of a sandblaster, knocking the heaviest equipment rolling, and pulling gear right out of hands that, even in the warmest gloves, soon become too cold to move. From March to

November, sea ice effectively isolates the continent from access by ship, even as darkness falls. If an accident were to occur at that time, nothing could be done for at least six months, while the oil steadily seeped, leaked, or gushed out.

Counterpoised against the harshness of the climate is the fragility of the ecosystem. The waters surrounding Antarctica are the world's richest and liveliest, and the marine life depends on a factor that has been taken for granted for millions of years: the cleanliness of its sea. "Studies persistently report that the animals worst affected by oil spills are those which, like seabirds, regularly move in and out of the water. Penguin and seal colonies would be extremely sensitive to even a small, isolated spill," according to Barney Brewster in *Antarctica: Wilderness at Risk*.

The impact of an oil spill would be devastating and prolonged in the extremely cold temperatures. Oil could take as long as fifty years to degrade. More toxic substances would take longer still to evaporate. Even without an environmental disaster, routine oil extraction would involve steady contamination by pollutants that are harmful to marine life in even very high dilutions. Contaminants frozen into sea ice would gradually work their way out for years and years. Damage to the nutrient-rich seas that flow northward could have an adverse effect on the organic life in other oceans.

Offshore oil exploitation would also require substantial onshore facilities, which would be in direct competition with wildlife for the limited amount of snow-free land available and would produce additional environmental disturbance to the region. The effect of seismic surveying could disrupt whale feeding and reproductive behavior and could also affect seals, fish, and other marine organisms.

By 1988, the Australians became concerned that if there were an oil or mining disaster, they would be left with the cost of cleaning up even though they had not benefited from the mining. Soon, France also began to have doubts about the wisdom of mining and oil drilling in Antarctica, thanks in large part to a vigorous antimining campaign led by Jacques Cousteau. The prime minister announced that France would not sign the minerals convention and instead supported permanent protection of the Antarctic environment. Australia quickly announced the same intent. Because those two countries had veto power, their refusal meant the convention had run aground.

∾

THE PRO-MINING COUNTRIES, including New Zealand, were furious. New Zealand's Labour Government issued statements that Wallace and other environmentalists exposed as ambiguous and contradictory. "I became the hatchet woman of the New Zealand environmental scene. I was the one who took the flak and delivered the flak.

"There's a tension between campaigning and being an academic. There's a lot of pressure not to be out there on the radio all the time. While it's tolerated, it's also regarded as not quite appropriate. On one occasion, after we'd put out something about one of the statements, the prime minister came on the morning radio saying 'Cath Wallace is putting this information around that's misinformed, malicious, and mischievous.' Meanwhile, I had to go back to the university and see all those colleagues who heartily disapproved of what I was doing.

"I was the one who went in there and scrapped with the officials, did the really hard talking. Once, after the prime minister had said he was in favor of a permanent ban, the officials said, 'That was just the prime minister saying that.' In other words, they were refusing to talk about implementing the prime minister's announced policy. So we'd have these incredible standoffs. And it was an election year. The members of Parliament and party people would get really angry at me. There was a lot of personal anger and hate directed toward me. And it was pretty tough. You had to really hone your nerve and just keep on pushing and never give in to this personal anger and stuff. But you just can't take all that sort of personal shit without having it affect you to some extent."

She confronted the prime minister with the fact that while he was saying one thing about mining and environmental protection of Antarctica, his officials were saying another. He fumed and was affronted at the very thought of officials undermining him. "Mr. Prime Minister," Wallace said, staring him down, "that is the case." She laid out the examples.

Finally, on a late-night television news bulletin, the prime minister announced government support for permanent protection of the Antarctic.

And just as the convention was running aground in Antarctica, the *Exxon Valdez* ran aground in Alaska, pouring millions of gallons of crude oil over the coastline, demonstrating in the most tragic way that oil and ice do not mix.

∞

"I'VE HAD TO FIT CAMPAIGNING in amongst all my other real work, with endless skimping on it—such as not doing as much publishing as I should. At times I've taken a couple of weeks off to go to the other side of the world to be a lobbyist. It has meant not having much of a social life, skimping on relationships with friends and family, skimping on the sorts of relaxation that you normally have. I come home from a day at the university and, if I'm not completely wiped out, go straight into trying to do this environmental stuff."

In the United States, environmental work supplies a few low-paying jobs. In New Zealand, it is all volunteer effort. In fact, it costs Wallace because many of the expenses, such as "phone calls around the world at one hundred dollars a whack" come out of her own pocket.

In 1986, Wallace began to feel terribly tired and exhausted. Thinking she might just need a break, she went on a hiking trip in the Nelson Lakes. "On the sixth day I felt absolutely terrible and eventually crawled my way out to discover I had glandular fever. It just wiped me out. I gave up a lot of things in 1986, but not the Antarctic. It seemed to me that I just couldn't give that one up. That was just too important to me. I knew that we were making progress, and knew we had to keep the impetus going.

"I didn't realize, actually, how bad it was going to be when I got this damned disease. I mean, they said you need a bit more rest. So I sort of said to myself, 'I'll go to bed an hour earlier.' Actually, I woke up some days, and by the time I'd taken a shower, I was so wiped out I had to go back to bed. But there were some of these diplomatic meetings going on, so I went. I would sort of just go out to a reception or something and then fall back into bed, then crawl out to go to the next thing.

"The funny thing is it completely blows the brain cells. All your con-
nectors and certainly your short-term memory just get really blown.
I had that for about four months. It was a really terrible time, and there
were some pretty hairy moments when I'd be really scrambled in the
brains and someone like the Secretary for the Environment was ringing me up. I remember once lying there in bed trying to have a rational conversation."

Typically, Wallace laughs at herself as she tells a story. But after three
years of such activity, she admits her doctor "got very cross with me.
He said I had made it go on much too long by doing all that."

∾

IN 1991, when Wallace was awarded the Goldman Environmental
Prize, worth NZ$100,000, her colleagues at Victoria University seemed
truly delighted, though one of them was heard to say: "Fancy giving
her all that money for being such a nuisance all these years!"

Wallace was at first reluctant to make the trip to the United States
to receive the award; she would have to miss an important meeting on
the Antarctic in Madrid, and besides, she "didn't have any respectable
clothes." But in the end she realized that the enormous press coverage
offered her an even more important prize: the opportunity to further
expose the Antarctic issues, particularly to people in the United States.

∾

MEANWHILE, the United States and Britain caught a new wave of inspiration and proposed a moratorium on mining rather than a ban, with
a convention to review the moratorium at the end. And in October
1991, the treaty countries agreed to a Protocol on Environmental
Protection that establishes a ban on mining for fifty years unless all twenty-six voting members of the treaty agree to lift it. After fifty years, any
one of the voting members can request a review conference on the
ban. At the end of the review, the ban can be lifted only by agreement
of seventy-five percent of the voting countries. In diplomatic circles, the
document is considered to be a masterly compromise between the
countries that support a permanent ban and those that oppose it.
Wallace, however, considers it a pretty coarse sort of agreement.

She points out that the moratorium would in fact be relatively easy to remove, compared to a permanent ban. Worse, though, the ban does not take effect unless and until the domestic governments of all twenty-six nations ratify it, which could take years. "So far, all those signatures do is signal intent to put into domestic legislation the substance of the Environmental Protocol. Only when all twenty-six treaty countries have done that, does the protocol take effect. Until then, we've got no ban at all. There are a multitude of international agreements that have never gotten past the signature stage and been ratified. The Environmental Protocol is extremely vulnerable. It could easily go by the wayside, if we don't keep the pressure up to really make countries ratify it by making it domestic law, quickly. If even one of the twenty-six countries decides that other things on their agenda are more important, the protocol doesn't happen."

Within the United States, for example, there has been a history of policy positions formulated in liberal internationalist terms being gradually eroded as the pressure of special interests takes hold. Wallace believes the ideal solution to the situation is still not really being considered. She believes in the concept of creating an Antarctica Treaty Park with no mining and no disturbance of the sovereignty claims, with environmental controls on science, tourism, and other human activities, and with administration by the treaty nations.

This scenario is actually pretty much the way things have stood since 1961, long before the first Antarctica Treaty minerals convention meetings began. The world park concept would merely strengthen the aims set forth in the original Antarctica Treaty. Specifically, that document prohibits activities that might endanger peace, and Wallace believes that the treaty states should acknowledge that their own attempts to take possession of Antarctic resources have already endangered peace in the region by introducing rivalry for resources where sharing of data once prevailed.

∾

EVERY QUESTION THAT INVOLVES ENERGY SUPPLY inevitably ends up with the same answer: Conservation is by far the cheapest and safest source of energy. Wallace's arguments stress the idea that the current huge demand for fossil fuel is not an unchangeable fact of life. The demand for oil is the result of poor conservation. "Ultimately, if we don't find ways of limiting our demand and creating better fuel efficiency—dealing with the imbalance between demand and supply by addressing the demand side instead of the supply side—people will behave like junkies, drilling and digging until we're absolutely history anyway." In short, we are at the end of the earth—literally—looking for more supplies, when what we should be doing is first limiting our demands, particularly in the United States, where energy use per capita is 6.4 times the average in the world, and sixty-three times greater than in low-income countries.

"I do think there is enormous scope for the United States to diminish your use of energy without substantially diminishing your standard of living," Wallace says. From the sidewalk café table, she gestures toward the street clogged with cars and trucks. The roar of their large engines has been constantly interrupting our conversation. "You may, of course, consider some reduction in your standard of living as well," she adds with a smile. "But before you have to do that, you can at least look to major efficiency gains. I say this coming from New Zealand, a country that has also been profligate in our use of energy. I believe there is substantial scope for both the United States and New Zealand to cut back on energy use. But the difference between the U.S. energy fleet and the vehicle fleets in New Zealand, or Europe, or wherever you care to mention, is just so enormous. The United States owns thirty-five percent of the world vehicle fleet. If the United States would, just for once, get real about the costs of the energy it's using, then you could basically solve the whole problem." As she says it, a car engine drowns out her words.

Wallace proposes a number of strategies for influencing demand. Some of them are regulation based, and some of them are market based. "We should certainly be looking to develop prices that actually reflect the true environmental costs and benefits. And that means that the United States must seriously join the move of other countries and start adding into energy prices the cost of damage to the environment. Regulation might include greenhouse gas law permits, with allocations to various nations of the world on the basis that everyone has a right to a clean and intact environment."

The current interest in the greenhouse effect centers around rising levels of carbon dioxide gas, owing to the burning of fossil fuels and the destruction of forests. There is evidence to suggest that changes in carbon dioxide levels in the past could have contributed to the ice ages. Antarctica provides a crucial laboratory for studying such effects, by measuring the amounts of the gas in air bubbles contained in the ice. With a depth of eight thousand feet of ice, representing millions of years, a wealth of information is preserved in Antarctica. Remote from civilization and its industrial and urban pollution, Antarctica is an ideal baseline from which to measure changes in the world's atmosphere and environment.

ༀ

ANOTHER CRUCIAL SCIENTIFIC UNDERTAKING in Antarctica is the study of the ozone hole. The ozone layer in the atmosphere shields life on earth from the damaging effects of ultraviolet radiation. Increased ultraviolet radiation not only harms humans and other animals, but also has far-reaching effects on all of the environment, right down to the plankton, the primary source of production in the food chain of all the oceans. "Of course, we don't completely understand all the effects of the interruption, decay, and degradation of our biophysical systems," says Wallace. "But we do know that the exchange systems between the atmosphere and the oceans is essential for all of us, humans and non-humans. And we do know that these changes seem to be irreversible."

Depletion of the ozone layer was first noticed in an Antarctic survey in 1981 and later confirmed by satellite observations. Since then, the size of the hole has steadily increased at an alarming rate. It is widely accepted that the increase is mainly due to the presence of chemicals commercially used as coolants in refrigerators and air conditioners, as propellant in aerosol containers, and as a blowing agent in the manufacture of foam.

∾

MANY NATIONS ARE EAGER to reap the harvest of Antarctica's ecosystems. Krill, the foundation species for all of Antarctica's wildlife, is their primary target. Krill is a shrimplike crustacean about three inches long, with high protein value. Harvesting krill means competing with all of Antarctica's wildlife—including the great whales, already near extinction.

Yet some scientists and fishing experts believe krill could be one of the world's largest untapped food resources. "One of the things that people throw at you is, 'How can you rich, Western, affluent, middle-class New Zealanders go around saying let's not use these resources when there's that whole Third World starving?' I was quite intimidated by that argument until I went to a grass-roots conference in Tunisia in 1988. A lot of black Africans there were working at absolutely rock-bottom, village level with societies torn apart by armed conflict and total collapse of their ecosystems and the economic structures that depended on them. When I talked to that group about Antarctica they were more supportive than anyone. They understood in a way that I had not, until then, that the poor were not going to benefit from Antarctic exploration." The spoils will go directly to the nations with the most advanced technology: the industrial nations.

It is difficult to predict how quickly the new Antarctic krill fishery could develop, but a possibility of rapid buildup exists. Meanwhile, there are proposals for hunting penguins, and some companies seem interested in killing seals again.

∾

WALLACE HAS FINISHED HER TEA and she looks forward to using the few minutes left in the afternoon to visit the art museum next door. Her plane for the long trip back to New Zealand leaves early the next morning.

"It very important to take the campaigns to the public. Ultimately, when people are properly informed, they will make the right choices. Not everyone, of course, but enough people, in a democracy, to come out with the right options.

"Because, all else aside, Antarctica is enormously important as a symbol that there is one place we will not just go rape and pillage. Preserving it as a wilderness is a sign that there's a little bit of the globe that we'll leave to itself. I simply believe that nature does have rights and that humanity has got some obligation to be a good neighbor on the planet. I really reject the idea that the whole planet is put here for us to use. But I do have quite strong faith in the general populace. When things are explained to them, they really do make the hard decisions."

∾

For more information, contact Catherine Wallace, ECO, P.O. Box 11-057, Wellington, New Zealand, or Antarctica Project, 707 D Street SE, Washington, D.C. 20003.

Jeton Anjain

Making Waves

JETON ANJAIN

Marshall Islands

 THE SOUND OF ROLLING WAVES is heard all over the island. Villagers rise with the sun and wash their faces with rainwater stored in a tank. Columns of smoke start to plume from each little house, where villagers burn coconut shells to cook breakfast. By the time the rainwater in the kettle boils, glimmering sunshine bathes the island. The village scene is dominated by a white church with blue and pink trim.

A calm turquoise lagoon teems with reef life. Men keep their outrigger canoes ready to go fishing at a moment's notice. The women fish from shore, tying coconut leaves in a long line to make a kind of net.

The island (and village) of Rongelap, is the southernmost and largest village on a string of thirty-six coral islands that ring the lagoon, which is roughly one hundred twenty miles in diameter. The islanders canoe to one of the nearby islands to catch turtles, to another island to catch crabs, and to yet another island to pick coconuts. They also eat pandanus, breadfruit, bananas, papayas, fish, and clams. Although a limited diet, it is well balanced and nutritious. Coconut, for example, in various stages of its growth, contains a complete assortment of vitamins; it is a complete food.

The people say, "Rongelap means everything to us." One of their hymns begins, "I love my home island, where I was born / I will never leave it / This is my home, my only home / And it is better that I die on it." In their native language, there is no word for "enemy."

On the morning of March 1, 1954, many villagers were away. Some had gone fishing; some were at school on other islands, and others were just elsewhere. Eighty-two people were in the village when, according to John Anjain, the mayor at the time, two suns rose. "I was awake and drinking coffee. I thought I saw what appeared to be the sunrise, but it was in the west. It was truly beautiful, with many colors—red, green and yellow—and I was surprised. A little while later, the sun rose in the east. Then, some time later, something like smoke filled the entire sky, and shortly after that, a strong, warm wind—almost a typhoon—swept across Rongelap." This report was published in *Day of Two Suns*, by Jane Dibblin.

The schoolteacher, who shared coffee with the mayor that morning, noted: "The heat was threatening. It stung and burned our exposed skins. I could see some signs of movement as everyone withdrew from the terrible heat." Then came "a tornado-powered wind sweeping through our land, twisting coconut trees, uprooting bushes, smashing windows, doors, and overturning one house. . . . Thatched roofs of most houses were blown out." This report was published in *Eyes of Fire, The Last Voyage of the Rainbow Warrior*, by David Robie.

Several hours later, powder began to fall on Rongelap.

∾

THE ISLANDS IN THE CENTER OF THE PACIFIC OCEAN were formed millions of years ago by volcanoes erupting from the sea bed. The volcanoes peaked above the ocean's waves, and coral began to grow around them. Though the volcanoes slowly sank back into the ocean, new coral grew on the older coral, creating a reef that collected broken coral, which, pulverized by the sea, became an island of sand. A string of islands surrounding a central lagoon where a volcano peak has been is called an atoll.

Rongelap is one of these, part of the archipelago of the Marshall Islands that includes twenty-nine atolls and five single islands, scattered over nearly a half-million square miles of sea. In the middle of the Pacific, in the Tropic of Cancer, every island that is blessed with water, coconut trees, and a large, quiet lagoon is inhabited. The ancestors of the Rongelap people are said to have come from Southeast Asia, or perhaps from southern Pacific islands, thousands of years ago. They traveled by canoe, using the moon and the stars to navigate in the unknown sea.

On their islands, they began drawing detailed maps of the wave patterns around them. The navigators memorized the patterns, and today's inhabitants can rely on feeling the waves against the sides of the boat to know exactly where they are. It is a precise system.

Not much is known about the the Marshall Islands before the Spanish arrived with Magellan in 1520. Our written history charts colonial powers like tides, bringing trade, missionaries, and disease (syphilis and smallpox were particularly deadly to the islanders). Germany bought the Marshall Islands from Spain in 1885. The Germans were driven out by the Japanese in 1914. The United States took the islands from the Japanese in 1944, after more than two years of some of the bloodiest battles in the Pacific during World War II.

As a result, each generation of the Marshall Islanders, who speak ten different native tongues, speaks a different second language. Great-grandparents speak German, grandparents speak Japanese, and parents speak English. Now, some children do not learn the native languages.

In 1947, the United States and the United Nations signed a trusteeship agreement for the Marshall Islands, along with some twenty-two hundred other small islands and atolls with a total land area of less than fifteen hundred square miles and a population of seventy-six thousand—the area is called Micronesia. The United States promised to protect the health of the inhabitants, to guard against loss of land and resources, and to promote economic advancement and self-sufficiency. In return, the mandate of the trust allowed the United States to "fortify" the islands. In other words, the United Nations gave the United States approval to annex the islands for military purposes.

The trust was a handy piece of paper for the government to carry in its back pocket, but in fact, a year earlier the United States had already selected Bikini, one of the northernmost atolls in the Marshalls, as the site for a series of atomic tests and had removed the 167 islanders. The islanders were small, brown people who wore few clothes and fewer shoes. "Primitive they are," said an article in the *New York Times*. "But they love one another and the American visitors who took their home." The article was titled "The Strange People from Bikini." Atomic testing began right away. One particular test stood out. It tested more than atomic theory or military might; it has come to test the entire system of the U.S. government.

On March 1, 1954, during the height of the Cold War, the United States exploded an H-bomb called Bravo, on Bikini. The bomb was equivalent to seventeen megatons of TNT. It was one thousand three hundred times more destructive than the bomb dropped on Hiroshima and was specifically designed to create a vast amount of lethal fallout. The military knew that morning that the wind was blowing in the direction of Rongelap.

∾

"IN THE AFTERNOON something began falling from the sky upon our island," says John Anjain. "It looked like ash from a fire. It fell on me, it fell on my wife, it fell on our infant son. It fell on the trees and on the roofs of our houses. It fell on the reef and into the lagoon.

"We were very curious about this ash falling from the sky. Some people put it in their mouths and tasted it. One man rubbed it into his eye to see if it would cure an old ailment. People walked in it, and children played with it." The white powder continued to fall until late afternoon, and it piled up in a shallow drift.

Later in the afternoon, a seaplane landed, and American soldiers came to the island. They looked around. They glanced into the tanks of rainwater. They said, "Don't drink the water," and without saying much else, they left.

But the islanders had already drunk the water. That night, children cried and screamed, complaining of body aches. They and the grownups vomited and had diarrhea. Soon they were too weak to move. On the evening of the second day, a seaplane arrived with two men who brought some strange machines. They stayed only about twenty minutes, and they took some readings of water catchments and soil, then took off again. "They really did not tell us very much." The machines were Geiger counters checking for radiation.

On the third day, an American destroyer made its way through Rongelap's calm, blue lagoon and headed toward the village. Through an interpreter, the villagers were told that they were to move immediately. They were not to take anything at all other than the clothes they were wearing. The military put the villagers on the destroyer and sailed away. On board, the villagers were told to throw away their clothes; they were given bathing suits or underwear to put on. At the U.S. military base on Kwajalein Island, the Rongelapese joined other Marshall Islanders who had been exposed. Nine out of ten of the Rongelapese had severe burns. In *Day of Two Sons* by Jane Dibblin, one man reported, "My fingernails came off and my fingers bled. We all had burns on our ears, shoulders, necks, and feet." Their hair was falling out.

Tests showed that sixty-four of the eighty-two people who had been on the island were exposed to amounts of radiation equivalent to more than half of a lethal dose. The exposure included deeply penetrating whole-body gamma irradiation, internal radiation emitters inhaled or swallowed, and direct radiation from radioactive debris on the body.

On March 11, the Atomic Energy Commission made this public statement: "During the course of a routine atomic test in the Marshall Islands, the United States personnel and 236 residents were transported from neighboring atolls to Kwajalein Island according to plan as precautionary measures. These individuals were unexpectedly exposed to some radioactivity. There were no burns. All were reported well. After the completion of the atomic tests, the natives will be returned to their homes."

Atomic tests continued on Bikini and another atoll for four more years, during which time the natives were homeless. Radioactive material was scattered into the atmosphere on each occasion, adding to the contamination of Rongelap and the rest of the area. In all, a total of sixty-six nuclear tests occurred in the Marshall Islands between 1946 and 1958 in the Cold War race for weapons superiority.

During that period, the military moved the Rongelapese from place to place several times. The people didn't really know what was happening or why; no one bothered to explain much to them. The only surety in their lives was the annual visit from military doctors who studied them and made lots of notes but did not offer any treatment.

Jeton Anjain, the younger brother of the mayor, believes the military deliberately allowed the people of Rongelap to be exposed to the fallout of Bravo so it could study the effects of radiation. It seems possible, as we now know that at about the same time the Pentagon used U.S. citizens for experiments they were told were medical treatments. Doctors irradiated the testicles of healthy prisoners and poor people, mostly African-Americans. The doctors have testified that the experiments occurred in the interest of national defense. If such experiments had been conducted in a Nazi concentration camp, we would have called them war crimes and prosecuted the experimenters.

A leading Atomic Energy Commission scientist suggested in 1956 that the people of Rongelap should be returned home to test the human uptake of radiation in a contaminated environment. He noted that the people in the northern Marshall Islands provided a unique research opportunity because the area "is by far one of the most contaminated areas in the world," and, "while it is true that these people do not live, I would say, the way Westerners do, as civilized people, it is nevertheless true that they are more like us than the mice." A newsreel called the people "simple savages."

∞

MEANWHILE, ON THE STREETS OF NEW YORK CITY, Tokyo, London, and other cities and small towns all over the world, the Bravo test sparked protests against atmospheric nuclear weapons testing. "Ban the Bomb!" picketers shouted. Mothers stood on street corners collecting signatures to appeal for an end to nuclear experiments. The public outcry included noted scientists. The antinuclear movement began.

The U.S. government's initial response was to try to minimize the health risks of fallout caused by weapons testing. Partly in response to this pressure, the military in 1957 told the Rongelapese they could go home.

When they returned to Rongelap, it looked much the same as when they left it. The only noticeable difference was that the houses the military had built for them were on stilts. The Rongelapese suspected that it was to keep them away from what they called the "poison" (radiation) on the ground. But, happy to be home again, they quickly returned to their old life. About two hundred people who had been away from Rongelap at the time of the fallout returned as well. One of these was Jeton Anjain. He had left Rongelap in 1949 for higher education. After schooling in Guam and the Fiji islands, he obtained his dental degree in 1954. He returned in 1957, working for the government of the Marshall Islands, and began spending about three months a year on Rongelap.

Village life resumed its ancient pattern. The men caught fish, and the women took care of their daily chores. The military told them it was safe to eat anything they wanted except the coconut crabs. Yet when they went to pick food, they were surprised to find much of it had changed color. The arrowroot now burned their mouths.

They were visited regularly by a large, white ship that brought doctors. A jeep would cruise around the atoll, collecting people for examination. The Rongelapese complained of diseases and ailments they had not known before the fallout: stillborn babies, miscarriages, retarded growth of children, and many cases of thyroid abnormality. The doctors collected specimens of blood and urine but treated no one.

Atmospheric nuclear testing in the Pacific ended in 1958. Since then, the United States and Britain have carried out hundreds of underground nuclear explosions in the Nevada desert. The very next year, though, the United States began to test the next generation of weapons, the missiles that carry the nuclear explosives to their target. The tests were fired from California to the islands and lagoon of Kwajalein atoll. Nearly all long-range missiles, from the MX to the Minuteman, have been tested on Kwajalein. The military base there grew more important.

At the same time, a strong feeling against colonialism was sweeping the world: in Africa, the French and British were granting independence to former colonies at such a rate that it appeared the United States would soon be the only nation left administering a trust territory. And the quality of that administration was being questioned. In 1960, an official U.N. visit to the Marshall Islands reported a deplorable lack of economic development in the U.S. Trust Territory.

President Kennedy foresaw a problem if the United States did not clean up its act in Micronesia, but he was also determined to maintain the convenient military testing ground. Testing sites had only gotten harder to find as the antinuclear movement managed to release more and more information to the American public about the effects of fallout. Kennedy wanted to move Micronesia into "a permanent relationship with the United States within our political framework," according to Jane Dibblin in *Day of Two Suns*. After some study, in 1963 he began implementing a plan to allow the people of Micronesia to vote and make "an informed and free choice" about their future political relationship with the United States. The plan was designed to ensure "a favorable vote" and involved a quick infusion of cash and an election while the cash was still flowing. After that, the area would be reopened to Japanese investment and U.S. subsidies would be cut off. Toward that end, in 1963, economic aid doubled to $15 million.

In addition to cash, to encourage loyalties to the United States, Micronesian leaders and students would be given scholarships to U.S. schools, and Peace Corps volunteers would be sent to the Pacific. Kennedy had established the Peace Corps in 1961 to provide interested countries with trained personnel. The goal was to encourage a better understanding of Americans and to encourage a better understanding of other people by Americans—all worthy causes. Now, the Peace Corps was sent to Micronesia in droves. At one point, the ratio of Peace Corps volunteers to Micronesians was nearly one per hundred. The Peace Corps's intent in Micronesia was a little different than in other host countries. The volunteers were to foster favorable political attitudes toward the United States and to report on all activities and attitudes that might bear on the outcome of an election.

However, what some of the Peace Corps volunteers saw and reported on—to the public—was U.S. government abuses of the Micronesians. Some Peace Corps volunteers used their skills as lawyers, educators, and community activists to assist the Micronesians in asserting their rights.

U.S. aid continued to mount: $30 million in 1969.

&

THE GOVERNMENT IN THE MARSHALL ISLANDS is a combination of British and American models grafted onto an old society. Many of the elected leaders are former royalty in flower-print shirts. The people are still loyal to old ties and traditions. For example, President Amata Kabua, is also an *iroijlaplap*—a king of kings. By virtue of wealth, class, position in industry and commerce, confirmed by a plebiscite, his authority is unshakable. The traditional social bonds of the society hold him strongly in place.

The Marshall Islands' Parliament, the Nitijela, however, is more open to new leadership. On Rongelap, in 1969, the people turned to the mayor's younger brother, Jeton Anjain, to represent them as a senator in Parliament. Jeton Anjain was a dentist, and they thought his training and education would help them make a case about all the strange illnesses and birth defects they were experiencing. "Of course, I didn't understand about the weapons," Anjain says. "I didn't even know what radiation was. I started to learn. I started to read reports."

Anjain is the kind of person who is sensitive to anything that will contribute to his goal, and he sees people in terms of what they can do to help a project. As the new senator, he was soon in touch with Peace Corps volunteers and former volunteers who were forming organizations to support radiation survivors. "I started asking questions of some American friends of mine: What is radiation, and why are they monitoring the health of my people? . . . I started to ask: the United States is a very big country, how come they don't do their testing over there?

"And they said: 'Because they don't want to hurt their own people. That's why the Marshall Islands was selected. Because there are fewer people, and they say fewer things. If we hurt these people, who cares? They won't tell the world what we are doing.'"

From 1969 to 1975, the United States concentrated on getting a favorable vote in Micronesia. The U.S. withdrawal from Vietnam increased the need for secure bases in the Pacific. However, under pressure to decide, the various groups within Micronesia began to splinter. The Marshall Islands, which had the highest yield of copra (dried coconut, valuable for its oil), as well as the largest tax and wage revenue from the military base on Kwajalein, was reluctant to share its wealth. The Parliament decided to split off and established the Republic of the Marshall Islands. Soon, Micronesia consisted of three separate nations. "I now realize," Anjain says, "that allowing Micronesia to split up has made us much weaker when it comes to negotiating with the United States."

By then Anjain had made many long plane flights to Washington, D.C., to plead the case of the people of Rongelap. He had climbed the long steps of Capitol Hill many times. He learned about lobbyists and consultants; he carefully watched the successful leaders on the hill and took on the image, the mannerisms, and the presentation style necessary to be taken seriously and to get his message across. Now, he wore business suits.

In 1977, Anjain was able to secure some congressional compensation for radiation survivors. He used part of the compensation money to employ lawyers, scientists, lobbyists, and political consultants in Washington, D.C. He said, "I'm not very popular with my people because of that money. They think I'm wasting their money. They wanted to spend it on themselves." But Anjain was by then fully committed to his cause. Nothing and no one was going to stop him—even the people he was fighting to protect.

∽

BY 1982, the Atomic Energy Commission had changed its name to the more socially acceptable U.S. Department of Energy. The department had published a study conducted four years earlier, which ranked the different Marshall Islands according to their radioactivity. It showed that some inhabited parts of Rongelap were still as "hot" as parts of Bikini, where the Bravo bomb had been dropped. Bikini was still considered to be too dangerous for human habitation. The northern Rongelap islands, where the people gathered coconut, pandanus, breadfruit, fish, birds, and fresh water were as contaminated as Bikini. In other words, for at least four years the Department of Energy had known that for twenty-five years, the Rongelapese had been eating and drinking poisoned food.

By then, one-third of the Rongelapese who had been on the island on the day Bravo fell had died of cancer and other diseases previously unknown to them. The women, who had been so fertile before, were now regularly miscarrying or delivering babies so astonishingly unformed—lacking bones, with brains exposed—that they coined a term for them: jellyfish babies. They were born dead or died soon. Of those who survived, many had bad hearts and lungs.

When they saw the information in the Department of Energy study, the Rongelapese realized they had been lied to for twenty-five years. Department of Energy officials insisted that all test results had been published in scientific reports, but informing uneducated, unworldly people about medical complexities was often impossible. According to Roger Ray, the Department of Energy's project manager for the Marshall Islands from 1972 to 1985, "I know Senator Anjain, and if I told him something in picocuries per gram, I'd get a blank stare."

The military doctors said, "We couldn't educate them. They don't even have a word for radioactivity."

Nor a word for "enemy."

The military doctors told the Rongelapese not to eat food from the northern half of the island. But if the food-producing half of the island was now known to be deadly, how could they continue to live there? "While we might understand the quarantine" said Anjain in *Eyes of Fire*. "I'm afraid the lagoon fish, sea turtles, and coconut crabs in our diet don't understand it as they move around freely and end up in our dinner."

Fear began to drive some of the people away from Rongelap. Those who stayed became terribly afraid for themselves and their children. The idea of leaving Rongelap was dreadful, especially for the older ones who remembered three years of exile after Bravo. In 1982, though, torn between their homeland and their children's future, they came to the conclusion that they would all have to leave their atoll until the radiation was gone. But where could they go? Where could they get funds to pay for the move? To build new houses? To feed themselves?

Close relatives on a nearby island offered to give them the island of Mejato. One of the few parcels of uninhabited land in the center of the Pacific Ocean, it was small, half desert, and surrounded by rough seas. The basic traditional foods—breadfruit, banana, and pandanus—did not grow there. A few coconuts did, but not nearly enough. The Rongelapese knew they would have to struggle to survive there, but they decided it was better than being slowly poisoned to death. It would have to do for the time being.

They pressed Anjain to ask Parliament for money to pay for the move. "I went to the Parliament requesting the Cabinet to seek something from the U.S. government so the people could be removed from Rongelap Atoll to someplace that we feel the people of Rongelap and their children could live in peace without fear." The Parliament passed a resolution requesting $3 million, only eleven percent of what the Rongelapese had calculated it would actually cost them to move. The Parliament was cautious because, by the early 1980s, the Marshall Islanders had become accustomed to a way of life they could not afford. Heavy dependence on U.S. aid had made most of the island leaders toe the line. The early Kennedy plan was working.

"The resolution was passed unanimously, but after that, everybody was silent." Anjain told them: "We were led to depend on U.S. assistance, and now we're afraid to stand up for our rights in case the Americans step on our heads and push us back down." Anjain, then Minister of Health, resigned that position in protest, though he remained a senator.

He went to the bank on Guam and asked for a personal loan of $10,000 to fight the nuclear issue. They gave him the money, which he used to make trips to Washington, D.C. He appealed to congressional committees to relocate the people of Rongelap. "The first time, they just looked at me and said, 'Who is this man?'" They saw a short, brown man in a cheap suit, with thick glasses and an even thicker accent. The traditional Marshallese culture does not include written reports and statistics. Anjain did not, therefore, have figures with which to impress scientists on what had happened to his people. "But I just kept punching. Every year, I kept bothering them." He took out more loans, a total of $70,000, to support the work. He made monthly loan repayments out of his meagre salary as senator.

At home, the other members of Parliament called him paranoid. "They tell it to my face: 'You are a stupid man. You are a communist. You are a renegade.' They said 'You better keep quiet, you cannot do anything.' There was a time when I argued with the president. I said, 'What do you want me to do? Just sit here and let you step on my head, push me down in the mud?' I said, 'One of these days, Mr. President,

I will prove you wrong.'" He fearlessly took on anyone with opposing views. His inner optimism was bolstered by paying selective attention to positive achievements; what some people might call failure, he calls an incomplete success. To him, the glass is half-full, not half-empty.

In the fall of 1983, the long-planned election about Micronesia's future was held. The three nations of Micronesia voted in favor of a Compact of Free Association that purported to be a fifteen-year bridging arrangement until the islands were ready for complete independence. It really amounted to U.S. annexation of Micronesia for military purposes. Some eighty-five percent of the Rongelapese voted against it.

The compact awarded the Marshall Islands $150 million for radiation survivors' claims, but in exchange, it wiped out lawsuits claiming damages of $7 billion pending in U.S. courts. Some $37.5 million was to be paid to the Rongelapese over the next fifteen years, but President Kabua claimed one-third of that belonged to him according to ancient harvest traditions.

Anjain's people were becoming sicker each day they lived on Rongelap. The Marshall Islands Parliament refused to act. The U.S. Congress refused to act.

When a friend suggested that he contact Greenpeace for assistance, Anjain says, "I didn't know who Greenpeace was. But he said they were people who were fighting the same fight I was." Anjain works fast and efficiently, and he does not mind cutting corners around authorities to get the job done. He looked for a phone.

∾

GREENPEACE BEGAN IN THE EARLY 1970S as a loose environmental organization. It launched an eco-navy with a fishing boat that left Vancouver in a brave attempt to stop a nuclear test blast by the United States on the wildlife sanctuary of Amchitka Island. Though the test went ahead before the boat arrived, the publicity Greenpeace generated encouraged the Atomic Energy Commission to abandon the rest of the blasts. The organization continued to create publicity campaigns based on a philosophy of nonviolent, direct action. Protesters sailed between the harpoons and the whales; they dyed seal pups' coats green to make them commercially worthless. In so doing, Greenpeace created worldwide controversy, which started millions of people thinking, talking, and acting.

In 1977, Greenpeace decided to buy an old trawler for a campaign to save whales in the North Atlantic. The World Wildlife Fund provided money for the ship they named the *Rainbow Warrior*. Painted with a rainbow and a dove carrying an olive branch, the ship campaigned against whaling by Iceland, Peru, Spain, and the Soviet Union. Greenpeace grew; by 1984, it had nearly 1.5 million members in fifteen countries.

That was the same year the United States fired a missile from California that was intercepted by one fired from Kwajalein and President Reagan's Star Wars program was declared possible.

Greenpeace had planned 1985 to be the Year of the Pacific, with the intention of creating symbolic demonstrations against U.S. Star Wars testing at Kwajalein and French nuclear testing farther south. The organizers intended to tie in the health problems of "atomic" veterans —the approximately two hundred fifty thousand former U.S. servicemen who had been exposed to radioactive fallout from nuclear testing programs between 1945 and 1962. When Anjain called and asked Greenpeace if it would help move 320 radiation survivors, the request fit right into their agenda. They made plans with Anjain to move his people.

"The people looked to me to find a way to save them," Anjain said in *Eyes of Fire*, "but they didn't really believe a ship would come." When the *Rainbow Warrior* arrived in Honolulu, Anjain boarded her for the trip to Rongelap. Sailing into the lagoon, with Anjain on the main deck, the ship was met by a small, rickety motorboat with eleven Rongelapese women aboard. From the stern they flew a banner saying, "*Ba eman kabjere*—We love the future of our kids." The women sang a welcoming song, then took the visitors ashore for a small ceremony.

The islanders had built an arch of coconut wood and braided pandanus leaves, covered with hibiscus flowers. Across the arch was another banner with the same affirmation: "*Ba eman kabjere*—We love the future of our kids." The crew was decorated with floral crowns and sweet-smelling leis and presented with coconut drinks as the women sang more songs.

Behind the ceremony site, several houses already had their roofs and walls torn down and stacked in neat, labeled piles, ready to be taken to their new home.

Anjain made a brief speech to introduce the *Rainbow Warrior* crew and to recap the island's tragic history since the Bravo fallout. "American scientists have been lying to us for thirty years about the radiation on our islands. The poison from the Bravo monster bomb is still being felt today. Our people suffered then, and we are still suffering from radiation diseases, such as thyroid tumors, cancer, leukemia, birth defects, stillbirths, and miscarriages. Now, as we all decided, the time has come for us to leave for Mejato Island. For the sake of our children and our grandchildren. . . . It will be hard, but we'll find a way to survive," he said in *Eyes of Fire*.

On Sunday, May 19, 1985, the Rongelapese held one last church service. Christmas decorations still hung in the room. According to *Eyes of Fire*, the pastor said, "It is a sad moment. But remember what is happening to us is rather like the biblical deliverance of the Israelites from Egypt." The women sang with tears about their homeland. Outside the church window lay the gravestones of those who had died of radiation illness.

After church, everyone spent the day taking apart the rest of the houses and loading them onto the *Rainbow Warrior*. About twenty tons of supplies were ferried out to the ship in small motorboats. They carried building material from their former homes, generators, furniture, kerosene lamps, tools, and trunks of clothes and gear. Shortly before dark, the *Rainbow Warrior* took aboard the first nuclear refugees—about seventy-five old people, pregnant women, and mothers with young children. The *Rainbow Warrior* weighed anchor, and no one looked back; the islanders kept their eyes ahead. The ship traveled through the dark, navigating by an ancient Marshallese "wave map."

After unloading, the *Rainbow Warrior* returned to Rongelap for three more loads of people and about eighty more tons of materials. The pigs and chickens, though, presented a problem. For one thing, there was no food for them on Mejato. For another, they might be contaminated. The islanders decided not to take the risk. They left the animals behind. They padlocked and shuttered the church. It and the gravestones were all that was left in original form. On Mejato, the islanders began building temporary shelters and a new village.

∾

GREENPEACE ENSURED that the evacuation received publicity around the world. The foreign minister of the Marshall Islands said, "The Government has indicated its support for the evacuation by a unanimous resolution of the Nitijela. The involvement of Greenpeace means an opportunity for some international scrutiny of a problem that has plagued us for a long time—one that the United States refuses to acknowledge or recognize. The people don't want to live on a contaminated atoll, and there is an alternative home for the time being."

However, Ambassador Harvey Feldman, U.S. representative to the United Nations Trusteeship Council, told the council the exodus had been instigated by outsiders who had misled the islanders about radioactive contamination on the atoll. Feldman said there was "simply no new scientific information, either radiologically or medically" to support the move.

Anjain quickly replied that the evacuation had not been prompted by any outsiders. "It was instigated by me and my people as a result of the American nuclear testing program. Secondly, we don't need the most brilliant scientists to come and tell us we're not sick. We know we have had health problems on Rongelap from the beginning—we are having them today, and we will have them for the indefinite future."

Next, the U.S. government claimed it had not been advised of the move, despite the fact that Interior Department officials had listened since early 1984 to a series of Rongelapese delegates testifying in congressional hearings about their plans to evacuate their atoll.

∾

THE RONGELAPESE LIVE under basic survival conditions on Mejato. U.S. food aid is essential to keep them from starvation; at best, the people live on canned tuna, white rice, canned pears or peaches, pancakes, or doughnuts made with white flour, sugar, water, and fat. But sometimes the ships are late, and there is not even canned food to eat on Mejato. It is not uncommon for two meals a day to consist of a small amount of white rice and milky coffee. Furthermore, the health and safety of their homeland is still uncertain.

Anjain continued to make powerful friends in the United States by aligning himself with groups of citizens who live near the Nevada Test Site and nuclear weapons plants in Washington and Ohio. One friend, Ohio Senator John Glenn, pointed out that the Department of Energy's weapons division, not its environment and health division, was overseeing efforts to clean up the Marshall Islands and to treat the residents. Internal memos obtained by Glenn's staff indicated the weapons division had taken over the Marshall Islands program in 1982 as part of a plan to resume atmospheric testing of nuclear weapons. Not only that, but the department doubled the annual radiation exposure considered acceptable on Rongelap. Glenn managed to have the Marshall Islands transferred back to health experts in October 1990. That little bureaucratic change made all the difference in the world, Anjain found. "People I talked to, they treated me like I am a human being," he said. "We want only an answer to two questions: Is our homeland safe? What is in our bodies?"

By the summer of 1991, a U.S. congressional committee appropriated $3 million for independent radiation studies, cleanup of Rongelap, and ultimately the resettlement of the people. "If the report says some cleanup should be done, then there is another part we will be fighting for. We will go back to the U.S. government."

Anjain, now seriously ill with cancer himself, returned to Mejato and "made a little celebration. I tell the young guys, we go fishing. We make food. Let's treat these old people. And they were singing and dancing, and some were praying. They were really happy," he says with a proud smile.

His power has been the ability to hang in for twenty years of hard, lonely, sometimes horribly boring work; he has outlasted the U.S. Department of Energy. "I feel like I have done something. I don't blame anyone for not agreeing with me." But he points out that ten years ago, he told the president of the Marshall Islands that he would prove him wrong. And "I have done that," Anjain says with a chuckle.

His efforts have won him the Right Livelihood Award for 1991 and the Goldman Environmental Prize for 1992. "Receiving all these awards, I feel that I am the happiest man alive. For me and my family, we think it is the sweetest thing that has ever happened to us, especially my children. They are very happy. They understand what I have been through." Anjain, raised a Protestant, says, "I believe in God. I know there were guardians given to me by the good man up there."

∽

THIS STORY IS ONE of the most disturbing in this book. It has forces us to confront the horrible cruelties one group of people can perpetrate against another. In this case, the perpetrator is the U.S. government. The story also brings up the terror of the possibility of nuclear war. The term "psychic numbing" was coined in studies of Hiroshima survivors, and it means not wanting to know; it means blocking our natural reactions of fear, anger, and grief in the face of such enormous despair. It is tempting—to me, and possibly to you—to "numb up" in order to try to deny this story and others like it. The enormity of the grief and pain seems overwhelming. But if we can allow the grief and pain of the truth to surface, anger can surface too, and with it, the energy and the will to make changes. The nuclear powers of the United States, France, and Britain have much invested in the continued colonialization and destruction of the Pacific islands. Kwajalein Missile Range is essential to the development of new U.S. weapons; if we did not have Kwajalein, we would not be able to test long-range weapons over open, largely uninhabited areas of the earth's surface. The United States has invested $1 billion in the Kwajalein Missile Range. Not only would it be costly to replace, but finding another small nation willing to relinquish its land would be a difficult task. Kwajalein Island houses three thousand expatriates in what looks like a typical American suburb. Along with the palm trees and manicured lawns, there is a nine-hole golf course, baseball fields, a bowling alley, and two swimming pools.

Meanwhile, hundreds of thousands of radiation survivors are battling in U.S. courts for compensation. Being forced to pay for our mistakes as a society is hardly the point, though. The struggle is not "out there," but inside each of us. The first painful step is to acknowledge that reality—to refuse to go numb. We have to recognize that no amount of radiation is safe, and nuclear weapons are not acceptable.

☙

You can reach Senator Jeton Anjain, at Republic of the Marshall Islands. P.O. Box 1006, Majuro, Marshall Islands 96960.

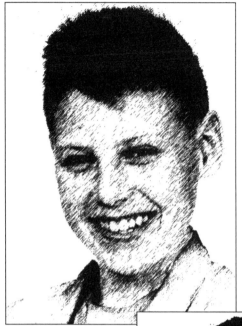

Roland Tiensuu

Eha Kern

Teaching Children Well

EHA KERN/ROLAND TIENSUU

Sweden

 SHE HAD BEEN an elementary-school teacher for fifteen years when she began to feel "a little hopeless that I was not doing more than teaching my pupils to read, write, and count when there were so many problems in the world that needed to be solved." A kind, gentle woman who speaks English with a strong Swedish accent, Eha Kern thrives on helping others. She teaches pupils seven, eight, and nine years old in a rural village in southern Sweden. Surrounded by farmland and forests, most of the houses and the school are painted rust-red.

"I decided to start influencing my pupils to work with international understanding. I wanted to let the children know of other cultures and how they worked, so we invited people who had lived in other countries to come to the school. A person came from Bali and told them about the rain forest. And then the children started to ask me questions about rain forests." They were fascinated by the strange and beautiful animals that live in rain forests of the world: jaguar, ocelot, spider monkey, sloth, golden toad, armadillo, and tropical birds such as the parrot, macaw, and resplendent quetzal.

"There were lots of television programs about the rain forest at the same time. The children learned that all this could be gone within twenty years." They were saddened to realize the forest might not survive long enough for them to ever be able to see it. One of the students, Roland Tiensuu, asked Kern, "Why can't we buy some rain forest so there is some left when we grow up?" All the children liked the idea.

"And then, just more by accident," says Kern, "through a friend that I had in Stockholm, I met Sharon Kinsman who was a biologist in Maine. She knew about the Monteverde program to buy rain forests." Kinsman, a biology professor from Bates College in Lewiston, Maine, had studied plant reproduction at Costa Rica's Monteverde Cloud Forest Preserve, a luxuriant, montane cloud forest in Costa Rica's high, cool mountains.

In Costa Rica, every year 125,000 acres of forest are cut and cleared, today mostly for banana plantations, but previously for farms and cattle ranches. At this rate, soon only five percent of the country's rain forest will be left outside of preserves. "I have a very, very narrow answer to, 'What can I do?'" Kinsman says. "And that is, 'Save enough now so that we can go out in fifty or one hundred years and make the earth green again because we will have a few pockets where there's forest left.' I do have a vision of a period of an ugly, sad world. It can be made green again, but not if we lose the species. . . . If you can, share your money, and you can save a piece of forest that will be protected forever. I see it as a race against time."

Kinsman gave a rain forest slide show to the students and told them about the Monteverde Conservation League, which had been started the year before, in 1986, to buy and preserve areas around the reserve. "It was one of the most fantastic days that I've ever spent," says Kinsman. "They did songs and dances for me, and then I did the jungle slide show. They loved it. Everything was translated for them, and they were patient for hours to hear all about the animals. They drew pictures of them and remembered every word I said about quetzals and golden toads."

Roland helped organize the other students to raise money for the project. Kern reports, "They said, 'If we start, maybe others will follow. If they don't, at least the piece we have bought will be left, and it is better than nothing. Let's try.'" They decided that their first effort would be to put on a performance and sell tickets to their parents and other villagers. For the performance, they created "earth peace dwellers"—small handmade puppets of creatures that live in trees and protect them from chainsaws. They wrote poems and songs: "We will never give up," they sang. "The animals have a right to their homes, and we want clean water." After the performance, they sold books and paintings and raised $300, which, at that time was enough to buy twelve acres of Monteverde rain forest. The date was November 6, 1987, Kern remembers. Everyone, including Kern, was impressed. Excited by their own success, the children started thinking of other ways to raise money, such as holding a Christmas bazaar and selling Christmas cards.

"Then they realized they couldn't do it alone, so they started to write to other schools to ask them to help. And to the Swedish television to ask them to announce that you can buy rain forest." At first, they did not get any answer from the television stations, but they refused to be discouraged. They simply wrote again. "And then there were little, little pieces on television. And then other schools started to call. It took about half a year before it became more known in Sweden that you could do that. And then, it started to grow in some way, and then every television program wanted to tell about it, and everyone wanted to help."

A skillful teacher, Kern saw the potential in her students and was able to bring it out. "We had what we call a brainstorm. You tell all the ideas you have, and there are no bad ideas because someone else can turn it into a good idea. So I just wrote everything up that the children were saying." They arranged rabbit-jumping contests, pony rides, bake sales, lotteries, and markets. When they had no more ideas, they sat and sang some of the songs they had made up about the rain forest. Then they thought maybe they could go around and sing their songs and ask people to donate money to buy rain forest. "That's always worked. They have even stood in the middle of Stockholm and sung their songs." In addition, they thought of writing to rich people to ask for help, and some of the rich people responded. They created a little newsletter and sold subscriptions, and two girls sold their toys. "One boy who was involved died in an accident. His parents asked friends not to send flowers, but instead to donate money to purchase rain forest in his name."

The forty children in the class that year, Kern still believes, were "very, very special," particularly sensitive, bright, and motivated. "And they understood that one person cannot do so much. We have to do this together, and we have to make others help us. They said very early that if we start, perhaps others will help us in Sweden, and perhaps children in other countries will help us, and then perhaps we can make something big." Kern challenged them to do their best, and they challenged and inspired her in return.

"They are very, very shy children when you meet them, but not when they want to talk about the rain forest. It's very fascinating to meet them in that way. Because the rain forest, it's their idea, and they wanted to do it. And they think that it's maybe succeeding, it's going very well." Those first forty children raised about $30,000, which they sent to the Monteverde Conservation League. By February 1992, twenty-three thousand acres of tropical rain forest on the Caribbean slope of the mountains had been purchased with funds donated by children and adults in twenty-one countries around the world. Land that had been targeted to be cleared for pasture is now returning to cloud forest. The area is called the Bosque Eterno de los Niños—The Children's Eternal Forest. When the Monteverde Conservation League consolidated that area with other of its holdings in February 1992, the children's forest grew to thirty-five thousand acres. The league employs forest guards to patrol the protected forest and other staff to work in environmental education in the communities around the forest. For $100 you can purchase an acre of land or put a forest guard on the trail.

"As the area's population continues to rise," says Lisa Wirtanen, formerly of the Monteverde Conservation League, "there is tremendous pressure to cut down more and more rain forest. The truth is, there are countless plant and animal species dependent on the continued dedication and resolve of these children."

∾

COSTA RICA LIES as close to the equator as Sweden does to the North Pole. Whereas Sweden has long enjoyed its status as one of the most prosperous and progressive nations of the world, Costa Rica has only recently emerged as the strongest democracy in Latin America. Costa Ricans are mostly middle class, educated, and literate; and they have worked persistently for peace and economic stability with their neighbors in Central America. In 1987, President Oscar Arias proposed a peace plan for Central America that was adopted, with modifications, by all the Central American governments. For his efforts, he was awarded the Nobel Peace Prize that year. In 1988, Costa Rica celebrated the fortieth anniversary of its constitution: forty years of free elections, free press, democracy, and survival without an army.

However, Costa Rica, the size of West Virginia, has a rapidly growing population of about three million. The country has cut half its forests in the past forty years, and before the year 2000, it will have used all forests not in parks and reserves. Much of the forest was not even used as timber, but was burned to clear pasture and farmland to graze beef for export. The figures would be far worse except that in the 1960s, Costa Rica began protecting forests with a remarkable national park system. The intent was to protect at least one example of every type of landscape and ecosystem in the diverse country, from the active, steaming volcanoes to the dry tropical forest; from the rolling wet, lowland to the cool, high cloud forest. (The U.S. national park system, by comparison, represents only about half of our ecosystems.) Because of the broad ecological range of the parks, conservationists had to fight an equally broad range of destructive forces: loggers, miners, ranchers, government, development, bureaucracies, and other interests.

In the early 1970s, Costa Rica became aware of the problems of sea turtle slaughter, dwindling quetzal populations, endangered species, and deforestation. In response, the park system grew rapidly and well; it serves as a fine example to other tropical and developing nations. Costa Rica has set aside twelve percent of the country for a national park system. Another fifteen percent of the nation is in forest reserves or under other protected status. In *The Quetzal and the Macaw: The Story of Costa Rica's National Parks*, David Rains Wallace writes, "If history continues, power will reside with societies that have conserved their resources, not with those that have spent them. Costa Rica has limited resources, but if it manages to conserve twenty-five percent of its forest in parks and ecological reserves, and another twenty-five percent in commercial timberlands and extractive reserves—as its leading conservationists propose to do—it may well become a 'super-power' of a new kind."

Most of the parks shelter thousands of bird and animal species; in Monteverde, there are thirty species of hummingbird alone. In Costa Rica's parks, you can watch sea turtles come ashore to lay eggs in the sand; you can snorkel on coral reefs; walk up to thermal springs of boiling mud; and watch waterfalls tumble out of the rain forest beside the road.

Costa Rican park system administrators keep a sharp eye on the United States and Kenya, where national parks have created multibillion dollar tourist businesses. According to Wallace in *The Quetzal and the Macaw*, Mario Boza, the first director of the Costa Rica national park system, wrote in 1969: "East Africa, by having more vision than us in this field, increased it annual income from tourism by fifteen percent. What couldn't our country do, being closer to the main source of tourists in the world?" (By which he meant, of course, North Americans.) Boza and other administrators knew that stimulating the local economy was the key to making conservation popular. However, the park administrators were equally determined to maintain the integrity of the ecosystem itself. The system was working so well, that in 1981, Boza published a little book entitled *A Decade of Development* that serves as a kind of field guide to the establishment and administration of a park system in a developing country.

In the 1980s, coffee prices dropped; the beans had been the riches of the country since the late 1700s. At the same time, gas prices shot up. Foreign debt had grown rapidly, and Costa Rica began to spend most of its income on paying the interest on that debt. The country fell into economic decline. The park service had to cut staff, and inflation gobbled up about eighty percent of the buying power of its budget between 1980 and 1986. During the same period, deforestation had increased. It was time to increase the fund-raising effort.

One innovative solution evolved in 1987: the debt-for-nature swap, backed heartily by President Arias. The way it works is fairly simple: A creditor nation forgives a debt, or receives a fraction of its worth, in exchange for Costa Rica's setting aside land. For example, in 1990 Sweden forgave $24.5 million in Costa Rican debt in exchange for the preservation of 210,000 acres for the Guanacaste National Park.

The Monteverde Conservation League had been established in 1986 to preserve and protect rain forest. A nonprofit organization of Costa Ricans and North Americans, the league is recognized by the Costa Rican government as a legal association, and both the World Wildlife Fund and the Nature Conservancy channel donations to the organization. The league buys and protects rain forest in northern Costa Rica and assists local efforts in education, sustainable agriculture, and reforestation. It was to this organization that the Swedish schoolchildren sent their donations.

∾

IN SWEDEN, Kern organized Barnens Regnskog—Children's Rainforest—a Swedish nonprofit organization dedicated to raising funds for rain forest preservation. As a result of Kern's guidance of Barnens Regnskog, there are now more than six thousand schools in Scandinavia and the rest of Europe involved in raising money to save the rain forests, an effort that has so far brought in $2 million and purchased nearly twenty-six square miles at Monteverde. One classroom began posting a picture of a quetzal on the wall for every area saved, until the students estimated they would paper the room four times, which would be "a terrible waste of paper."

"When television started to tell about the rain forest children," says Kern, "we were drowning in letters. Schools wanted to help, wanted to see slides, wanted information about the rain forest." Her husband, Berni, an amateur photographer, put together some old slides he had from visits to Panama and Bolivia, and even used slides from a small forest in their own community (without actually admitting it was local jungle) and showed the slides all over Sweden on his days off. "All the campaign was administered from our kitchen," Kern says. "Sometimes there is little time left for sleeping."

Barnens Regnskog, now one hundred thousand children strong, has inspired children in twenty-eight other countries to form their own rain forest conservation groups. Children's Rainforest U.S.A. reports activities in thirty-five states. A similar organization in Japan is called Nippon Kodomo No Jungle; it has been raising awareness in Japan—more difficult than in some other countries—and influencing the Japanese government. A growing movement in England is called Children's Tropical Forests-U.K. To date, the worldwide children's groups have come up with $2.5 million. "I am so fascinated," Kern says. "I think they are, too, to see how much we can do when we make something together."

For their efforts, Kern and her pupils were honored with a visit to their little red schoolhouse by the king and queen of Sweden. And in 1990, President Oscar Arias invited a delegation from Barnens Regnskog to visit Costa Rica. Kern, her husband, student Roland Tiensuu, and nine other children made a three-week trip. For most of the children, between nine and eleven years old, it was their first plane flight. "Once we got up there, so many thousands of feet in the air, the children started crying. First one did, then soon all of them were crying."

In Costa Rica, the Swedish kids went to stay in the homes of Costa Ricans. "That first night, they were all crying for their mommies. But soon we were visiting the rain forest, and they forgot all about their mommies," says Kern. In parkas and rainboots, they tramped through the Monteverde forest. Later they met with President Arias.

"By the time we got back on the plane, now the children were all crying because they didn't want to leave." That reaction has been repeated by many of the tens of thousands of nature tourists who visit Costa Rica each year and who are moved by the tropical beauty and peace.

In 1988, half of the tourists interviewed said they had visited natural sites, parks, reserves, and refuges. Visits to seven of the principal national parks increased by fifty percent in two years. Tourism accounted for about thirteen percent of Costa Rica's export income—bringing nearly as much foreign revenue into the economy as bananas.

❧

KERN CONTINUES TO TEACH HER CLASSES about the rain forest, and the original pupils still return to participate and raise funds. They plan to expand their purchases to other countries such as Belize, Guatemala, and Thailand.

Kern says the children have become more aware of the environment of their homeland as well. "Suddenly they see that we also have something that is very valuable. When you start talking about something that is far away, you suddenly see what is close with other eyes." Sweden suffers from problems of acid rain drifting over from sulfurous British air. "They learned it's not just the rain forest; it's how different systems work. And if you take a little piece away from one system that is in the circle, then you destroy the circle. So they realize it's a global thing we have to think of, that everything works together."

ᐁ

For more information contact: Barnens Regnskog, PL 4471, 137 94 Vasterhaninge, Sweden.

Children's Rainforest U.S.A., P.O. Box 936, Lewiston, Maine 04240. (Donations are tax-deductible.)

Monteverde Conservation League, Apartado 10165-1000, San Jose, Costa Rica. (A donation of $100 purchases an acre of land, and a donation of $25 or more includes a year's subscription to *Tapir Tracks* newsletter in English or Spanish. You can become a Rain Forest Partner with the Bosque Eterno de los Niños with a donation for forest patrols, community education, tree planting, or land purchase. Make checks payable to Monteverde Conservation League.)

Michael Werikhe

Step by Step

Michael Werikhe

Kenya

Devoted conservationists often resemble spiritual devotees, offering up their lives for some greater good—whether it is the annihilation of mortal suffering, or the survival of an ecosystem. Michael Werikhe's devotion takes the form of a pilgrimage. But instead of traveling toward a sacred place, he walks away from one. The place is Kenya—Eden, you might say—where once a vast garden thrived in harmony. Werikhe's particular object of devotion is the black rhinoceros.

"The rhino is a unique animal," says Werikhe. "It represents life itself." To him and others living in eastern, central, and southern Africa, the black rhino is a sacred symbol, the African equivalent of the American bald eagle. Preserve it, and the essence of a people and its land endures. "My simple way of getting the message across, because of the lack of funds, was to take what I call the gospel of conservation to the people." Like Saint Paul bringing the gospel of Christianity, Werikhe walks to spread the word.

One of the most prehistoric-looking creatures still left on earth, the rhino is currently also one of the most endangered because of poaching for its horn. Rhinos, second in size only to the elephant, are slaughtered and their massive carcasses left rotting in the African sun with only one part missing: the horn, ripped out of the snout.

Werikhe's devotion sprang from direct experience. After graduating from high school in the late 1970s, he took a job near his home in a sprawling Mombasa warehouse that contained the Ivory Room of the Kenyan game department. His job was hardly the ivory tower type, however. It fell to him to sort and weigh elephant tusks, rhino horns, and zebra skins for auction. (The Ivory Room was once a tourist attraction and is now permanently closed.) "Some of them had been confiscated from animals killed by poachers, some had died of natural causes. But each week, each month, the numbers increased." He saw and touched these atrocities, and he heard stories that turned his stomach. "For a year, I was subjected to that kind of stuff. It reached a point that I could not take any more of it—I was so distressed that so much poaching was going on and so little being done, I opted to resign. But before I resigned I made a promise to myself and to my sisters and brothers, that I would try to fight for the wildlife in my own capacity." He chose the most endangered of African animals as his special cause.

In 1982, Werikhe set out from his hometown of Mombasa—a provincial seaside city of small factories and workshops, with an important harbor that handles trade from the outside world with Kenya and East Central Africa—to walk three hundred miles, through the villages and towns on the road to Nairobi, the country's capital, telling people along the way about what was happening to the black rhino. "I just walked into villages. I took a python with me for company, and today I think I owe a lot to that snake. I remember I'd go into a village, and there would be two or three people around. The moment I pulled the snake out of the bag, there would be fifty to one hundred people. And they would just stand there and listen to what I had to tell them. I might start talking about snakes and telling them about how they are, in my view, man's best friend in rural areas. They contribute a lot to the biological control of rodents and other destructive animals. If we could just learn to respect them, we would be doing a lot of justice to ourselves and to Mother Nature. A lot of them understood the relationship and appreciated that snakes were very important. And once they related to the snakes, I could bring the conversation around to rhinos.

"At the end of the talk, I would request them to assist me with food and a place to sleep. It was too risky to carry money around with me. And, truly, people would say, 'Well, we can give you this, and we can give you that.' They even went so far as to say they were ready to give food to the snake. This is unheard of in Africa. Snakes are generally associated with evil and are hated. It really touched my heart that these people became concerned, not just with my affairs, but were concerned also about the snake I had with me."

Werikhe was greatly encouraged by his first trip. "Because I feel it is very important that the ordinary man out in the village and in the street should be made aware that he, too, has a role to play in the interest of the environment. So I thought I should get their views. Now, these are very down-to-earth people. Did they have the same feeling that I have about wildlife? And I discovered, as a result of the walk, that the people were very, very interested, and they wanted to do a lot more. I think that first walk helped the authorities and the ordinary man understand that for conservation to succeed, there has to be a dialogue, and we have to work together. Before you can go anywhere, you've got to start at home."

Werikhe kept walking, and eventually he reached millions of people around the world, including presidents, princes and princesses, and kings. He has met with the president of the United States and the president of Costa Rica, and he received a letter of support from Prince Philip of Great Britain. "This is not a problem that concerns just one place, because nature knows no man-made boundaries. In Kenya and other parts of Africa, we view wildlife as part and parcel of our heritage," says Werikhe. "We believe if we were to lose the elephant and rhino, we would lose far more than only two species. What is going to happen is the total disintegration of the wildlife in that part of the world. We're going to see a chain reaction that will affect many other species, big and small, and eventually their habitat will mostly disappear. And, of course, in the final analysis, man himself will be the biggest loser."

As Diane Ackerman, the American poet and scientist wrote in the *New Yorker,* "So many animals vanishing may be an indication that we're not far from the brink ourselves. Human beings could be among the fossils that future life forms speculate about one day—if they do speculate—puzzling over our tragedy as we puzzle over the dinosaurs.'

If we'd like our species to hang around awhile, we must be vigilant about what we're doing to other species, because evolution is a set of hand-shakes, not a list of winners." Or, as Gregory Bateson writes, "The horse isn't the thing that evolved. What evolved actually was a relationship between horse and grass."

Awareness of this kind of relationship prevails in native African religions south of the Sahara. They accept the presence of a universal life force as part of the natural order. They emphasize living in harmony with the universe and preserving harmony by maintaining proper relationships with all beings. Separating religion from other aspects of life serves to distort rather than clarify its meaning. This bush religion is not very different from the ultramodern "Gaia hypothesis," developed in the 1960s by James Lovelock of the Jet Propulsion Laboratory. From that shrine of high technology, where he was studying the atmosphere of Mars, he saw that Earth and its atmosphere constitute a symbiotic network of all living things. He fused his scientific understanding of the hard sciences with an ancient religious theme, and called it Gaia, after the Greek earth goddess, Ge. Gaia is a living, breathing body of which humanity is a small part; she is Mother Earth. The notion of a female, nurturing goddess is as old as civilization; but during medieval times, Christianity and male-dominated society severed human society from its relationship with Mother Earth, from that which is most human and healthy in each of us.

Though we are pushing ourselves toward extinction when we obliterate another species, the planet will do just fine without us; there is no need to "save the planet." Even in the event of an atomic holocaust, planet Earth will keep on spinning, perhaps putting down another Ice Age for a while to purify the place and gradually, over a few million years, warming to the idea of living creatures again. In the Gaia hypothesis, the planet itself is indestructible, and yet so infinitely complex that each microbe is necessary. We meddle at our own peril when we wipe out even a flea: We are meddling not only with our continued survival, but with our continued sanity.

"The reason why we have so many wars and misunderstandings among ourselves," Werikhe says, "is because we've broken loose from the great design of Mother Nature. And as a result of that, we've become too combative, and we've lost our powers of reasoning and tolerance. We've reached a very dangerous stage. The problem of pollution, the depletion of the ozone layer, the warming of the planet, these are signs that all isn't well. What are we going to do? We need to get down to basics. We need to reevaluate ourselves. Changes need to take place from within, not from outside. We need to cut ourselves to size and stop being arrogant. We are just animals, like other animals. If we're able to save the rhinos, then we'll be able to save whatever is coexisting with the rhinos, right from the elephants to the smallest microorganism that forms the ecosystem of the savannah." Even, perhaps, ourselves.

Werikhe maintains a "simple belief that there is a superior being around me, around us, in the universe . . . and that being, that force, has the power to influence events. Nobody understands that force very well. Some people call the superior being God, some call the superior being Allah. But I communicate with that force in my own way, and I get satisfaction knowing that I'm contributing something to it, helping events that are part and parcel of nature."

∾

WERIKHE DESCRIBES HIMSELF as much like the rhino: "We're both shy, sensitive, and nearsighted." In Werikhe's case, those qualities are endearing; when he speaks to an audience, they can see he has to struggle to put himself forward for what he believes in. In public talks, his chest is so full of the struggle between intense stage fright and an even more intense determination not to let that stop him, that he has no space left for ego. The audience sees a selfless, determined, and very intelligent, small, lean, young man, eyes magnified by thick glasses. When a bit of humor breaks the surface, it sounds funnier than it is; when a ray of personality shines through, it feels warm. Because the audience loves him, they come to love the black rhinoceros.

For a shy person, Werikhe does a bang-up job of drawing crowds and cameras. In May 1991, the *New York Times* listed under "Social Events" Zubin Mehta's final concert at the Philharmonic, a celebration of Cole Porter's 100th birthday, and a cocktail reception for

Michael Werikhe at the Central Park Zoo. The ticket price for the Werikhe event was three and a half times that for Porter.

The next month, Werikhe led a fund-raising group on a walk from the Central Park Zoo to the Bronx Zoo. Walking down 194th Street in the burned-out borough of the Bronx, Werikhe had hundreds of beautiful people behind him, marchers in fluorescent T-shirts, bicycle shorts, and athletic shoes. The neighborhood folks clustered on the sidewalk and watched the parade go by while trying to figure out what the fuss was about. The beautiful people marched to a high-school cheer nearly as old as the prehistoric rhino itself: "Give me an R!" "Give me an H!" and so on, until they put it together, and what's that spell? "RHINO!" The local denizens did not seem to be too familiar with anything called a rhino. (Wino?)

One follower came to New York from Arizona for the occasion because Werikhe is his "patron saint." Werikhe himself was, as usual, pretty cool about it all and walking at a good clip. Having already covered 3,400 miles in Africa and Europe, and being in the middle of a 1,500-mile walk in the United States and Canada, he had trekked almost ten miles that day. And, he says, "I don't like walking." He turns the money he raises, more than one million dollars so far, over to rhino conservation projects and continues to live on the paycheck from his job at home in Mombasa. In order to get time off to walk and talk for the black rhinoceros, sometimes five months at a stretch, he works seven days a week the rest of the year.

He has walked through Kenya, Tanzania, and Uganda—picking up malaria and dangerous tsetse fly bites along the way, as well as picking his way around a war in Uganda. He's trekked across five countries in Europe—over the Alps in Italy, under snowfall in Switzerland, through Germany's Black Forest, across the flat farmland of the Netherlands, and down London streets. Walking as far as forty miles a day, giving interviews in the evening, he has won the backing of the Discovery Channel, has been the subject of a documentary on CBS Television, and has been featured in *Time*.

The adoption of his cause by so many diverse people is heartening because, he says, "The initial years were frustrating and difficult. They were just a nightmare because when I started off, people thought I was crazy. It was very painful trying to get them to understand. Some were calling me names. I'd go to an office, and some shut the door in my face. That was really bad. People like officials. People from different social scales. I think being single-minded was the only thing that saved me. If I had a weak mind, I don't think I would have made it. I would have just changed my mind and picked up something else. But the sheer fact that some people were opposed to the idea made me determined to prove I wasn't crazy. I had to prove they were wrong. But now it's all changed. And it hasn't only changed for me, but it's changed for many others. Awareness has built up. I'm very happy that I paid the price for others."

∾

"THE RHINO DOES NOT ENJOY THE LOVE AND ATTENTION of the elephant simply because it is not as pretty or as social as the elephant," says Werikhe. "But it's still a unique mammal. It's beautiful in its own way, and I think it requires as much attention and respect as the elephant." The black rhinoceros is the more common of the two African species, the other being the white rhinoceros. Neither one is white or black. The white species is slightly paler in color than the other, but both are dark gray-brown. The name of the white rhino may have come from the Afrikaans word *Weit*, meaning "wide," referring to the fact that its mouth is broader than the darker, or black, rhinoceros. The latter has a prehensile upper lip that is long and pointed, an adaptation that aids its life as a browser. It usually feeds on the leaves and shoots of shrubs and bushes.

Behind the lip, the first of two horns protrudes an average of eighteen inches—but it can grow to four feet. It is composed of a solid mass of closely packed vertical fibers like hair. The black rhinoceros uses its strong front horn in combat, to gore or club an opponent, and as a tool to snap small branches off tasty trees. The second horn, further back on the head, pops up about seven inches. Occasionally the black rhinoceros grows a third horn.

Rhinoceroses have weak vision, but their senses of smell and hearing are acute. The poor eyesight is said to be compensated for by the presence of small birds that travel on the rhino's back, eating ticks and other small bugs, and sounding an alarm in times of danger. "I have witnessed on more than three occasions," says Werikhe, "the tick bird's shrill calls alarming a slumbering rhino to its senses."

Standing about five feet at the shoulder, measuring thirteen feet from tip to tail, the black rhinoceros weighs as much as two tons. Only the white rhinoceros and the elephant are larger land mammals. The black rhinoceros spends its entire solitary life in extremely limited home ranges. The area varies from less than three to more than twenty square miles. If a stranger trespasses, the rhino invariably attacks.

The daily routine of the black rhinoceros includes a walk around the home range for feeding, a nap in its accustomed bed during the day, and a visit to a nearby watering hole in the late afternoon. The black rhinoceros is most active at night and between early-morning and late-afternoon snoozes in sand or dust-filled depressions. Not a bad life.

The homely beasts form no close pair bond; they are polygamous and polyandrous. Breeding occurs at any time of the year. Several males may be attracted to a female in estrus, and a good deal of charging, snorting, squealing, and jousting takes place—with little damage done. The female accepts any or all of them. The bull mounts the cow as many as twenty times during several hours before actual copulation occurs, which lasts about half an hour. This behavior may have contributed to the legends of the aphrodisiac value of rhinoceros horn. Each female gives birth about every twenty-seven months. She continues to suckle the calf until shortly before the next one is born.

Black rhinos were once found over most of Africa south of the Sahara, roaming the bush by the hundreds of thousands a century ago. By the mid 1960s, they could still be found throughout most of their range, but their numbers had been reduced to between seventy thousand and one hundred thousand. The population had suffered large losses because of measures intended to control the tsetse fly—which can be carried by the rhino. In the late 1970s, poaching for the horn escalated, and fewer than thirty thousand remained. Today, only thirty-six hundred are left. Kenya, which boasted a black rhinoceros population of between seventeen thousand and twenty thousand in 1965, has only four hundred fifty now.

"The rhino has been here for more than sixty million years," says Werikhe. "According to fossil remains, there were once more than thirty species of rhinos, which were found from North America to other parts of the world. But, as a result of the changing climate, they could not cope, and with evolution many were phased out. If rhinos are to disappear, I think we should allow that process to be influenced by their evolutionary factor, but it should not be accelerated by man. For man to accelerate the extinction of such a unique mammal is a crime against nature. Right now, it's not an evolutionary problem as such. It's a man-caused problem."

Preserving the black rhino depends, at this point in history, almost entirely on stopping illegal killing of the animal for its horn. The rhino is rarely, if ever, hunted for meat. The Maasai tribe, which today lives in an area that supports most of Kenya's wildlife, are cattle herders who do not kill game for food. Historically they hunted a few animals for decorative or ceremonial purposes: ostrich head plumes, monkey-skin anklets, ivory earplugs, and the lion mane helmets that once identified a proven warrior.

For hundreds of years, African natives have killed small numbers of rhinos for their horns, which are bought by Asian traders and sold in Asia as an aphrodisiac; records of this commerce date from the first century. A recent, dramatic increase in the trade has threatened the black rhino with extinction—to no purpose, since, despite the suggestion of its shape and angle, the rhino horn cannot raise any more than the hopes of those with low libidos. "The horn is not a true horn at all, just compact hair, much like fingernails," says Werikhe, who recommends that a man worried about his potency might just as well chew his own fingernails.

While popular folk myth in Asia recommends the powder of the rhino horn for a range of ailments from backaches to high blood pressure, no scientific evidence exists that rhino horn has any beneficial effect on humans. Nonetheless, the medical uses of rhinoceros horn are deeply embedded in Chinese and Japanese culture. To help save the black rhinoceros, we have to embark on what will probably be a long and difficult period of education and persuasion.

In North Yemen, the rhino horn brings in big profits as well. There, horns are carved into daggers and worn as status symbols. Again, the use is deeply embedded in the culture. The most important badge of an adult Yemeni Muslim man is the ceremonial dagger presented to him when he is eleven or twelve years old and considered a man. The belt, the sheath, the dagger handle, and their decorations indicate the man's place of origin, social standing, and family wealth; they also identify those who claim descent from the Prophet. Every Yemeni male must have his ceremonial dagger to signify manhood and dedication to the Muslim faith. The dagger is used in ceremonial dances and is a symbol of trust in disputes brought before the sheikh. The material of the dagger handle has varied over the years, but when oil prices shot up in the late 1960s and early 1970s, and the country became flooded with wealth, the handle of choice became the most expensive in the world: black rhinoceros horn. In 1986, a well-finished horn handle costs about $20,000. Many conservationists are working with the North Yemen authorities to persuade people to use other materials. If the trade can be stopped, by diplomatic or any other means, the future of the black rhinoceros would be more hopeful.

Ͻ

THE RHINO WAS AND STILL REMAINS one of the most fearsome of the African beasts. One of the old hunters, Colonel Steadman, wrote about the rhino in *Wanderings in Africa*: "Whilst the native hunter pursued and wounded one of these formidable creatures, his horse was killed under him by one lunge of the terrible long horn. Before the rider could release and shoulder his gun, the beast came thundering at him again, and thrusting his horn into the chest of the dead horse, threw it and the rider who still bestrode the saddle, clean over his broad back. And then, with a triumphant grunt, trotted off into the forest's impenetrable depths."

Huge, terrifyingly dangerous, and unpredictable, the rhinoceros charged even at trains going full speed. Perhaps with good reason: After all, it was the railroad that brought foreigners, technology, and capital to Africa; the tracks cut a wound that bled the old life out of the continent. The white men exterminated animal populations so they could have living-room trophies, to clear land for "progress" and plantations. They also encouraged a general contempt for wild animals, which they saw as competitors of cattle and as carriers of the tsetse fly. In Uganda, Zambia, Zimbabwe, and Tanzania, the solution was to destroy the bush and slaughter the wild creatures in a vain effort to render these regions safe for men and cattle. Between 1944 and 1946, under orders from the colonial Kenya game department, John A. Hunter recorded shooting 996 rhinos to clear the land southeast of Nairobi. (To his credit, he also recorded some doubt about the wisdom of the policy.) Within a matter of a few years more, the European's paradise became a part of the modern world. A generation ago, humans had to be protected from the beasts; today the beasts must somehow be protected from us, or the next generation will know them only as history.

∾

SCIENTIFIC KNOWLEDGE of the black rhinoceros dates back only about twenty years, when fully trained and experienced field biologists first began working at research stations and universities in East Africa. We have been handed most of our ideas of the rhinoceros from the tales of hunters, explorers, and adventurers who, in general, considered the rhino a relic, a warm-blooded dinosaur that had outlived its time. The rhino was dangerous largely because of its unpredictability; it was apt to charge when another animal would hide. Its best defense was a good offense.

Peter Matthiessen said in *The Tree Where Man Was Born:* "The rhino will often thunder past its target and keep right on going until, at some point in its course, having met with no obstacle and having forgotten what excited it in the first place, it comes to a ponderous halt." Surely whoever or whatever it was thundering down upon felt the old heart come to a ponderous halt for a moment as well.

Still, according to Matthiessen: "The relative menace of what hunters know as 'the big five'—elephant, rhino, buffalo, lion, and leopard—is a popular topic of discussion in East Africa. . . . For people like myself who lack experience, it is purely a subjective business. I fear all five of the big five with all my heart, but I have the least fear of the rhino, perhaps because one may leap aside with a reasonable hope that the rhino will keep on going. Unlike the other beasts of the big five, the rhino, with its poor vision and small powers of deduction, is only anxious to dispel an insupportable suspense, and is probably as frightened as its foe."

However awesome its innate defenses, the rhino is no match for modern weapons. Poaching has become a paramilitary operation carried out with semiautomatic weapons, chain saws, axes, and razor-sharp *pangas* that can lop off a horn with one swipe. Despite the fact that game hunting of any kind has been illegal in Kenya since 1976, "We've lost more than ninety-six percent of our black rhino population in the last twenty or twenty-five years," says Werikhe. The rhino is now the most endangered species in Africa.

"There have been severe drought conditions in recent times, and, coupled with human encroachment of the range, they have taken a toll. But poaching has been the biggest factor. The poachers with assault rifles can kill as many as they want." Though they risk five years in jail for killing a rhino, Werikhe says, "These people are ruthless. We've lost many law enforcement officers as well." When a rhino horn can be sold in Asia for $18,000 a pound (nearly four times the price of gold), the heartless individual in the wild would hardly hesitate to blast a game warden who stood in the way. As a result, Werikhe says, in about 1988 Kenya adopted a "shoot to kill" policy against poachers, and more than thirty have been killed. "It is very painful to kill, but our national heritage is at stake." And national economy, one might add. Kenya earns more than $450 million annually from tourists who come to see the wild animals. The locals realize it is in their own best interest to live with the vagaries of wild animals if a percentage of the tourism revenues are shared with them—a concept called "sustainable utilization."

"We have, since independence [in 1963], been involved in a big campaign to preserve our wildlife," says Werikhe. "For the last five years, tourism has been our biggest foreign exchange element. We see wildlife as a value. We see wildlife as our second mother."

∾

WERIKHE PICKED UP ENGLISH at home and in school and speaks it fluently, with only a slight accent. "I got my degrees in the bush. You don't have to have a degree to be a conservationist. You don't have to be really well educated. All you need to do is ask yourself what you can do in order to improve the quality of life for all. I believe for conservation to have any impact, for conservation to work at any level in any given situation, you have to involve the ordinary people. You have to make them understand that they are part and parcel of this great design of nature. If conservation is to make an impact, we have to look into the welfare of the people who coexist with nature."

Werikhe works with children whenever he can, frequently visiting schools near his stops; he believes "children have a magical way of getting things done. And I think it's fair and proper that they too should be given a right to participate in conservation or environmental issues. After all, it's their world, too. I think it's wrong to underrate their power because kids can influence this issue. Given the right information in the right way at the right time, they can do a lot of good later on."

While Werikhe hikes across foreign continents, his employer supports his efforts by giving him extended leaves from his job. Werikhe is in charge of the environment of the compound at the Associated Vehicle Assemblers (AVA), where cars from Japan and Western European countries are assembled. In addition to being responsible for keeping the compound clean, he has spent the past seven years reforesting twenty acres around the plant. Today, indigenous trees, bushes, and shrubs cover a formerly barren landscape. The garden serves as a living example to the surrounding villagers. "They can see the difference and thus cooperate to the extent that they don't allow their livestock to graze on the site, which is not fenced." In return, AVA provides the villagers with discarded packing crates for firewood, and, again in return, the villagers give Werikhe useful tips on the traditional use of certain local trees and shrubs.

"My employer has helped me a lot, and I hope there'll be more companies in other parts of the world that will come out and support environmental programs. I think there is no other company in the world that has done so much for rhinos as the company I work for."

Werikhe also has the support and understanding of his family. When he travels, his wife and two daughters wait patiently at home. The first daughter was born while he was walking through England. "I'm always on the move. I think that's the price that I have to pay."

There have been other prices as well. The international poaching industry is a small, highly efficient organization of perhaps two to three hundred people, Werikhe says. "I have made enemies. Unfortunately, they are very powerful, and they know me very well—but I don't know them. I know if they had the chance, they would harm me. I equate it to the drug situation because the poaching trade is so well organized that one government alone cannot eradicate it. It's a global problem because of the international market, and it requires global attention. But I believe that as long as I'm careful and don't overexpose myself, nothing will happen. But I rarely go out in the evening. I've changed my life in the sense that I used to hang out in coffee places, and now I can't do that. If I'm not doing a project, I go home and spend time with my kids, read, and listen to music. I have to be very careful. If somebody I don't know calls and wants to meet with me, I have them come around to my place of work, where there are a lot of people around."

Although he says he has not received any actual threats to his life, Werikhe has received some "funny phone calls" and letters. But he refuses to be frightened. "Life is often a risk. You can't please everybody in this world. Whatever you do, it will not always be right to everybody. I have made enemies. But I have met a lot of wonderful people, too."

ॐ

WERIKHE ADDRESSES A LUNCHEON CROWD of 1,500 environmental lawyers, activists, and students gathered at the oldest environmental law student society in the United States and delivers his message. A few of the slides of gory mutilation are difficult to view after lunch, but in all, the audience loves him. Before the applause has ended, Werikhe begins pulling out of his knapsack Kenyan cloths and baskets, which he announces he will be selling on the law school steps to raise funds for the black rhino preservation effort. And with that, he moves from the dais to the marketplace.

Within moments, the celebrity looks no different than dozens of other campus vendors selling earrings, bagels, newspapers—or native goods for a righteous cause. Certainly a more egotistical campaigner would never consider performing so humble a task himself. But self-contained and single-minded, Werikhe displays no embarrassment. In the first few minutes, one woman sticks $10 in his pocket, and another sympathizer pays $20 for a cloth, which he does not really want and almost immediately gives away. By the end of the day, Werikhe has raised $300, a sum that goes very far in Kenya. Rather than humbling himself, he probably sees this simply as less strenuous than walking for money. His walks raise funds from the registration fees people pay to join him and from the pledges walkers earn for their footwork. But the money does not go directly to the projects; twenty-five percent or more is needed for administration and publicity.

The black rhino conservation effort needs money to erect fences around African preserves to keep rhinos in and poachers out. The funds help improve the water systems for rhino habitats and also help relocate animals to safer preserves. "Rhino sanctuaries are a new concept in conservation," Werikhe says. "Although rhinos are very territorial, sensitive animals that hate being uprooted, ultimately they are better off moved into these protected areas." For one thing, it is easier for them to find mates this way. "If we don't pair them up, they could spend their lives looking for a friend." Money is needed, too, for better communication systems and transportation for park rangers, who are ill-equipped against poachers armed with fast-firing AK-47 rifles. And some of the funds go for education projects.

Werikhe is hopeful about the rhinos' future in Kenya. In 1990, for the first time in decades, there were more births than deaths among Kenya's black rhinos: twenty-eight new calves were added, a five percent increase over the two previous years. In 1991, eighteen were born. It makes Werikhe feel that "the tide has turned in our favor. But we've got a long way to go. I won't be satisfied until I see twenty thousand black rhinos in Kenya."

However, Werikhe is very encouraged. "I think it clearly shows that if we mean business, if we really are committed to objectives, something good will come as a result. I think now it's just a question of us keeping the ball rolling. I am very optimistic about the future." The success in Kenya contrasts sharply with the fate of the animals in the neighboring countries of Chad, Sudan, and Zaire, where they are now extinct. Those countries have no Michael Werikhe, no pilgrim traveling the earth, spreading the gospel of conservation and humanity's essential bond with its own planet.

"I am happy that I have managed to make a small contribution and helped to bridge a small chasm," Werikhe says. "I'm happy that people appreciate whatever my contribution is. There is a euphoria that comes when your system is at peace with your surroundings and yourself, and you don't feel tired the way you do when you are given a job by somebody else."

∾

Werikhe asks that donations to help save the black rhinoceros be sent to the East African Wildlife Society, P.O. Box 20118, Nairobi, Kenya.

Colleen McCrory

Standing Up for Trees

COLLEEN MCCRORY

Canada

WHEN SHE FIRST STARTED OUT to save a piece of wilderness, Colleen McCrory thought, "I'll just tell them how nice it all is, and they'll give us our parks." She was concerned about proposed logging and mining in the mountains that had been her childhood playground: the Valhallas Range in British Columbia—untouched slopes, waterfalls, ancient cedar forests, unique plant communities, large lakes loaded with trout, as well as wildlife including mountain caribou, goat, and grizzly bear. The area encompasses a complete range of British Columbia landscape, from Slocan Lake cupped in the valley to the mountaintops, all still in pristine rain forest condition.

Many people are not aware that a rain forest grows in Canada, but in fact, British Columbia receives as much as 180 inches of rain a year and has a true temperate rain forest, part of more than two thousand miles of Pacific rain forest that still stretches from Alaska to Northern California. In addition to being immense, this forest is astoundingly rich, even more productive than tropical rain forests. Whereas a tropical forest grows about 185 tons of vegetation per acre, a prime Pacific Northwest forest grows nearly ten times as much, some 1,800 tons per acre.

The Pacific forest also grows much larger and older trees—huge red-woods, pines, cedar, and hemlock.

The Pacific Northwest forest is essential habitat for thousands of species of animals and billions of dollars worth of fish. But equally important, the Pacific Northwest creates about thirty percent of our planet's rainfall. Yet the Pacific Northwest forest is now only a fraction of its former size; in the United States, about ninety percent has already been cut. Canada has not made so great a dent yet; it has cut only sixty percent of its forest. But at current rates of cutting, we have about only twenty years' worth left—as much as eighty years, if we are really careful. The question is: If who is really careful? Most of this forest is owned by the public.

ᐤ

McCRORY AND HER FRIENDS formed an organization to raise public awareness about the value of wilderness, especially the Valhallas Range. "I didn't bring any special training or skills to what I did," says McCrory, "just a concern about Canada's wilderness and a desire to do something about it. Anyone can be a concerned citizen." She started by volunteering to be secretary. However, a high-school dropout, she claims to have been "the worst secretary ever. So I switched to fund-raising. I put on dances and made food. I made homemade apple juice—picked all my own apples, squeezed all the juice—and homemade tortillas for three hundred people at a time. Then I thought of going to Vancouver to expose this issue to the media a little bit more." She took the bus on a fourteen-hour trip from her home in New Denver. "I'd never done any media work before, so when I got to Vancouver, I just ripped the yellow pages listings for television and radio stations out of the phone book and caught city buses around Vancouver. I walked in and asked to see key people."

Continuing to ascend the pyramid of movers and shakers, McCrory and the group, by now named the Valhalla Society, next went to Victoria, the capital of British Columbia, to lobby. They rented a room in the Empress Hotel, one of Victoria's best-known landmarks, where tourists flock each afternoon to enjoy British-style high tea. "We called up the provincial ministers and invited them to come over. To our

amazement, all but one of them showed up." She began taking the 5
A.M. bus from New Denver to Victoria every two weeks, to knock on
doors of cabinet ministers. Frequently, she had to take along her
youngest child, two-year-old Shea. Carting stacks of files and clippings under one arm and Shea under the other, she made her way
into ministers' offices. "We'd just sit in offices until we got meetings."
Once inside, Shea played with his toys on the legislators' desks while
McCrory lobbied.

"I would hear the technical jargon of the forest industry: 'timber
supply areas, public sustained-yield units, clear-cut logging, cubic
meters'—and all of that was Greek to me. At first, it made me feel like
there was nothing I could do." But Colleen McCrory does not give in
to feelings of hopelessness. "I would rather die trying than not try at
all. One thing I've always found is that a door will open somewhere."
Or, more correctly perhaps, some time. "I lobbied for the Valhallas for
eight years." At last, in 1983, the Valhallas Provincial Park was created. It is thirty miles long and as beautiful as world-famous Banff
National Park.

"The key thing is," says McCrory, "when you take on an issue, any
issue, you have to follow it right through. You can't let go of one little part of it. As soon as you take time off, if you don't answer a letter or go to a meeting—or whatever you're following up—your issue
can be lost. It's not that these issues are so overwhelming or difficult
for government. It's making the changes that are difficult. You have to
follow it right through to the change."

According to conservationist and author Farley Mowat, "Colleen
did not start the campaign to save the Valhallas from destruction by
the so-called 'forest industry'—but it is no exaggeration to say that she
won it. It is often thus. Without one person who is prepared to sacrifice everything to the cause, who is prepared to put the rest of his or
her life on hold until a million phone calls are made, until a hundred
demonstrations are organized, until a thousand letters are written,
all the earnest support of others devoting occasional effort to the
cause will come to nothing. Every movement needs a workhorse-cum-
martyr-cum-slave."

McCrory attacked the issue with dogged persistence and won one
small victory after another by fearlessly plodding forward. Her style

lacks flamboyance; she does not try to charm or entertain or even to convince with her passion or enthusiasm. She merely states her case, calling up facts and figures from the mountains of data stored in the back of her mind. No brilliant analysis, just nearly perfect eight-second sound bites that news editors love. Television news broadcasts cut from the big, blustering, bullying opposition to feisty Colleen McCrory spitting out the one telling fact in response.

Her face displays lines beyond its years, the commemorative notches of a lifetime of outdoor activity, hard work, and hard times. In a way, she has come to look like the cause she is championing. She is tall for a woman, so most of us have to look up to her; her silver-blue eyes remind one of a clear mountain lake; when she smiles, it is like a map of mountainous British Columbia unfolding.

The province is composed almost entirely of a mountain chain called the Cordillera that was formed when crusty plates of the earth's surface collided, buckled, folded, and rode over each other up and down the western margin, from Alaska to the tip of South America. In British Columbia, the Cordillera settled into three main ranges: the Coast Mountains in the west, the Rockies in the east, and the mountains and plateaus of the interior system. The Valhallas Provincial Park lies in the southeastern portion of the interior.

∾

MCCRORY HAD BECOME CONVINCED that British Columbia's ancient forests were in the final phase of liquidation. "If industrial development continues on its present course, British Columbia could be devastated within twenty years," McCrory said ten years ago. Corporations and environmentalists are engaged in the last great arm-wrestle over a pot of resources that will never come around again. The forests of Canada are being consumed at a rate of twelve acres per second. Logging in Canada is expected to double over the next few years.

But after the long fight for the park, the little Valhalla Society was dead tired and deeply in debt. "I thought we'd all retire," McCrory says. But McCrory is not the retiring type. "I had some great contacts. I'd learned how effective people could be when they work together, and

I knew the lessons of the Valhallas could be applied in other places. I'd already been helping with the fight for a national park in the Queen Charlottes." McCrory had never been to the Queen Charlotte Islands, more than one thousand miles from her home; and lobbying for a national park had to be done in Ottawa, Ontario, the nation's capital—another place she had never been. One day in 1984, she was on a plane returning to Vancouver from the Atlantic provinces (where she also had never been before—she went there to receive the Governor General's Conservation Award), and the airplane stopped over in Ottawa. She left the plane, determined to get an appointment with the federal minister of the environment and talk to him about the proposed national park on Queen Charlotte Islands. Carrying her suitcases, she strode onto Parliament Hill. At the end of the day, she had made no progress and had missed her plane home. She was determined to stay in Ottawa until she saw the minister, but she had nowhere to stay. She talked a security guard into giving her a lift to the suburban home of her local member of parliament, for whom she had helped campaign. He was not at home, but McCrory convinced one of his children to let her sleep on the couch, which is where the M.P. found her.

By late the next night, McCrory was meeting with a very tired minister of the environment in his office. She showed him pictures and told him about the islands' unique plants and animals, about the eagles' nesting densities, and about the eleven species of whales and thousand-year-old trees. "It's the Galapagos of Canada," McCrory said. "It's an ecological treasure."

"How much will a park cost?" the minister asked.

In other words, what price for treasure? A century ago, John Muir campaigned to save Yosemite Valley by rhapsodizing about the sacred quality of wilderness that enriches one forever. Today, the issue of riches has become much more literal. Twenty years ago, even ten, wilderness advocates could still campaign by talking about the intangible values of solitude, silence, remoteness, uninterrupted naturalness, and a sense of sanctuary. Today, environmentalists also have to be able to talk about tangible values. Nearly everyone agrees that wilderness is priceless, but coalitions of decision makers weighing the trade-offs of industry investment, job security, and tax revenue need to be convinced by detailed analyses of the value of tree-farm licenses, timber licenses, and unamortized facilities. Environmentalists have had to sharpen their pencils.

In this case, McCrory did not really know the cost, but she knew major forest companies had to be compensated for losing potential revenue. She took a wild guess and said, "Twenty million dollars."

To her complete astonishment, the minister said, "Then we should be able to do this."

To her further astonishment, when she consulted the key environmentalists on the issue, they said her figures were just about on-the-button correct. There followed a three-year chess match of negotiations between the federal and provincial governments about the proposal, a process that was interrupted by federal elections. Everyone could see the players were going to change, and McCrory decided to be ready. She and other environmentalists did some political arm-twisting and got two letters confirming that, if elected, the Progressive Conservative Party, led by Brian Mulroney, would support the establishment of a park that would include the southernmost part of Queen Charlotte Islands, called South Moresby, as well as many of the small islands. They were elected, and, in 1987, a federal-provincial agreement officially designated South Moresby a National Park Reserve (subject to still unsettled native land-claims), the first national marine park in western Canada.

Within a week of the signing of the agreement, Farley Mowat received a call from McCrory. Her phone and electricity were about to be disconnected for nonpayment of bills. He bailed her out with his credit cards. "Few people realize that working as a grass-roots environmentalist often means perpetual poverty, and our victories almost never bring any alleviations of that poverty," says Mowat.

∾

McCRORY'S HOME IS IN NEW DENVER, a village of about eight hundred people, in the Slocan Valley. Canadian small towns such as this so resemble the American small town of the imagination that filmmakers producing *Superman* used one for Smallville, U.S.A., the hometown of the hero. McCrory's father was a prospector who never managed to strike pay dirt, yet her mother took in three foster children in addition to the nine of her own, and fed everybody on deer meat and macaroni. The kids attended school across the street and played in the mountains, exploring, picnicking, and paddling on the lake. Of course, the large family always required help from the kids with the chores. "But she'd have her chores finished by seven in the morning," says her sister Kathy, "and I was standing around the washing machine all day." By the age of eleven, McCrory was also helping the family by working as a waitress and chambermaid. She quit high school to marry and soon had three children. She occupied herself with gardening, baking, pickling, canning, and preserving, as well as helping her husband peel logs for the house they were building together.

As she became involved in the Valhalla Society, her dedication to it became more single-minded. "Although I loved being married and having that life, I knew I had more work to do," McCrory said recently during a visit to an office on the waterfront of San Francisco. She was dressed for the city, in a loose skirt and wearing a jacket of unconstructed linen the color of redwood bark, that framed a linen blouse embroidered with blue flowers. "I knew that whatever my work was, I couldn't do it in my relationship. I knew that I had to leave everything. I had just spent five years building a log house, but I knew I had to walk away from all of that. If I stayed where I was, something was going to die inside. My husband was a very nice man, but we weren't meant to be together anymore." She moved with her children to a little house at the lakeshore. It was heated only by a wood stove. "With my eleventh-grade education, I didn't know what I was going to do to survive, but I had to follow an inner feeling. I'll know when it's time for me to leave or to take a different direction from this, too."

Soon, in between lobbying, she was running her own little store in New Denver. Calling it the Valhalla Trading Post, she sold clothes, jewelry, camping supplies, and books, and took orders from the Sears mail-order catalog.

"Then a very peculiar bird named R. L. Smith, from the town of Sandspit—the pro-logging stronghold of the Queen Charlotte Islands—and editor of something called the *Red Neck News*, decided to make Colleen and the Valhalla Wilderness Committee the object of his attention." Says Farley Mowat, in *Rescue the Earth! Conversations with the Green Crusaders*: "Previously he had attacked the Haida Indians of the Queen Charlottes and local members of the Islands Protection Society for their environmental stands, but Colleen was a bigger target.

"The *Red Neck News* attacked the Valhalla group with such venom and hurled such unfounded charges and vitriolic abuse at Colleen that local logging interests in the Valhalla Valley were incited to organize a boycott of her store. A rock was hurled through her front window, and her children were threatened at school. Some members of the Valhalla Wilderness Committee were beaten up, and others were threatened."

McCrory says, "The *Red Neck News* accused us of vandalism, terrorism, used words like arson—really serious accusations. There were so many rumors burning, we couldn't put them all out. People I'd known and worked with all my life bought the stories. The gossip was just growing and growing and growing.

"People in the corporations were paying for these stories. The writer publicly stated he got his money from the logging company. Yet when someone libels you like that, you have to take it upon yourself to get lawyers and raise money and prosecute them. Unless you have a lot of money, you can't do much about it.

"People began to hate us. They hated my group in particular—not only in my community, but all over the province. I felt the scorn and anger of people in the community. At social functions where there was drinking, suddenly an angry logger would come over to me, saying 'What are you doing trying to take away our jobs?' Ultimately, that kind of hatred leads to violence.

"And it led to a boycott of my store by the entire logging and mining community. As it dragged on, I was losing thousands of dollars. I thought I'd lose my house. I mounted an incredible debt. After two years, I had to sell out my stock and close the store. And I still owed fifty or sixty thousand dollars.

"I thought I'd quit when that happened, quit and move out of town. But I kept reminding myself that it was my obligation to stand up for the environment. I wasn't doing anything wrong. I mean, our work is mainly educational! We do a lot of slide shows! But I went through a very helpless feeling, a feeling of failure, failure to communicate my message, which I had worked years on trying to do.

"But I always believed that people would help me out. And they have. At the right time, at my most difficult times, I've always had someone come forward to help. The World Wildlife Fund raised money for me. Someone I don't even know donated ten thousand dollars. That got the debt down, so my payments were reasonable, and I've somehow come up with that payment every month. So I've always believed that if you're doing the right work, just keep doing it, and don't worry about the consequences."

Though the financial ruin hurt McCrory, the social alienation was far worse. She was raised in a large household and thrives on having lots of friendly people around. "It was the most painful time in my life. And it happened because corporations have such a stranglehold on things. What the logging contractor did with the *Red Neck News*—what it was geared up to do—was to have people hate me by saying, 'she's taking our jobs away.' Now the corporations have formed a movement to throw hatred at the environmentalists by pointing a finger, saying we're to blame for job losses. I call them corporate gangs. What I went through is just an example of what other communities are going through. Whenever we want to have an area preserved, they say we're taking jobs away. They say, 'The environmentalists are going to close you down. They're going to close the whole province down. They want to make the whole province a park.' They call us environmental extremists—at best—or environmental parasites. They say we should be charged with treason for trying to take jobs away. This movement has grown all over British Columbia in a very big way. It's also starting to happen in other provinces."

The logging communities and the loggers know that they are losing jobs; they can see it with their own eyes, but they do not always know why. "Unfortunately," says McCrory, "they don't focus on the fact that jobs are being lost because of mismanagement or automation. All the technical changes in the industry have led to larger facilities with fewer jobs." In 1977, the industry required 10.12 workers to process one million board-feet of wood. Ten years later, it needed only 8.2 workers to handle the same amount.

"Right now we have a twenty- to thirty-percent unemployment rate in parts of British Columbia," says McCrory, "and it's only going to get worse because the logging jobs are going down. But the Valhalla Society has always tried to work out job strategies. Only once did we save a forest and lose jobs—we lost thirty-five jobs there. In comparison, we've lost one hundred thousand jobs in British Columbia due to automation in the industry over the past ten years."

In addition to automation, overcutting is a serious problem affecting employment. Government as well as industry officials expect timber yields to drop by at least twenty-five percent as the old-growth trees—trees that took two hundred years to grow—run out. Already, sixty percent of British Columbia coastal old-growth forest is estimated to have disappeared. At the present rate of destruction, virtually all unprotected coastal old-growth forest will be gone by the year 2020.

Anyone who has ever driven through a U.S. Forest Service forest has seen the sign "Land of Many Uses." The basic assumption behind official U.S. forest policy—where it can be said to exist—is that public forests should be managed for multiple purposes: for recreation, for timber, and for wildlife habitat. But British Columbia's forest service is very different. "Unlike the United States Forest Service, British Columbia's forest service makes no pretense of managing its public forests equally for timber and for other uses," wrote Catherine Caufield in the *New Yorker*. "The single goal of its timber management is to create a prosperous timber economy. Instead, by allowing overcutting, it has contributed to the destabilization of the timber industry. In the past decade, jobs in the province's timber industry have declined by twenty-five percent, partly because of automation, partly because of a slump in the market, and partly because in some areas old-growth timber has run out."

∾

AN OLD-GROWTH FOREST is really many forests laced in a sophisticated interdependency. Under the towering evergreens hundreds of years old live other trees, shrubs, and herbs on several levels of growth and at different stages of their life cycles. The ecosystem is so complex and intertwined, in fact, that the old-growth forest of the Pacific region continues to defy precise definition, but experts generally agree that true old-growth forests contain large, old living trees, many layers of vegetation, large standing dead trees, and large dead trees on the ground and in the streams. Every part of the old-growth tree, from the tip to the roots, is home to a large community of plants, birds, mammals, and insects. After a thousand-year-old tree dies and falls to the ground, it will continue to support forest life for four hundred years more. Dead and down trees provide nutrients, water, and shelter; and they help prevent soil erosion.

To survive, the forest has to be able to spread out across a range of elevations. You cannot save the forest without the trees, and the survival of the forests depends on protecting the diversity of trees as well as a diversity of land forms. In the Pacific Northwest, the unchallenged giant is the Douglas fir. Known to some native peoples as the "real tree," it can reach two hundred feet tall; specimens six hundred years old are not uncommon; record Douglas fir are twice as old and nearly three hundred feet tall. Other characteristic species include the Western red cedars of coastal British Columbia and the hemlock of Northern California.

Half a century of clear-cutting and road building by both countries has already left North America with only fragments of forest. Clear-cutting is a practice of felling all the trees in a large area. Only stumps and "slash" (branches and other residue) remain. In theory, the clear-cut region will be naturally reseeded by remaining trees. Usually, in practice, the area is burned or bulldozed to remove the slash, and then foresters replant with seedlings. In theory, clear-cutting can be an appropriate logging practice. It has advantages over selective logging, in which only a few trees are taken out at a time. Clear-cutting is more economical. Also, some species of trees, such as the Douglas fir, do not grow well in shade and therefore may not come back after selective logging. Selective logging requires repeatedly intruding in forested areas with roads and heavy equipment. (The U.S. Forest Service is the biggest road builder in the world.) In addition, selective logging harms the forest's genetic stock by removing the biggest, straightest trees—the best specimens—and leaving behind the stunted, scrawny trees to reproduce.

However, despite the theories, the fact is that after nearly fifty years of intensive logging, the industry has not been able to take large amounts of timber out of the forest without damaging water quality, wildlife, and the forest's capacity for regeneration. Clear-cutting, as it is practiced today, is a destructive, ugly practice. Clear-cut areas never return to their former grandeur—either as scenery or as timber. Clear-cutting has already marched through the more accessible valley floors and onto the steeper hillsides, where the devastation is both more visible and more dangerous. As clear-cutting spreads uphill, it aggravates soil erosion and eventually leads to thunderous, crushing landslides. In British Columbia, there is no legal limit on the size of clear-cuts. One whopper covers more than one hundred eighty square miles and can be seen from space by the naked eye.

This valuable timber is being cut in vast quantities and at a breakneck pace. And for what? Douglas fir that have taken centuries to grow are used for scaffolding for construction, for concrete forms, and for other disposable materials in construction. Valuable trees are pulped to make paper and synthetic fiber. This type of high-quality timber does have valid uses—for objects that require good wood: furniture, paneling, musical instruments, lamps, and doors. Using Pacific Northwest forests for pulp and fiber is like using fine linen for toilet paper.

Of course, this kind of clear-cutting cannot last forever. Sooner or later, the forests will disappear, followed immediately by the timber industry. Already, the first symptoms of the death of the industry are showing up, and industry apologists blame them on environmentalists. Once again, Catherine Caufield writes: "The shortages and suffering have already begun. The fate of the whales and of the whaling industry presented the world with a similar problem. The question was a simple one: Should a species be exterminated to postpone the inevitable collapse of the whaling industry? The choice we now face is less extreme. Unlike the whaling industry, the timber industry is not doomed; change, not death, is inevitable. The question for us now is: Shall we destroy our ancient forests to postpone this change for a few years?"

"This is our last opportunity to preserve what has taken eons and eons to create," says McCrory. "We have to be the generation that sets these forests aside for hundreds and hundreds of years. This is it. Once they're logged, they're gone forever. We'll never get this opportunity again."

∾

LOGGING HAS BEEN THE CHIEF INDUSTRY of British Columbia in this century. Since the introduction of railways in the early 1900s, most of the province's forest products were sent eastward by rail or shipped to the western United States. Then the Panama Canal was opened. It became profitable to ship the products all the way to Europe, and the industry expanded rapidly. Today, most of the timber cut in British Columbia is exported to Japan (which lost almost half its timber resources after World War II when it ceded its timber resources to the victorious allies—Manchuria to China and Sakhalin Island to the Soviet Union).

Forestlands in Canada are managed very differently than in the United States. Although more than ninety percent of British Columbia's forests are owned by the public, and under the Canadian system they are the responsibility of the provincial government, this does not mean that they are managed for the public's benefit. The British Columbia Ministry of Forests can license private companies to log and manage large tracts of public forests in perpetuity, with very little supervision from the forest service and with virtually no public input. In Canada, with a huge land area and a population density of only six people per square mile, there seemed no end to the bounties of nature.

Most of the data on public forests in Canada, including the amount of timber cut in each licensed area and the price the government charges licensees for logs, are kept private, on the theory that companies have a commercial right to confidentiality. Therefore, it is nearly impossible for private citizens or environmental groups to check the government's or a private company's claims about the state of the forests. Licensees are required to adhere to vague management plans that are public documents, but the plans can be amended in private, without public notice. Not only that: If the licensee or the government violates the management plan, citizens have no right to take them to court.

The most valuable of Canadian timber licenses are "tree-farm licenses," which include perpetual rights to large areas of forest. The tree-farm license is free to its holder and can be bought and sold like any piece of property; it can be worth billions of dollars. And if the government does anything to reduce the amount of timber that can be cut on a piece of land by more than five percent over a period of twenty-five years, it must pay the holder of the license for lost future profits. Again, according to Catherine Caufield, writing in the *New Yorker*, "The Ministry of Forests sets the allowable cut of each licensed area on the basis of forest inventories, which the licensees carry out periodically. In general, the inventories do not exclude all areas that are inaccessible, environmentally sensitive, or valuable for wildlife, scenery, or archeology, or that have uneconomic timber.

"Neither the province nor the timber industry claims that logging at present levels is sustainable."

In other words, "It's a total sellout," says McCrory. "Alberta has leased away nearly all of its northern forest; in Manitoba, a single company—Repap—has control over twenty percent of the province. We're going to clear-cut our forests, kill our rivers, perhaps alter our entire northern ecosystem and our native cultures so foreign investors can make a short-term profit." Many of the jobs that might result from logging forests of British Columbia do not stay at home; they go to workers in other countries, principally Japan, Korea, and Taiwan where the timber is processed. These are the so-called value-added jobs that occur after the tree is felled. The *Globe and Mail* has reported that "a stand of 16 aspen, 16 meters high, fetches tree royalties of about $1.40 in Alberta. In Manitoba the royalty paid by Repap will be roughly $2.48. That same aspen converted to bleached kraft pulp is worth $950 in the hands of a company like Daishowa. The paper refined from that pulp is worth between $1,300 and $2,000. In other words, Daishowa, by shipping seventy percent of its Alberta pulp to paper mills in Japan, could recoup its $550 million investment in just three years."

McCrory believes that timber should not totally dominate the economy and that one key measure ought to be diversifying the economy by strengthening tourism. "The industry claims the issue is jobs versus the environment, when really, a healthy environment provides jobs. Wilderness tourism in British Columbia has grown by thirty-eight to forty percent in the last couple of years. It's the fastest-growing industry in the province." A government study of the Valhalla region, for example, showed that the costs of logging would exceed harvest benefits. By contrast, preserving the area would result in $16 million in new capital investment, $3.4 million in annual tourism revenue, and 229 permanent jobs.

༄

To answer the other accusation—that she wants to turn the entire province into a park—the Valhalla Society and a network of other environmental groups, acting as a coalition called Canada's Future Forests Alliance, has produced a map that clearly outlines areas it wants protected. If all the areas proposed as additions to British Columbia's park system were adopted, the total area of the parks would comprise thirteen percent of the land base, compared with the current 5.24 percent. (The United Nations recently recommended preserving from twelve to thirteen percent of each nation's land.) Most of the current parks are in alpine or subalpine regions and consist almost entirely of rocks, snow, and ice that could not be used for anything else, even logging. As in the United States, the parks in British Columbia have usually been preserved for their awe-inspiring scenery rather than for their development potential. Under the existing park system, approximately two percent of provincial forests cannot be logged. Under the coalition blueprint, about five percent of the forests would be preserved from logging.

"We wanted to get beyond the situation where we were fighting one battle after another in isolation from the total picture," says McCrory. "This is a system plan that has taken us five years of research. Even though the Valhalla Society put it together, it's based on input from a collection of grass-roots organizations, wilderness groups, forestry groups, and native groups—about four hundred organizations all together."

Pointing to the map where proposed and existing parks are shaded in green, McCrory says, "Every green dot represents files and files of information about statistical and ecological significance. There are one hundred twenty-two park proposals. We have whole valleys that can be saved—not just fragments of a river or a little watershed. These are the last large wilderness areas, not only in Canada, but in the world.

"The Valhalla issue made us aware of other issues in British Columbia. I thought the work would end with the Valhalla Park, but it was only the beginning. It's a lifelong commitment now for all of us."

This is the way, in fact, that most environmentalists become involved in the effort to save forests. "The battle to preserve what remains of our ancient forests is not driven by science or economics or an abstract respect for natural systems, though all those do play a role. It is driven primarily by passion for a place," writes Catherine Caufield in the *New Yorker*. "Across the Pacific region, people have fought to save their patch of forest—the one they live near, the one they know, the one they walk in or camp in, the one that overlooks their town, the one they see every day. What has now come to be referred to as 'the ancient-forest movement' was not started by professional environmentalists in Washington, D.C., for some theoretical or bureaucratic reason. It was started and is being carried on by scores of local groups."

McCrory, who thrives on mobs of people, has found her talent: networking and public speaking. She has become so effective at generating public support that she has been accused of exploiting the news media. "At each press conference, McCrory reveals her 'shock and dismay' at some new 'environmental crisis,'" one newspaper report complained. McCrory responds that her words are real, the situation is out of control. Hearing in her heart chain saws speeding through one irreplaceable forest after another is what keeps her on her feet and moving.

She travels to talk to media, to visit government officials, and to speak (as well as listen) with people in the communities that will be affected. Logging operations are moving farther and farther into the wilderness because the areas near population centers have already been logged. Most of the population of Canada crowds around the cities and towns on the 49th parallel, where the logging industry has cut already cut just about every last stick it can. Logging operations move on to more distant areas, where communities are isolated and less informed. That is, less informed in some ways. Many of these communities are native people who, McCrory has found, are well informed in other ways. "They can tell you what a lot of this means. An elder spoke about a dark cloud coming over the north, a vast area of darkness. They know a lot about what's coming to their areas."

It was while speaking in Alberta that she first learned that $4.5 billion worth of pulp mills were being built in northern Alberta's boreal forest. She spent the next six months traveling across the country to investigate, and she discovered more distressing news. "Without any public debate, forest operating licenses have been negotiated with industry, in most cases on a perpetually renewable agreement for up to twenty-five years for all the productive forested land across the nation."

The boreal forest grows in the subalpine zone, just below the polar cap of the globe, and stretches like a necklace across Canada and around the northern regions of the world. The trees—vast stands of aspen, birch, poplar, larch, spruce, fir, and pine—grow slowly because the soil at their roots thaws for only a short period each summer. It can take a century or more for a boreal forest to regenerate after cutting— if it comes back at all. It constitutes twenty-five percent of the world's remaining forests. Because the forest generates oxygen, "I call it the lung of the earth," says McCrory. Clear-cutting, which used to be called "a scar on the face of Mother Nature," is now a knife to her lungs.

Trees pull carbon dioxide out of the air and store it in humus, peat, and other organic material. Experts now believe that more carbon is stored in the boreal zone than in all the world's tropical rain forests combined. When the soils and peat bogs are exposed to air and sunlight after logging, they release carbon dioxide into the atmosphere. If too much of it is released, it acts like an invisible blanket to trap heat and creates the greenhouse effect that is warming the planet.

"Approximately forty new pulp, paper, and sawmills are being built or expanded across Canada's boreal forest, and all are being developed without the public hearing process," says McCrory. "Some of the largest pulp mills in the world are being built in Canada without any studies of the potential impact. There has been no meaningful consideration for the communities directly affected. To feed these new huge mills, logging in Canada is expected to double over the next few years. Thousands of miles of new logging road systems are being constructed so that logging and pulping the last forested lands can begin."

During her travels, McCrory says, she has slept on nearly every couch in the country. She organized Canada's Future Forests Alliance, an umbrella group representing one million people across Canada; it seeks a moratorium on new development projects in Canada's forests. Conservation groups from nations in the former Soviet bloc and from the United States are discussing joint projects to protect the remaining boreal forests.

"There are all kinds of things people can do. One simple thing is to take recycling more seriously. Buy one-hundred-percent recycled paper. Don't buy white paper or bleached paper. If you have to use white paper, use unbleached white paper. Be a lot more aware of packaging in stores.

"The key changes are going to come by people becoming involved at the grass-roots level. People need to know you can still link up with workers who are legitimately concerned. Once you work on one issue together, then you can work on another issue together, and then you're friends," McCrory says with a simple common-sense approach. "It takes years to make those friends, but we're beginning to do that in British Columbia despite the incredible odds against us. We're doing a lot of work right now with the fishermen's union, which is losing jobs because of the loss of rivers and key areas on the coast of British Columbia for salmon spawning.

"The governments of the world are so intertwined with industry that we're going to all have to insist that decisions go back into the communities—and be a participant in the decisions. A lot of companies have gotten a lot of free money from our tax-paying dollars, and we have precious little time to turn things around. That money could be put into very creative projects in the community."

∞

Contact the Valhalla Wilderness Society at Box 224, New Denver, British Columbia, VOG ISO, Canada.

Wadja Egnankou

Taking the Heat

WADJA EGNANKOU

Ivory Coast

 THE TEMPERATURE IN ABIDJAN, the capital of Ivory Coast, averages 80°F with eighty-
five percent humidity—hot, damp, and
uncomfortable. Likewise, the current political and economic climate of the country—
almost no one feels comfortable. The country swelters in heat and
anxiety and, for the past decade, has been hoping for a change.

President Houphouet-Boigny has ruled Ivory Coast since 1960,
when the nation declared independence from the French. He has been
known to take whatever measures he thinks necessary, including violent or illegal ones, to ensure the continuation of his rule. For two
decades, a certain kind of stability has resulted from the dictatorship,
but now the country may be headed toward drastic change. Severe economic recession has begun to affect even the elite.

Houphouet-Boigny's ideology is materialism, and his early success
impressed even those who questioned this goal and the president's
tactics for achieving it. Between 1960 and 1979, the gross national product grew by nearly eight percent per year, a stellar figure compared with
the minimal or negative growth rates often found elsewhere in Africa.
In 1984, income averaged $1,100 per person per year, one of the
highest in Africa. Ivory Coast's relative wealth attracts immigrants from

neighboring countries, some two million people so far, who now make up about one-fourth of the black population and seem willing to take the least-skilled, lowest-paying jobs. More than two hundred thousand Europeans, mostly French, fill top management positions and control most of the money. The majority of Ivory Coasters, segmented into dozens of tribes with little sense of national identity, subsist by farming and fishing.

Roughly half the people of Ivory Coast still live in the countryside, where they wear native dress and follow ancient traditions and customs, including magical arts. In forest villages just a short drive from the superhighway, magicians of the forest are believed to have fantastic powers. Some can convert themselves into pure energy—go to Paris, have a conversation, and come back without moving from the spot—they send doubles. Sorcerers can make themselves invisible and set houses on fire. Prophets can identify evil spirits and banish them. Rumors of human sacrifice persist.

Ivory Coast's population of 10.6 million people includes some sixty different tribes, each with its own language—in a country the size of the state of New Mexico. More than sixty percent of the people continue to honor African beliefs and religious practices and have not turned to either Islam or Christianity, the two main imported religions.

The president's development program, based on a vision of continued economic growth, has been ambitious. But many of the projects are little more than monuments to presidential ego. The most striking of these: his ancestral village of Yamoussoukro, one hundred forty miles inland from Abidjan. In 1983, Houphouet-Boigny declared Yamoussoukro the capital of the country. Because the actual government bureaucracy remains in Abidjan, he ordered that a superhighway be built between the two. The entire former village of Yamoussoukro has been incorporated into the grounds of the new presidential palace. An artificial lake has been created on one side of the palace and stocked with crocodiles (Yamoussoukro had no crocodiles before) in what seems to many to be a signal that uninvited guests are not welcome. Every afternoon, a man wearing a skullcap and a flowered gown feeds the crocodiles fresh meat and a live chicken. Tourists photograph the spectacle.

The surrounding African fields of bush—unused common land and wild trees—have been organized into plantations where mango, avocado, and pineapple grow in straight rows. Inside the new city, the land has been leveled and outlined with avenues as wide as jet runways. Extravagant modern buildings have sprung up and still await full occupancy, even as they decay from lack of maintenance and from the humidity that seeps into everything. One of the most extravagant buildings, costing some $175 million, is Houphouet-Boigny's pet project: the Basilica of Our Lady of Peace. The world's largest Roman Catholic cathedral, it features a dome larger than that of Saint Peter's, in Rome. After church on Sunday, the citizens can head out to the only golf course in West Africa; the president has suggested that his people take up golf. The golf club is attached to the twelve-story Hotel President, complete with swimming pool. The hotel, like the offices, awaits full use, although its engineering keeps it pumped full of well-chilled air, creating an almost museumlike feeling.

Misfortune struck in the late 1970s, when world prices dropped for coffee and cocoa, the nation's principal cash crops. Timber exports, the third-largest source of foreign exchange, declined because of continued overexploitation. Meanwhile, the cost of imports rose. Foreign borrowing to finance money-losing development projects sent Ivory Coast's debt skyrocketing far beyond its ability to repay. Houphouet-Boigny, now more than eighty years old, surely must be disappointed that his country has slid from a shining example of one of Africa's most stable and prosperous nations, to its current state of struggle and loss. The people are disappointed, too. In the last few years, protests, demonstrations, and riots have occurred, and even leading members of the establishment are voicing discontent (although carefully). Ivory Coast has an atmosphere that encourages great caution as well as private outrage. Dissent is not tolerated, and reports are widespread of political prisoners jailed for years.

The president stays in power, in large part, because of his ancestral royal heritage. The people still feel loyalty to that tradition, to the social bonds of their society. A World Bank official, Ismail Serageldin, has pointed out that societies with strong social bonds usually offer the people few opportunities, but societies that offer a lot of opportunity, like the United States, usually place lower value on social bonding. The worst case is to have neither. "If we trade bonds for options and do not succeed economically, we risk catastrophe," says Serageldin.

Within this complex and grim political context, Wadja Egnankou, a humble college professor at the country's only university (founded in 1963), spends a lot of time looking over his shoulder, always wary of government spies, because he is considered subversive. It is an indication of the degree of repression in Ivory Coast that such a figure would be considered subversive: He is the country's only academic expert on mangrove forests and has been a lone voice in the struggle to protect them and to help local communities.

Handsome, with a small, compact body, Egnankou looks to be an intelligent young scholar. He smiles beautifully and almost compulsively, keeping his mood up with imagination and mental play that easily finds pleasant things to appreciate, whether a beautiful building or a beautiful woman. He radiates a kind of charm that makes people take to him easily and that may have been cultivated as a first line of defense to keep him out of trouble. Sitting beside me on an airplane flight from San Francisco to New York, wearing jeans and a sweatshirt, he bears more resemblance to a naive college kid than to a firebrand. In Ivory Coast, however, the military elite considers college kids to be pampered rich brats. When university students rioted in 1991, a military assault team attacked their dormitories.

Egnankou understands English better than he speaks it, so we converse through a translator for our in-depth discussions. With the caution that characterizes political survivors, he politely declines to discuss with me the political aspects of his campaign to save his country's mangrove forests. However, that still leaves much to be said, and he is eager to say it.

∾

THE COASTLINE OF IVORY COAST consists of sandbars and low, sandy islands built up by heavy surf and ocean currents. Behind these barrier islands, lagoons form natural inland waterways for light craft, but entrance channels to the ports have to be dredged. The harbor at Abidjan, one of the biggest ports in West Africa, is man-made. At the turn of the twentieth century, fishermen paddled canoes through the waters surrounding Abidjan, then a sleepy fishing village of about seven hundred inhabitants. Today, cargo ships and cruise ships ply the same waters.

Mangrove forests thrive in the waterways of coastal creeks and river mouths, where fresh water meets salt water, between high- and low-water marks, in rich, silty soil. The trees may reach seventy-five feet, but most are usually between twenty-five and forty feet tall. They form dense, bushy stands with tangles of stiltlike roots exposed at low tide.

Until very recently, coastal mangrove forests have been considered "wastelands" by planners and administrators. The forests looked like hot, mucky, mosquito-ridden messes. They were valueless, and developers thought the best approach was to drain them, clear them, and build on them—make them pay.

Today we know that the mangroves are profoundly useful ecosystems. They create a kind of living alternative to elaborate engineering projects. Coastal mangroves protect Ivory Coast from the tropical storms of the Atlantic Ocean, and they defend the tropical rain forests that grow down to the shore. Mangroves also control soil erosion, one of West Africa's worst problems. In addition to the tangible services they provide, mangrove forests maintain and repair themselves—an important consideration in a developing country.

Globally, mangrove ecosystems are thought to contain only about eighty species of trees and shrubs. But they provide habitat for more than two thousand species of fish and reptiles. In Ivory Coast, the mangrove forest is home to manatees, sea turtles, crocodiles, and numerous reptile and bird species—including parrots and touracos. The mangroves play a critical role in the food chain, serving as a nursery for many kinds of fish, a main source of protein in Ivory Coast.

The mangroves' economic value as fish habitat was demonstrated by a model on the opposite side of the world from Ivory Coast, on Marco Island off the southwest coast of Florida. Considered to be a prime development spot in the mid-1960s, Marco Island's watery mangrove forest was cut to make room for a network of sea-walled canals and expensive homes. The development worried many people, and studies revealed that these mangrove forests had great unsuspected economic value. Mangrove forests were far from wastelands;

they allowed people to derive income that averaged $4,000 to $30,000 per acre, from fishing, tourism, and recreation. The mangroves' value to commercial fisheries is one of the most compelling arguments for saving these coastal forests. University studies showed that seventy-five percent of Florida's game fish (a $5-billion-a-year industry) and ninety percent of its commercial fish, lobster, and shrimp (another $165 million a year) depend on food from mangroves at some point in their lives. In 1976, the Army Corps of Engineers stopped further building and saved more than two thousand acres of mangrove swamp.

The mangroves are a virtual food factory, with an assembly line that begins with leaves falling from the trees. Three tons of leaves fall per acre per year; as the leaves decompose, they are eaten by larval crabs, shrimp, and mollusks. These are then eaten by larger shrimp, clams, and lobsters, which are eaten by even larger fish, which become food for people.

The mangrove has other economic uses as well. In West Africa, its leaves serve as fodder for camels, the light wood is used in carpentry or for fish-net supports, and the wood makes excellent fuel.

But economics aside, the mangroves are beautiful and wondrous. Egnankou says, "When you go into a well-developed mangrove forest, it's like walking into an air-conditioned house. In the water, you can see the fish right there at your feet. You see birds, all sorts of animals—it's like a paradise. When I travel through the mangroves, I feel very happy."

Egnankou believes that one hope for the future of the mangroves lies in eco-tourism, a new industry that has succeeded brilliantly in several tropical countries. In Trinidad, for example, the Caroni Swamp park has become a popular recreational area, yet it required little development—only the small cost of providing relatively simple access for visitors. Costa Rica's national parks, too, have preserved tropical ecosystems through eco-tourism and profited in the process. Egnankou tells villagers, "You are living in paradise here, and you're destroying it and wasting it. There are people—tourists—who would come and pay a lot of money for you to be a guide for a day." Egnankou envisions tourists coming to stay in typical coastal houses made of clay and raffia palms, with sand floors, where they would live like the villagers: swimming in the lagoons, fishing, relaxing by day, then making music and dancing at night.

The image of contemporary eco-tourism contrasts sharply and compellingly with the environmentally hostile tourist development favored by the president: international hotels identical to all the other international hotels in all the other former colonial territories of the world. For example, in Abidjan, along the lagoon, in the garden of the Forum Golf Hotel, artificial rocks and hollow, plastic elephants (the elephant ivory trade gave the country its name) surround the swimming pool, around which French-speaking women—mostly the wives of visiting businessmen and technicians—sunbathe topless. Children gleefully slide down the water chute. African security guards in uniforms stand sentry. The white sand of an artificial beach has been mounded over a concrete retaining wall two or three feet high above the lagoon. Ironically, here and there, in sheltered places—in the lee of boats, against the concrete wall— small mangroves still manage to sprout in the tainted lagoon water, as though asserting their natural right to the place.

The current government has plans for an elaborate seaside resort that would destroy ten thousand acres of coastal lagoons to the east of Abidjan. A city for 120,000 inhabitants would be built, along with an international exhibition complex, luxury accommodations, entertainment facilities, plus an amusement park and an animal reserve. At present, the plans exist only on paper.

ૈ

EGNANKOU RUNS HIS CAMPAIGN to save mangroves on next to nothing. Even such minor expenses as air-mail postage and photocopying costs are major items and can be afforded only at personal sacrifice. Though Egnankou is a university professor, he must struggle to make ends meet, just like most of his countrymen. When you ask him what his work involves, he says: "I spend time preparing lessons, working on research, and thinking about how to get resources." The big-ticket expenses, such as a car to get to the mangroves and a canoe with a motor to get around them, are rarities only supplied when visitors come and ask him to show them the mangroves. It is really only then that he can afford to do some of his own research. "I should go to the field every month, but because I don't have funds, sometimes I go only three times a year."

Although Egnankou was trained in techniques for remote-sensing and for reading satellite images to help inventory forests, he lacks the most basic kind of personal computer and software for this work. He has an entire program for conservation of the mangrove forests, but the lack of resources makes it hard to implement. "It's kind of haphazard," he says. Nevertheless, Egnankou's program has four stages.

First is sensitization of the people who live in or near the mangrove forests. The second is inventory of the mangroves and other aspects of the mangrove forests. The third is mapping the mangrove forests, and the fourth is starting fish plantations in the mangrove forest.

In the first stage, he teaches the people about the mangrove forest and how it works, how to keep it nurturing the fish. "I go to the village and get everyone together—the old people, the young people—and show them slides and explain," Egnankou says. The people live because the fish live; the fish live because the mangroves live. This concept is supported by local religions that emphasize proper relationships with all beings as a key to harmony.

Some people have been using poison or DDT to kill fish to sell in the markets. They do not understand that they risk poisoning anyone who eats the fish. Nor do they understand that overfishing will have bad results: "For the next two, three, four, or five years, there are no fish; the people are poor again. They have to realize that the water is like their plantation. Once they realize that, they don't want to poison it."

Although Egnankou is well aware of the modern method of fish farming by raising fish in basins and releasing them to harvest later, he says this method is too expensive for Ivory Coast. "You have to have some sort of capital to get the starter fish and to feed them." Instead, he encourages a traditional fishing method called *acadja*: "The natives build a trap surrounded by mangrove sticks. The mangrove sticks start decomposing and become natural bait. Little fish come to nibble the nutrients, go inside, and can't get out. The people wait three or four months, until the fish are big enough to harvest. But if the mangroves disappear, the fishing method will disappear."

∾

EGNANKOU WAS BORN IN FEBRUARY 1961, the fourth in a family of six boys. His father died when Egnankou was too young to even know him. How his mother managed to raise the boys, Engnankou says, had to do with God's help. A bright student, encouraged by his uncle who was a primary-school teacher in his hometown, Egnankou loved learning while his brothers "loved life: smoking, drinking, and dancing." Though he played soccer and enjoyed American movies such as *Rambo* (he has seen all of them) and *The Terminator*, he also excelled at school, where he skipped two grades and won scholarships. The scholarships he credits to God's help.

He first saw the mangroves when he was a boy of five or six years old, but it was not until he was studying in France at the University of Toulouse, where he majored in botany, that a teacher impressed on him their importance. He now holds a Ph.D. from the University of Toulouse. Since 1985, he has been a professor of botany and tropical ecology at the School for Science and Technology at the National University in Abidjan. He teaches there for half the year and pursues research the other half.

Because education is generally revered in Africa, Egnankou, born at the same time as his country's independence, has risen from a simple villager to a member of the respectable middle class. He has two small children and lives with their mother, though he is not married in the Western sense. Having attained the best of what French colonization had to offer an Ivory Coaster, he insists on sharing his education with his country, where forty-three percent of the population is fifteen or younger, and most are uneducated. What makes his work truly exceptional is the solitariness of his efforts.

Egnankou has no organization, network, or resources. He struggles to help the people of his country, despite a hostile political environment. He uses his expensive and high-status education to fight for the lowly mangrove swamps. Singlehandedly, he risks all he has gained to work for the betterment of his country and its natural resources.

∽

IN 1989, the Ivory Coast government applied for a loan from the African Development Bank (ADB) to finance the construction of a coastal road that would traverse the country's last largely intact mangroves and rain forest. Egnankou was asked to join an international team of scientists conducting an environmental impact assessment. His part of the study focused on the environmental impact of the road project on the mangrove forests. He analyzed the direct and indirect effects of the road's construction on the region's natural resource base. To mitigate the damage, he proposed that certain measures be carried out before, during, and after road construction. However, neither the ADB nor the government was willing to implement even minimal environmental protection measures. So they shelved the environmental impact study and began road construction.

Egnankou's work did prove very useful, however, in a case study prepared by the Environmental Defense Fund that documented the general lack of environmental consideration in projects funded by the ADB. The United States and other donor governments used the study to press for environmental reform at the ADB. Ultimately, the road was rerouted away from environmentally sensitive areas.

Egnankou believes that environmental and social issues are so tightly interrelated that they must be approached together. He has been a courageous critic of the state-run forestry agency, whose corruption was exposed by an independent audit in 1990. The audit, demanded by the World Bank, revealed that stumpage fees and other taxes collected by the agency had been paid directly into the private bank account of Ivory Coast's minister of agriculture. The minister had to resign before the World Bank would lend more money to Ivory Coast. But the basic forestry policies remained unchanged; the agency is still clearing tropical forests for plantations, even though Ivory Coast has been suffering from one of the world's highest rates of deforestation since the mid-1970s. Tropical rain forest areas have been chopped from an estimated thirty million acres in the early 1960s to fewer than four million acres today.

In the African rain forest, which covers a meager eight percent of the land, a host of biological wealth including one hundred varieties of trees, may be found in a single square mile: Balsa, rubber, mahogany, and ebony grow close together. But most of these forests were cleared for timber exports and for cash crops, mainly cocoa and coffee.

This large-scale cash crop production has reduced the amount of land available to grow food. Small landowners are forced into short-term slash-and-burn farming in forest areas. Farmers clear a small area of forest by slashing down the trees and burning them; the farmers cultivate the clearing for a few years, until the soil is depleted. Then they move to another patch, leaving the field to regenerate. It is a workable system of long-term rotation—where land is plentiful. But land is no longer plentiful. The severe depletion of Ivory Coast's forests has led to increasing drought conditions, which maximize the impact of the harmattan, a hot and dry wind from the Sahara. It is the familiar vicious circle, which has led to a precipitous decline in agricultural productivity that further threatens both food supply and export crops in many parts of the country.

Egnankou has pointed out that it is ecological and economical insanity to replace productive climax forests with monocultural plantations, which are highly vulnerable to disease; one blight can wipe out the entire plantation. Egnankou's program could reverse this trend. Only a fraction of the money now being spent by the forest agency would be enough to assist local villages in replanting deforested areas. This would not only stimulate the local economy but would also have long-lasting environmental and social benefits. So far, his calls have largely gone unheard—at home.

In 1992, Egnankou was awarded the Goldman Environmental Prize for his work. The prize includes $60,000 that should ease his strain for resources. The prize also conveys tremendous international publicity and prestige that has already afforded him some political clout. President Houphouet-Boigny honored him with a luncheon reception at the president's palace. While there, Egnankou had the opportunity to give a speech in which he described his work. Many observers on the local scene believe that Egnankou is now poised to become a major leader in the environmental and political movements of the country, as well as in other western and central African countries.

∾

Contact Wadja Egnankou at: Faculté des Sciences et Techniques, Département de Botanique, 22 B.P. 582, Abidjan 22, Ivory Coast.

Lois Gibbs

Mrs. Gibbs Goes to Washington

LOIS GIBBS

United States

 THE ISSUE OF TOXIC WASTE is one of the most terrifying—and mind-numbing—of all environmental issues. But even here, victories are possible. Communities all across the country have leaped into action, united in opposition to proposed hazardous waste sites, according to Lois Gibbs, founder and executive director of the Citizens' Clearinghouse for Hazardous Wastes. "If they didn't have a sense of community prior to the proposal, they developed it as a result. It's one issue that can bring all different people together," says Gibbs.

"The first time I saw it was in a little town in Louisiana. There was an African-American community, very poor but very together, a very tight community literally across the tracks from an extremely wealthy community of old Louisiana white folks. In between, there was a BFI [Browning and Ferris Industries] hazardous waste dump site, and BFI wanted to expand the site.

"The black community organized itself, and the white community organized itself, and we worked with them long distance on the phone. We said, 'You'll have to get together. You have resources to offer one another.' I went down there to a meeting at a wealthy white person's house, and here were these very poor black people sitting in there, and the two groups were talking to each other as equals. It was very impressive to see that happen.

"It was like, 'Well, Herbert, what do you have to offer? What can your folks do? What are your strengths? What are the abilities you have?' And Herbert was talking about, 'Well, we don't have much money, but we have lots of people we can turn out at the meeting. We'd be willing to help with fliers.' And the white community said, 'We know the business community in town, so we can get them to support us. We have some money, so we can help pay for fliers.'

"Here were two neighborhoods that would probably never have much in common—and they continue to work with one another now around other community-based issues. So that's one of the things that keeps us going. It's not just win or lose a toxic site. It's really effecting social change.

"Rarely a day goes by that someone hasn't called our office with a terrible, horrible story of tragedy befalling a family member. But on the other hand, we're in a really nice position to see communities win. And not only have they won their local issue, but they become an empowered group of people who are willing to move on and take on other issues. I guess we sort of see it as recolonizing the United States, community by community. Getting these folks who would not normally organize around anything, and seeing them set goals, go after them, and win. There are enough wins to balance out the tragedies."

One of the first goals set by the clearinghouse was to help local people prevent siting of new hazardous-waste landfills. Lois is proud that, "since 1978, there has not been one new commercial hazardous-waste site opened in this country. It has nothing to do with laws; you can build one tomorrow. But it's because wherever they try to build them, we were able to assist people in an educational way, a technical way, and an organizing way to say there are other things you can do with this waste. People have taken a stand locally saying, 'This is not a good thing, and this should not happen. Not in my backyard, not in anyone's backyard.'"

∾

IN 1972, Lois Gibbs and her husband, Harry, bought a little house in Niagara Falls, New York, and moved in, with their one-year-old son, Michael. The neighborhood consisted mostly of bungalows, many painted white, with neatly clipped hedges, freshly painted fences, and lots of trees. The Gibbs' house cost $40,000—an enormous sum to them, a working-class family who lived on Harry's take-home pay of about $150 a week. Proud of their achievement, they scrimped and put every extra penny they had into paying off the mortgage to build up equity—their entire savings and investment plan for the future. In 1972, real estate prices were escalating at a skyrocketing pace, and many financial advisers recommended buying a home as the best possible investment.

The rest of the neighborhood, not far from the Niagara River and a mile or two above the falls, was much the same. In the summertime, you could see men painting their houses or adding an extra room. "They were the type of men who protect their families and will let nothing hurt them," Gibbs says in *Love Canal: My Story*. Like most of the women, Gibbs had only a high-school education and wanted only to be the best wife and mother she could. In 1975, when Lois Gibbs was twenty-six years old, she had a second child, Melissa, soon nicknamed Missy.

At the same time, some twenty-two thousand tons of poisons were bubbling underground, beginning to cause cancer, miscarriages, deformed babies, and illness and death among children and adults. This was the now-infamous Love Canal, named after William T. Love, who had it dug in 1892 to connect the upper and lower Niagara River into a navigable channel that would also create a waterfall and provide cheap power. However, the country fell into an economic depression; Love had to abandon the project, leaving behind a partially dug section of canal. According to a history current residents have been able to piece together, the land was sold at public auction in 1920 and became a municipal and chemical disposal site until 1953. The principal company that dumped waste in the canal was Hooker Chemical Corporation, a subsidiary of Occidental Petroleum. The City of Niagara Falls and the United States Army used the site as well; the city dumped garbage, and the Army dumped chemical warfare material and parts from the Manhattan Project.

In 1953, Hooker Chemical, after filling the canal and covering it with dirt, sold the land to the Board of Education for one dollar. The deed contained a stipulation that if anyone incurred physical harm or death because of the buried wastes, Hooker would not be responsible. Soon after the land changed owners, home building began adjacent to the sixteen-acre rectangle that was once the canal. The families were unaware of Love Canal when purchasing their homes. In 1955, an elementary school was opened; it had been erected near the corner of the canal.

In the late 1950s, residents began to complain about children being burned, nauseous odors, and black sludge, but nothing was done. It was not until the late 1970s that the government finally decided to investigate the complaint.

In June 1978, Gibbs first read articles in the local newspaper about Love Canal and found out that the school where Michael attended kindergarten, the 99th Street School, was built on top of it. The articles listed the chemicals in the canal and described physical reactions to them: damage to the central nervous system, leukemia, and other blood diseases. Michael had started school the previous September and by December had developed epilepsy; in February, his white blood count dropped. The news surprised his mother, as the family had no history of these disorders.

Gibbs became convinced that Michael should go to another school, so she called up the superintendent of schools. However, the superintendent refused to transfer Michael; he did not believe the area was contaminated. Many people thought the newspaper reports had blown the problem out of proportion.

Until then, Gibbs had lived a sheltered life and believed in authority. But when the person who was supposed to be protecting the welfare of her child and four hundred other children refused to act, she felt betrayed and angry, she reported in *Love Canal: My Story*. The book is a kind of diary of her feelings, thoughts, and actions over the next two years, and is the basis for much of what follows in this chapter. "I decided to go door-to-door with a petition and see if the other parents in the neighborhood felt the same way. I had never done anything like this, however, and I was frightened. I was afraid a lot of doors would be slammed in my face, that people would think I was some crazy fanatic. But I decided to do it anyway."

It seemed to make sense to start at homes near the school, even though she did not know many people on that block. At the first door, "there was no answer. I just stood there, not knowing what to do. It was an unusually warm June day, and I was perspiring. I thought: 'What am I doing here? I must be crazy. People are going to think I am. Go home, you fool!' And that's just what I did.

"It was one of those times when I had to sit down and face myself. I was afraid of making a fool of myself, I had scared myself, and I had gone home. When I got there, I sat at the kitchen table with my petition in my hand, thinking. 'Wait. What if people do slam doors in your face? People may think you're crazy. But what's more important—what people may think or your child's health? Either you're going to do something, or you're going to have to admit you're a coward and not do it.'"

The next day, Gibbs went out on her own block to talk to people she knew, starting at the home of Michael's best friend. The father was at home, agreed with her, and signed the petition. It was as simple as that; Gibbs was relieved and pleased. She continued on to other friends' houses, going to the back door as she always did when she visited a neighbor. Each house took about twenty minutes. While some people had heard about Love Canal, others had not, so Gibbs gave background information and explained the situation. In the process, something began happening inside her. She realized she was fighting a real battle, and her habit of fearing what people might think disappeared. She thought clearly; she became courageous.

After several days and many houses, she went back to the first house, the one from which she had run away. This time the door opened; the man there understood and signed her petition right away. Then he showed her his front porch steps, which had separated from his house. The soil was sinking, but he didn't know why or what it meant. "He asked me if I could talk to anyone, or if I could see if someone would come out and look at it. I didn't know what to do. Because he was so concerned, I told him I would try, and I left." Her cause had begun to take on a slightly larger dimension.

"It was terribly warm and humid that day. The closer I got to the canal, the more I could smell it. I could feel it, too, the air was so humid. The odor seemed to hang in the thick air. My nose began to run, and my eyes were watering." She still doubted her own perceptions so much that when her body reacted like this to the underground canal, she thought, "Maybe I'm just oversensitive."

As she continued going from door to door near the buried canal, more and more people told her their troubles. "The more I heard, the more frightened I became. This problem involved much more than the 99th Street School. The entire community seemed to be sick."

That month, the New York State Health Department held a public meeting at the 99th Street School to discuss Love Canal. During the meeting, officials announced they were going to conduct environmental and health studies. About seventy-five people sat in the hot, humid auditorium; they could smell the chemicals buried beneath them. One woman said her dog's nose had been burned when it sniffed the ground in her yard. A man said the soles of his daughter's feet burned if she played barefoot in the backyard. Gibbs felt a chill. "This was a new danger, and a more ominous one," she says. Up until then, she had not actually seen any chemicals. Did this mean they were coming to the surface? The Health Department said it would take samples of the air, the soil, and the blood of people living there. Meanwhile, they advised people not to eat vegetables out of the garden.

Next, the city engineer discussed a plan to stop the chemicals from leaking. This remedial construction would make the backyards, the schoolyard, and everything clean again. The working-class audience had seen many an engineer's plan before and asked pertinent questions about the effects of underground springs, the depth of the tile drains, and the treatment plans. The city engineer had no straight answers. The audience became frustrated and angry; people walked out, muttering, furious. They did not understand, and they were frightened.

In the following days, Gibbs continued her canvasing. By now, she had contacted some one hundred homes without a single door being slammed in her face. But now, residents who had not attended the meeting wanted to hear about it, too, so what used to be a twenty-minute visit about a school petition took an hour or longer. She enlisted a friend, Debbie Cerrillo, to visit neighbors while Gibbs began meeting with members of the New York State Legislature, who gave her ideas about how to petition the state, see people, and get action. Gibbs came to understand the importance of the fact that 1978 was an election year, and she got in touch with U.S. Senator Moynihan's office.

Gibbs and a few neighbors went to see an environmental lawyer who was also an officer of the Sierra Club. "I had been in an attorney's office only once before, when we bought our house. I felt overwhelmed." The lawyer, though, was easy to talk to. He took the case, initiating a lawsuit against the City and the Board of Education of Niagara Falls, the Country of Niagara Falls, and the Hooker Chemical Corporation.

Gibbs ran into a new obstacle. Many residents did not want the investigation or the lawsuit to continue because they were worried about what might happen to their property values. Like Gibbs, their home equity was the only investment they had.

In July, the Health Department held another meeting. The night hung with humid, stagnant air, pervaded by the threatening, smothering smell of Love Canal. People said that in some houses the chemicals were coming through the basement walls. The Health Department's response was to tell those people to stay out of their basements.

One purpose of the meeting was for the Health Department to give out air-sample results for individual homes. And they did. But they did not include any information about what the numbers meant. Gibbs remembers that "one woman, divorced and with three sick children, looked at the piece of paper with numbers and started crying hysterically: 'No wonder my children are sick. Am I going to die? What's going to happen to my children?' No one could answer." The woman's panic started a chain reaction; other people became hysterical. Not surprisingly, the next open meeting of the Health Department for Love Canal residents was scheduled in Albany, three hundred miles away; very few residents could attend. Gibbs called the offices of the Health Department, Senator Moynihan, Congressman LaFalce, and Governor Carey to try to have the meeting moved, but she failed. She decided to go to the meeting herself. She asked her neighbors for their thoughts and questions to take with her. She tried to anticipate each potential objection from the Health Department and to have a response ready. Gibbs says, "I read all the articles I could find on the canal and its problems and about everything people had been talking about doing for the past couple of years. I learned as much as I could . . . about the chemicals in the homes and about their effects. I wrote out the questions I wanted to ask." Some of the articles horrified her because it became apparent that the Health Department and other officials had known what was in the canal for years. As early as 1976, Calspan, a private research laboratory hired to test in the area, had stated that dangerous chemicals were leaking out of Love Canal and made many recommendations, but none had been followed. Even still, she was doubtful of her own abilities: "I was intimidated by the meeting—me, Lois Gibbs, a housewife whose biggest decision until then had been what color wallpaper to use in my kitchen. Now, here I was going to Albany. It didn't seem real."

She, her husband Harry, and Debbie Cerrillo made a party out of the six-hour drive to Albany. Stopping at every rest stop, having coffee, and chatting stretched the trip to twelve hours. None of them had ever been to the state capital before, and when they arrived, they drove around to look at it. They were impressed by the government buildings, but they were depressed by the slums next to them. And they got lost. A policeman directed them to a nice hotel, but it cost a fortune: $40 a night. After all they had spent on gas, tolls, and coffee shops, they had only about $60 left among them. But Cerrillo had a credit card, and they decided they could all stay in one room. It was, after all, 3 A.M. by this time, and they were going to have to leave by 7:30 A.M. to get to the meeting. Lois stayed up going over some of her questions, to be certain she was prepared.

The meeting began with the health commissioner reading an order stating that the residents of Love Canal were not to eat food from their gardens and that the 99th Street School would be closed during remedial construction. Then he recommended evacuating pregnant women and children under two years old because the state was concerned about their health. That did it. Gibbs, furious, jumped up and said, "If the dump will hurt pregnant women and children, what, for God's sake, is it going to do to the rest of us?" Cerrillo lost her cool, as well: "My kids are over two. Are you trying to tell me my children are safe?" The meeting, which had barely been called to order, never calmed down. "I don't know what else they thought would happen when they said pregnant women and children under two should be moved. Did they think no one would notice it?" Only hours later, the Health Department agreed to hold a public meeting with all the residents the next day in Niagara Falls to discuss the situation. After the long drive back to Niagara Falls, still exhausted from the tense, emotional meeting and too little sleep the night before, the trio returned home to find hundreds of people in the street, screaming, yelling, and burning mortgages and tax bills in a bucket. Someone with a microphone was standing on a box asking, "Is Lois Gibbs back from Albany yet?" The crowd saw her and pushed her to the microphone. "I had never spoken to a group of people in my whole life. In high school, if I had to do a book report in front of the class, I would cut the class. I got up to the microphone and stood there looking out at about four hundred people. Some were pregnant women, some little children, some senior citizens. There were people of all ages, colors, sexes, and sizes. A pregnant woman was standing there crying, 'What's going to happen to me, Mrs. Gibbs? What's going to happen to my baby?' I certainly couldn't answer such questions. I tried to sympathize with them and to explain what I had learned—practically nothing. It was horrible to see all those people so afraid, helpless, and angry, not knowing what to do or where to turn."

The next day, her house was like Grand Central Station. "Before Love Canal, not many people came to our house, other than family and a few friends. Now I had residents, neighbors, politicians, and various important people. And I couldn't keep the floor clean. All those people, and my house looked like hell!"

That evening, the school auditorium was packed, standing room only, with residents who were already emotional even before the meeting began. The health commissioner had just started reading his order, when people started yelling, crying, and screaming; they were near panic. One man whose wife was eight-months pregnant started crying; his wife and his unborn baby were in danger, and he could do nothing about it. Gibbs had never seen a man cry before. The meeting lasted until well after eleven, and then a group went to Gibbs's house, where the press was calling. "I couldn't believe it. Me, what am I doing here? All I had wanted to do was move my child out of the school. I'm not the kind of person that does things like this. Why am I here? Why am I doing this? . . . The phones kept ringing, and people kept arriving. I went to bed about three-thirty in the morning. That's when everyone left. The press started calling again at six." The next day, it seemed like every television camera and every newspaper from coast to coast had come to town. The *New York Times* carried the story just before newspaper employees went on strike. Buffalo's four television stations were there.

Gibbs and her neighbors formed the Homeowners' Association, and they got about five-hundred fifty people to join for a dollar each, with further funding to come from donations, bake sales, and T-shirt sales. Gibbs was elected president and Cerrillo treasurer. The meeting lasted until eleven. "There were a lot of things to do when we got home. I had to put all the papers away somewhere, and we had to send a telegram to President Carter on behalf of the association. My head was spinning. I had so many things on my mind. I had a list of things that should have been done. It was the first time in my life I didn't know what I was doing or how I was going to do it. It seemed like weeks or months since I had seen my kids. My husband was getting upset with me. I was never home. Dinner was never on time. And three months earlier, I hadn't even known there was a problem! Residents were calling; the press wanted a comment. I feel embarrassed about some of the statements I gave then. I have a limited education, and my vocabulary isn't that large. I didn't know quite what to write or say. When anybody asked me for a comment, I felt inadequate." Gibbs began to get help with the statements and her public speaking from her brother-in-law, a college professor.

Meanwhile, in the area of the canal, barrels of black gunk were erupting to the surface of the ground.

In early August, Governor Carey came to Love Canal. At first, Gibbs was thrilled that the governor was coming; she had never imagined meeting, talking to, or being anywhere near the governor of New York. But when his plane was two hours late, she began to get annoyed. "There were a lot of other things I could be doing rather than standing around a parking lot in the hot sun. My house was a mess, my kids needed attention, my laundry needed to be done, and I had calls to return. The governor was wasting my time."

When the governor entered the public meeting, television cameras rolled, and he sounded very generous. He said the state would purchase the homes in the first and second rings nearest the canal and would relocate the people. "He even told the residents that if their basements were contaminated, and they had furniture in the basements, he would pay for that as well. When he said it, I was really excited that people were going to get out." Afterward, she found out the governor had promised more than he could pay for. Just a few days later, after the television cameras left town, state officials said they could buy only the homes nearest the canal, the homes located within the first ring drawn around the canal. Gibbs recalls, "They tried to tell us the governor didn't say he was going to move people from ring two."

The Federal Disaster Assistance Administration in Washington, D.C., called to ask Gibbs to attend a meeting at the White House the next afternoon, August 9. She had to borrow money from her brother-in-law to pay for the flight. To prepare for the meeting, a group stayed at her house until after midnight. She got up at 5:30 A.M. to make the plane. Fortunately, an official car met her at the airport because otherwise she would not have had a clue how to get to the White House. Gibbs remembers her reaction: "Just think: Lois Gibbs goes to the White House. How many people actually go to the White House on business, not as a tourist? And here I was!" In the Roosevelt Room, she felt intimidated and nervous in front of the officials and Congressman LaFalce, but she stumbled through her report. After about an hour, the congressman walked her to another building, where they met with finance and budget people. "I didn't understand one word. I didn't even know why I was there. People were talking a language I didn't understand, using initials and talking about finances." At the end of the meeting, a representative from the governor's office said the second ring of homes would be evacuated; the news would be released at a press conference. Obviously, the state officials must have made the decision well before the day's meetings. "Then it clicked. They were using me to make it look as if the community had some input." There was a press conference on the White House steps and another one in LaFalce's office. "I was so tired my eyes would hardly stay open. I almost fell asleep in the congressman's deep, red leather chair. I just wanted to go home and go to sleep. It had been a wasted day, a wasted trip, a waste of money, and a waste of my time." The leaders she had trusted were tottering around on clay feet.

The return plane was delayed by a thunderstorm, and then rerouted to Rochester, leaving Gibbs with plenty of time to think about why she was involved in all this. "I said to myself: 'You can't sit back and shut your mouth, Lois. You aren't the only one they're hurting. They're hurting hundreds of people. You have to get up there and do it, whether you like it or not, whether you have to push yourself or not, whether you stumble or not.'" When she got home and sat down at her kitchen table, she suddenly realized she had forgotten that the next day was Michael's sixth birthday. She had no gift, no cake, nothing. She had never dreamed she could forget her child's birthday. The next morning, Michael was in tears, and the phone kept ringing with reporters calling, while the association's lawyers came over with forms for the residents. In addition, some of the first residents to be relocated needed her help with problems. By 7 P.M., she had exactly half an hour to spend with Michael before running to a meeting.

∞

THE PEACEFUL, LITTLE COMMUNITY started looking like a disaster area. Many families were in the emotional and logistical chaos of evacuation. Heavy construction began, designed to contain the canal, and some of the first homes were being demolished. At one home, bulldozers plowed through the walls while the resident was still inside watching the start of construction on television. He had not signed any papers, yet his things were destroyed. The 99th Street School was closed to classes and opened as offices, with the Homeowners' Association occupying the former teachers' lounge. Across the hall, the Red Cross moved in, and the Health Department set up next door. Charity groups provided support as residents came through in droves, needing rent money for temporary quarters, food baskets, blood tests, and information.

While Gibbs and the association were scrambling to document residents' health problems so everyone could eventually be relocated, state officials "were treating us as if we were an inconvenience or the enemy or small children they didn't have to explain anything to. It was strange. I never thought government worked like that. I thought that if you had a complaint, you went to the right person in government, and if there were a way to solve the problem, that they would be glad to do it. I learned the hard way. No matter what they say, if you don't follow through and fight for something, it's not going to be done because they're not good for their word."

In the early fall, Governor Carey returned to Love Canal for about an hour, and Gibbs again heard him make exciting promises. "I still had the naive belief that the governor meant what he said. I ran down the hall to tell everybody: if you have contamination, and if you have illness, you will be relocated." Unfortunately, she had not pinned the governor down on a couple of crucial points, such as who would take care of them. It turned out he meant the United Way or some other voluntary agency, not the state of New York. But the voluntary agencies had long since run out of funds for the residents of Love Canal. And in his press release, he specified that residents who wanted to be relocated had to prove that their health problems were caused by Love Canal. This was virtually impossible to do. No bullets flew out of the canal and killed or injured anyone; strange and unaccountable illnesses did. The causes of these illnesses could not be identified, but they couldn't be explained by family histories or other natural causes either. When a map of the canal was overlaid on a map of the location of residences with illness, birth defects and miscarriages formed a perfectly straight line across the south; respiratory disorders to the north; central-nervous-system problems such as epilepsy in the center.

"This little boy had been playing baseball and football. He showed no sign of illness. All of a sudden, his body swelled up. He was hospitalized twice, and then he died. He had apparently been a healthy, normal child," reports Gibbs. The mother went to a stockholders' meeting of Occidental Petroleum. "The stockholders' meeting was held on the birthday of the board chairman, Dr. Armand Hammer. They listened to her politely and then went on with the board meeting and birthday celebration."

About this time, President Carter came to Buffalo, campaigning with Governor Carey and Senator Moynihan. "Debbie Cerrillo got up close to President Carter. When she tried to tell him about Love Canal, he shook her hand and smiled; but all he said was, 'I'll pray for you.'"

The work continued to take its toll on Gibbs's family life. "I wanted to be home in the worst way. But I could not give up what I was doing." She and Harry talked about moving away, but they could not afford to pay for the mortgage and rent, too. "We only owed five thousand dollars on this forty thousand dollar house because we had been paying down the mortgage. But we decided we were going to walk away from the house. We talked to the bank about it, and they said they would take away my husband's wages." He was making only ten thousand dollars a year. "So then we said, 'Okay, he'll just quit work, and we'll go apply for welfare.'" They went to the welfare office to pretend he had already quit work and see what the office would say. "They said we would not qualify for welfare because we had thirty-five thousand dollars equity in this house." The house, of course, was unsalable under the circumstances.

"So we said, 'Okay, then we'll declare bankruptcy and get out from under. Harry can continue to work, and we'll just start all over. We were young.' So we went to a lawyer to talk about declaring bankruptcy, and he said, 'Your only liability is the five-thousand-dollar mortgage. You cannot declare bankruptcy unless you go run up a bunch of bills,' which we would be happy to do. So we went out and tried to get a loan to run up some bills so we would have enough debt to declare bankruptcy. But nobody would give us a loan because our only asset was thirty-five thousand dollars in a house that was worthless. We were literally trapped there. Our families were all working-class people, and they couldn't put us up."

In addition, moving is itself an expensive process. The total bill—rent, moving company, new furniture—for a family of four could run into thousands of dollars that the Gibbses just did not have. "I went to my church, First Presbyterian, where I had taught Sunday school for years. They were unwilling to even loan to me—I wasn't asking for a handout, I was asking for a loan to relocate—and they said no. They didn't want to jeopardize funding for a renovation project that Occidental was supporting."

Families could move if they had some savings or relatives who could take them in, but they frequently split up because the husband would not leave the Love Canal house. Gibbs explains, "The house was the only thing that they ever had, and it was a symbol of their masculinity. They were supposed to be the protector and provider." A home is much more than expensive sticks and nails. Some of the people in Love

Canal had built their own homes and were proud of that. They had the security of a low-crime-rate community; they had children in school, and the children had friends they had known all their lives. Their homes were the center of their lives, their life-style, and their sense of community. When they had to relocate, they lost all of that. And in the midst of this loss and grieving, the old friends and neighbors they might have turned to for love and support were scattered across the country. The new communities did not always welcome refugees from Love Canal because of fears that they might be contaminated with something contagious.

"It's impossible to explain the emotional part of it. Impossible to explain the split in the family as a result of it, all of those stresses and tensions. It's hard for the general public to comprehend what it means. It's impossible to explain." As Gibbs continued doing media campaigns, the one question she could not answer with a satisfactory eight-second sound bite was, "Why don't you just move, Mrs. Gibbs? Why don't you just get up and move?" And it was the question the press and officials began to badger her with.

The families who stayed in Love Canal lived partly in denial, partly in cockeyed optimism. Maybe things were not as bad as everyone thought; maybe things would get better. If they stayed, they might die; but if they moved, they would have to give up everything they had worked so hard for. Many people had a difficult time deciding when enough is too much. The Gibbses could not afford to do anything but put every penny into paying off the loan, with the hope of being able to leave. The little home they had loved so much had become cold, dangerous, frightening—and a trap.

∾

IF THE RESIDENTS felt ignored by officials before the election, they were completely abandoned after it. Attempting to get attention, the residents started picketing during the freezing upstate New York winter of 1979. Gibbs was arrested for stopping a school bus. Being thrown into a jail cell was one more shock to her self-image, but after so many months of hard work, the main emotion she felt was relief at seeing a bed. "It felt pretty good to lie down and cover myself with a blanket. I had been getting up at five A.M. to make it out to the pick-et line, and I hadn't been getting much sleep. When I lay down and looked up at the ceiling, I saw it was made of asbestos. All I could think was, 'When is this ever going to end?'" It was a perverse version of the punishment fitting the crime. Protest an environmental disaster, and we will lock you up in one.

Released from jail, she continued to picket, then going into the office, then to meetings and to speaking engagements. Christmas, one of the most important days of the year to her, along with her children's birthdays, came and went. "I can't remember decorating the tree; I can't remember the children opening their gifts."

Gibbs was a guest on many talk shows, including "Donahue." She testified before Congress. Jane Fonda and Tom Hayden came to see the area and offer support. Congressman LaFalce was trying to have funds for cleaning up places such as Love Canal put in the new Super-fund Bill.

Her children were sick; they required hospitalization for unex-plained, life-threatening illnesses. Air samples showed that chemicals had migrated from the basement to the upstairs of her home. Benzene—known to cause leukemia and other diseases—and toluene—known to cause reproductive harm—were found. More than two hundred dif-ferent compounds had been identified in Love Canal, including at least twelve known carcinogens. In April 1979, the state reported that it had found dioxin in concentrations of 176 parts per billion in the canal. Toxic in only a few parts per billion, dioxin is a contaminant in trichlorophenol, of which there were more than two hundred tons buried in the canal. Hooker had admitted to burying some 21,800 tons of various chemicals. The extent of the chemical migration was unknown, but many of the air, soil, and water tests detected chemicals throughout a ten-block residential area, in the creeks, and in the Nia-gara River. Ten blocks is as far as the tests went; the chemicals could also be eleven, twelve, or thirteen blocks away. Less than a year before, adults had been walking around on the canal in shorts; children had been running around in bare feet. Now, workers who went on the site wore boots, gloves, helmets, and gas masks. In August 1979, the reme-dial construction in the hot, humid weather clogged the air with thick fumes, making the neighborhood smell like a chemical factory. Meanwhile, says Gibbs, "the newspapers were carrying stories about soldiers who had been exposed to Agent Orange, which contained dioxin, and were coming down years later with cancer."

Gibbs met with Governor Carey, away from the cameras and reporters for the first time, and he stonewalled her. "The way I talked to the governor didn't hit me until I got home. I talked to him as if he were an average person, not the governor of New York. I wasn't rude, and I wasn't vulgar; but I was very determined and very angry."

She made several trips to Washington, D.C., to contact as many people as she could at as many agencies as possible to seek federal help. She called the White House several times, trying to arrange a meeting with Mrs. Carter. Her secretary said her calendar was full.

ᘍ

LATE FRIDAY AFTERNOON, May 16, 1980, a representative of the Environmental Protection Agency (EPA) called Gibbs and said he had some test results to discuss with the residents; he needed her to organize a meeting the next morning. She and her group went into action on the phones. The next day, reporters started calling her at 5:30 A.M.; they knew more than she did. According to the news reports, based on leaked documents from the EPA, eleven of thirty-six residents who had been tested showed broken chromosomes of a rare type, which indicated increased risk of miscarriages, stillborn births, birth defects, cancer, or genetic damage that could affect their children and grandchildren. Over at the office, a crowd had gathered: news reporters, EPA representatives, residents, and doctors, all talking loudly. Television cameras were turned on. The EPA representatives met with the thirty-six residents. Most of the people were as confused when they came out as when they went in.

Rumors began to fly about what the state or federal government would do, but no one from the government contacted them. The first sign they had was Monday afternoon's newspaper headline: WHITE HOUSE BLOCKS LOVE CANAL EVACUATIONS. Word spread quickly through the neighborhood, and people gathered on the lawn in front of the Homeowners' Association office, where they became angrier and angrier. "Someone poured gasoline on a lawn across the street, forming the letters E, P, A. Then they put a match to it. The flaming letters drew loud applause and cheers from the crowd." People gathered in the street and stopped cars. The police arrived. Gibbs recalls, "Some people were throwing gasoline on trees and signs and lighting them. Others were beating their fists on cars entering the neighborhood and yelling at the drivers." These same angry demonstrators were mothers who had spent years teaching their children not to be destructive, not to play with matches. They were fathers who, a few months ago, would not carry a picket sign or withhold their taxes. The crowd numbered about three hundred.

Gibbs decided that attacking innocent passersby or police officers who were trying to do their jobs would only hurt their cause. She called the federal officials and told them they had better have another talk with the residents. "One thing I learned as a leadership person is that if you don't have somebody to focus anger on, you, as the leadership, will become the target." More than that, "I was as angry as they were! I was not going to take my children back to our house. It wasn't safe! I had almost lost Missy a few months ago because of a blood disorder, and I didn't want to go through that again."

By the time the EPA officials arrived, the crowd numbered five hundred very angry people. Once the officials were inside, the people started yelling, "We have them!" "Let's see how they like being trapped here!" The people encircled the building and declared the officials their hostages.

Gibbs no longer felt she had any control over the crowd. Besides, she agreed with them. Inside with the officials, "I decided to call Jimmy Carter's office. I said, 'We are holding two EPA officials hostage here, and we aren't going to release them until you release us from Love Canal.' Every media source in America and overseas was there: the first U.S. people holding hostages against the president of the United States." The association's lawyer and his partner showed up and asked Gibbs to let the officials go. "Every time I referred to the EPA representatives as 'hostages,' they told me not to use that phrase. It could cost me five years in prison. I don't think even our attorneys understood how desperate we were. Nothing we had done had gotten us out." Their children were sick, some had died, and their homes were worthless. It was dangerous to become pregnant. Relatives did not dare come visit.

And now the EPA said some residents had genetic damage. "How much can human beings take without rebelling?"

She talked with Congressman LaFalce, who was meeting with the president for dinner that evening; he said he would discuss the situation with the president. The hours dragged on, and then a heavily armed police team showed up, took over the building across the street, and took aim at the residents' heads. The FBI called Gibbs and "gave me seven minutes to release the EPA officials or they would rush the crowd." She knew by now that this was the sort of promise that government officials do keep. Looking out the window, she saw her friends and neighbors, pregnant women, children and the men who would protect them against any harm. She looked at the barrels of the guns pointed at her. She had to release the hostages, or there would be bloodshed and a riot. The FBI was on the phone with her a countdown: "Two minutes, Mrs. Gibbs." She caved in.

To stop the clock, she stepped outside, but she did not have any idea what she could say. The crowd was angry; the news cameras were whirring. Gibbs thought, "If I say one wrong word, it could be disastrous. If there was a God, and He had a miracle, I sure needed it then." She did not tell the crowd about the FBI. First, she told the reporters the people of Love Canal were tired of waiting for government, tired of being told their health was at risk. "We're not going to put up with any more of their bureaucratic bullshit!" The crowd yelled and applauded. She demanded an answer from the president by noon Wednesday. Then she told the crowd she believed they had made their point. President Carter would discuss Love Canal at dinner that night. "It's up to you what we do from here, but I think to continue to hold these two will hurt us more than it will help us." She asked for a show of hands, and although the vote was split about evenly, she announced, "The majority wants to let them go." She turned back to the reporters and cameras, saying, "But remember, we want an answer by noon Wednesday, or this will look like a Sesame Street picnic!"

Wednesday morning, Gibbs sat in the office calling one number after another in Washington, D.C., trying to find out what the government was going to do. Residents and reporters assembled. Just after noon, Gibbs finally reached the press receptionist at EPA, who read her a press release over the phone. As it was read to Gibbs, she repeated it to the waiting crowd and reporters. The release went on at length about the problems, the chromosome-breakage study, and the agency's concern for the residents. As Gibbs repeated what she heard, the crowd was silent, almost holding its breath. At last, Gibbs heard that all 810 families in the Love Canal community would be evacuated from their homes temporarily. They could leave immediately and live in any hotel, motel, or apartment they chose; the costs would be paid by the Federal Disaster Assistance Administration.

People began laughing, crying, hugging each other, dancing around. Someone brought a case of champagne, and corks popped. The office filled with flowers, fruit baskets, other gifts, and people. "It was a wonderful day, with more happy people than I had seen in the past two years."

∾

THE EVACUATION BROUGHT its own problems. Living in a motel or small apartment away from Love Canal added as much strain as it relieved. Space was cramped, and the future was uncertain. Children acted insecure, and marriages began to break up. The families needed funds to buy permanent homes.

Gibbs and other residents appeared again on "Donahue." Jane Fonda and Tom Hayden arranged a speaking tour of California for Gibbs. There, she raised enough money to pay for a busload of Love Canal homeowners to attend the Democratic Convention in New York City and to hold a demonstration, protesting the fact that President Carter still had not resolved this issue. She appeared on "Good Morning America" and accused the Carter Administration of refusing to act. In a presidential election year, this accusation had an effect. Less than two weeks later, she received a phone call that President Carter was coming to Niagara Falls and wanted her to be present when he signed an appropriation of $15 million for the state to purchase all the homes.

It was a major step forward, and Gibbs and the association did not want to appear ungrateful, but they needed more than that. Equivalent property values and home mortgage interest rates were much higher than what they had been paying; and they needed low-interest loans. Gibbs went to the convention center where the president was to sign the bill and learned he had no intention of meeting with her. He was only going to sign the bill. She sat down, uncertain how to proceed. The Secret Service surrounded her. Onstage with Senator Javits and Governor Carey, President Carter began his speech. When the president sat down with the governor to sign the bill, Gibbs knew that time was running out. She stood up, stepped into the aisle, and walked slowly to the front, where she stood until the president noticed her and invited her onstage. News cameras clicked, flashed, and whirred, but Gibbs found herself surprisingly calm. She thanked the president and went on to explain the situation. They talked about interest rates and mortgage money for about twenty minutes. "Every time Carter held my hand or put his arm around me, I thought, 'Boy, that's a good political move. America will love it.'" She had become as savvy as the savviest of them.

Soon after, "The Revitalization Committee was given money to buy homes, assist renters in their moves, and revitalize the neighborhood. The agreement between the state and the federal governments gave New York State $7.5 million as a grant and $7.5 million as a loan. The state hoped to repay the loan from the proceeds of a lawsuit against Hooker Chemical."

By February 1981, more than four hundred families had moved from Love Canal never to return. Hundreds more were building or looking for homes or preparing to move to apartments.

The president had signed the bill on the basis of the residents' mental anguish, not because federal officials acknowledged that there was a health problem at Love Canal. But there had been mental anguish. Small children suffered nightmares about "chemicals" or an imaginary "thing" attacking them. Moving in and out of temporary residences and schools troubled them. Parents lived with terrible uncertainty. When their child had a common cold, they worried that it might be the beginning of something related to toxic chemicals. They worried about cancer, birth defects, and other illnesses. Couples wondered if they really should have another child—or even their first—because of the high risk of stillbirths, miscarriages, and birth defects.

The Love Canal families are blue-collar, middle-class Americans who paid their taxes on time and voted in every election. They minded their own business, kept their houses and property neat, and spent most of their time raising families. They are different now. Gibbs says, "They now realize that government cannot be counted on to protect health, property, and well being without a battle." More than that, "Many have come to hate government because they have been hurt so badly, lied to so often, and treated so terribly."

They have changed their life-style, their values, and their priorities. "Our community was made up of families in which the man went to work and the woman stayed home and cared for the home and the children. You rarely saw husbands doing the laundry or cooking. But because of the canal crisis, the women did most of the work at the Homeowners' Association. In the evening, the couple shared household tasks. Before, most of the men came and went as they pleased, and the women stayed at home with the families and their hobbies. But because the women were active during the crisis, many found a new independence, which they have come to like. As a result, many women are now going to work or becoming involved in community organizations and in activities outside their homes."

That may be a positive change, but it occurred in thousands of other families across the country without the tragedy of Love Canal. "It would be nice to go back and live in that fantasy world," says Gibbs. "Now life is much more difficult because when you have to think about what is really being said and what is really being done and what you have to do about it, your mind works totally different."

Her marriage ended. "My husband never changed, but I did. I felt like I couldn't go back and be a full-time homemaker. I learned a lot from Love Canal, and I needed to share it with other groups in the country. We made a lot of mistakes, and we learned by the seat of our pants. It would be a terrible thing for somebody else to have to start from scratch again." She moved to Washington, D.C., with $10,000 and two kids, and in 1981 founded the Citizen's Clearinghouse for Hazardous Wastes. Its goal: "This will never happen to another person."

∾

THE CLEARINGHOUSE NOW has thirteen full-time staff members and from one to five interns or volunteers. Funding comes from foundation grants and member contributions; the organization will not accept government money or corporate donations. "One of the biggest problems with this particular issue is that it's not real fundable," says Gibbs. As an example, she notes the well-organized and usually highly lucrative direct-mail campaigns by Greenpeace. "I think everybody in the world has gotten one if not a dozen pieces from them. And when they did their direct-mail pieces around toxic waste, they lost money each time. Because people get this numbing effect: 'I just can't deal with it. I will give you twenty dollars toward the dolphins, which are sort of warm and fuzzy.' But for toxics, the public response is, 'This is just so tragic I can't deal with it.'" In addition, it is very hard to raise money because of all the corporate and governmental interests they go up against.

According to Gibbs, EPA estimates that around thirty thousand hazardous waste sites need to be cleaned up. "There are a little over a thousand that are the worst sites in the country. Their estimate of solid waste, basically garbage dumps, is somewhere around two hundred thousand. EPA—at best—is only studying the problem and making consulting firms very, very wealthy. But as far as actual cleanup and protection of the public's health, it's just plain not happening."

Nonetheless, not a single new commercial hazardous waste site has opened since 1978—not because of new laws, but because the public, assisted by the Citizen's Clearinghouse for Hazardous Wastes, will not let it happen. As a result, U.S. industries have become creative about other ways to deal with the waste. An estimated eighty percent of waste chemicals can be reused, or others can be substituted. "Many industries are beginning to reduce the amount of waste they are generating. A lot of them are using technology at the plant site itself to take care of the waste, so they don't have to transport it offsite. And there is plenty of new technology out there that is safer than incineration or land disposal."

Today, Gibbs firmly believes, "The average people and the average community can change the world. You can do it just based on common sense and determination and persistence and patience. Because there is this big, false premise that one must be an expert before one can make a difference. Or one must deal with it in a legislative, governmental-system sort of way. The world has never changed that way. If we look at the civil rights movement or the welfare rights movement or the unionization of workers—almost every time it's been done almost exactly the same way. Major changes have come from local people being angry and collectively speaking out."

❧

Citizen's Clearinghouse for Hazardous Waste, P.O. Box 6806, Falls Church, Virginia 22040, offers memberships for $25. Membership includes technical and community organizing assistance, a bimonthly magazine, and discounts on publications, seminars, conferences, and products from environmentally responsible companies.

Medha Patkar

Hell or High Water

MEDHA PATKAR

India

 THE LIFEBLOOD OF INDIA has always been her rivers. The rich flow of fresh water and fertile sediment was and is the basis of the wealth and culture of India, in both ancient and modern times. Farmers and fishermen, crafts-people, bureaucrats, armies, and priests live off the bounty of the river. Contemporary life still relates to the river. Before dawn, Hindus go to the nearest river to bathe and pray, ritually washing themselves with water drawn in brass pots or clay dishes. Every morning, people still gather at the river with bundles of laundry, which they beat against smooth stones before spreading colorful saris and white dhoties out in the sun to dry. Religious festivals call tens of millions at a time to sacred river ceremonies.

Some six thousand years ago, in northern India, the Indus River was the cradle of the earliest urban civilization on the Indian subconti-nent. (It became part of Pakistan in 1947.) Another northern river, the Ganges, is India's most sacred, still worshiped as a goddess. These great northern rivers originate in the mountains and are fed by snow or ice. The rivers of central and southern India, however, depend entirely on water from springs and monsoon rains that fall only for four months each year. The South is, therefore, generally drier and less populous than the North. Central India is crossed by three major rivers, including the Narmada, that flow from east to west and empty into the Gulf of Cambay.

In deep, hidden river valleys, such as the Narmada, something of the natural richness that was once India—when forests clothed more than half of the subcontinent—still lingers. Today, forests cover no more than eight percent of India; the trees that once protected the soil from monsoon rains are largely gone. The country suffers from cycles of drought and flood, a cycle of misery to millions.

∾

MEDHA PATKAR MEASURES barely five feet tall and weighs only ninety pounds, but she commands such a seemingly endless supply of energy, that if she decided to stop a bulldozer, I would bet against the bulldozer. But today the bulldozers lie a world away, in a remote river valley of western India. We sit in a luxury hotel room on Central Park South, New York City.

Patkar's graying hair is twisted into something resembling a bun. She wears a threadbare maroon and gold sari and falling-apart canvas shoes. When she enters the hotel lobby, she makes a striking contrast: any one of the floral arrangements looks taller, stouter, and better dressed than she. Curious people turn to stare. She does not seem to notice the staring or the luxury—or the incongruity of herself in it. The hotel merely serves as a temporary campaign headquarters, paid for by The Goldman Environmental Foundation as part of their prize program. They have brought her to New York City to publicize the movement she leads before she goes on to Japan to try to prevent renewed funding of the dam she opposes.

In the few hours she has been here, she has covered the queen-sized bed in her room with piles of papers and documents. Videotape cassettes are stacked on the bedside table and window ledge. Kicking the shoes off her dirty feet, she curls up on the bed to sit Gandhi-style: one foot folded underneath her, the other planted on the bed so the bent knee provides a prop for her elbow. Her wrists and arms are as thin as sticks, yet she gestures with grace as she talks.

Patkar speaks English with the fluid pitch of an Indian accent. Her words come forth with care, without hurry, but with intensity as her conversation streaks from the tiny village of Manibeli, in the Narmada Valley, where she works with the tribal people, through the tangled international interests involved in the dams. "It's a long story, how I really reached out from the village to the World Bank and legally got hold of their documents and found international supporters and their missions."

Patkar is a social worker with a master's degree from the Tata Institute of Social Sciences in Bombay. "I did my postgraduation in social work with a specialization in community development. And I pursued my doctorate studies with the theme of economic development and its impact on traditional tribal societies." She had fertile fields to study. In India, since independence in 1947, the construction of high dams has forced the displacement of millions of people—most of them tribal—uprooting their lives to serve an industrial vision of India's future. Compensation usually consists of a small amount of cash. Most of the tribal people displaced by hundreds of projects end up in urban slums or become migrant laborers in sugar-cane fields.

∾

BOMBAY HAS AN ALMOST INCREDIBLE DENSITY of population, more than one hundred thousand people per square mile. Frequently, several generations of a family must live in a single room. And these are working-class people, not slum dwellers. Nearly a third of the city's inhabitants have no permanent shelter, no running water, and no toilets. The famous Bombay slum called Dharavi is said (sometimes with perverse pride) to be the largest in Asia. Formerly a vast marsh, Dharavi is now jammed with shacks and lean-tos, the walls of one holding up its neighbor, side by side and back to back on black mud and garbage. Through the slum, narrow lanes curve out of view. At the edge of what appears to be a black lake, shiny with toxic oil, men, women, and children defecate. The stench of the place fuses with fumes from nearby factories (many illegal) that tan animal skins and cook chemicals; the stench mixes with the petrol-and-kerosene exhaust of vehicles crawling along the bordering streets. In the excessive sun and heat, the air burns your skin; you cannot breathe it through your nose—the smell is too nauseating. You take only the smallest possible whiffs of it through your mouth, and even then it rakes your lungs. This is the sight and smell of Dharavi from a cautious distance. Life at night or in its back alleys can only be imagined.

Dharavi and places like it are where most of the gentle river people of the Narmada Valley and their children would end up if the dam construction were to proceed. This is where Medha Patkar started her work.

"In Bombay, where I was working with the slum dwellers," says Patkar, "I realized that it is wrong policies and planning that resulted in the slums and shanty towns. The tribal people are displaced from their life support and turned out on the outskirts of the city. So if the problem is going to be tackled, it has to be at that end, as well. Also, on the basis of my knowledge of the economic development, I saw consumerism growing. I really feel angry to see the Western kind of consumerism growing."

In recent decades, Patkar's hometown of Bombay has emerged as India's premier financial city, a major center of trade and commerce; it produces more films than any other city in the world. Flamboyant and cosmopolitan, it is home to financial magnates, socialites, and movie barons. Marine Drive, curving along the seafront, sparkling with lights at night, is nicknamed The Queen's Necklace.

Behind it, this Riviera of the East meets Detroit. The city houses some five thousand factories, from cotton mills to chemical and fertilizer plants, as well as an atomic research center, several oil refineries, and thermal power units. The air has become heavily polluted with oil fumes and industrial waste, the water supply is dangerously limited and contaminated, the streets are choked with traffic, and fields and marshes are jammed with rural migrants who wander to the city in a steady stream. In the past decade, Bombay has gone from India's most prosperous and promising city to being its most precarious one.

"Now, how to really turn this backwards?" Patkar asks. "I began working with the tribal society, where there is still some kind of man-nature relationship, a nonconsumerist attitude and life-style. While working in the tribal areas, it became further clear to me that in the name of development of those very societies, they are being deprived of their capital." More than sixty million tribal people live in India, most of them dependent on land, forest, and river for most of their livelihood. The land, "owned" and used by them and their forebears for generations, fulfills sixty to eighty percent of their household requirements even today. Much of the land is harvested and grazed on a communal basis. These tribal peoples are strongly rooted in the region, with local gods and goddesses who created and named the rivers and forests around them. They have had hardly any contact with the outside world.

"It is mostly the poor who are made to give away their resources, cultural base, and even life, if so required, because it has become crucial and central to 'economic development' of society symbolized by rampant consumerism on one hand and the increasing percentage of the population being pushed and retained below the poverty line, on the other," Patkar has written. "It is an irony that the tribals and the rural poor—in whose name development action and projects are justified—are the ones who face the severe backlash of development."

"And what's more," she says, "not only are the tribals kicked out of their land and forest and river valleys, but the one who really takes it is destroying capital which is for all the world, which is limited, and which has to be used very carefully and sustainably, considering not just a few years, but generations. So it's neither justice to the tribals nor is it really rational, considering the future requirements of all the population. And this is the conceptual framework I'm working in."

A room-service cart for tea is wheeled into the room. Patkar takes a cup of tea with cream and looks for sugar. Surveying the cart, covered with a white tablecloth on which is a flower in a bud vase, a silver teapot, silver cutlery, china, water goblets, and a cream pitcher, she finds no sugar. She laughs. "In India, the more they love you, the more sugar they give you. Here they give you everything but sugar."

In large matters as in small, Patkar suffers from a constant awareness of the discrepancy between the way the world is and the way it should be. She is certain that correct information is enough to make people radically change their lives. Born and raised in Bombay, Patkar is the daughter of social activists. Her father is a former freedom fighter and trade unionist; her mother works with a women's organization. "So it's nothing great I'm doing, really. It's part and parcel of my life, my thinking and acting, since childhood. It would have been a wonder if I had not become an activist."

In Indian tradition, every good Hindu (eighty-five percent of the population) knows his or her duty from birth because each family, clan, and caste has its place and tasks. Most Indians, even modern intellectuals, share a belief in karma, an ancient Hindu concept that all individuals, whether insects or sultans, accumulate merit or negativity by their actions. After death, the soul will move along to inhabit another being, either higher or lower in the universal hierarchy, depending on the individual's spiritual advancement or regression. The way to ensure higher birth, or, better still, liberation from the endless cycle of rebirth, is to do one's duty without complaint or impatience, as best one can. One welcomes death as the release of one's soul and an opportunity for liberation, rather than as annihilation and loss, as it is considered in most Western thought. Dying for a righteous cause certainly aids liberation. These concepts, which we now associate most with the Hindu religion, emerged around the dawn of the Christian era, were folded into Buddhism centuries later, and greatly influenced Mahatma Gandhi and his chosen heir, the first prime minister, Jawaharlal Nehru. Though Patkar is an atheist, these concepts have undoubtedly influenced her, too.

One writer said of Patkar, "Amazing in her tolerance and the lack of personal comfort, she scurries like a mountain ibex, barefoot over hot river stones. She walks alone on dark nights right through the heart of the construction site which will devour her river and its people. The Punjabi guards gaze dumbly at her. A truck driver for the dam project said, *Usme to zaroor Shera wali vaas karti hai, yeh baat to saaf hai aur kuch ho na hon, hum sub log to unko bahut maante hain, par mera naam na lena.* 'We all believe that goddess Santoshi resides in her, and we respect her immensely, but don't use my name.'" In Hindu tradition, Santoshi Mata is the goddess of the victory of good over evil.

∾

THE NARMADA VALLEY DEVELOPMENT PROJECT IS the kind that makes engineers' hearts race. Plans include the construction of 30 major dams, 135 medium-sized dams, and 3,000 small dams on the Narmada River and its tributaries. The project is one of the largest water resource projects ever undertaken in the world. The monumental scale of the operation and the stupendous stretch of the work seem to the engineering mind entirely admirable. The first stages, called the Sardar Sarovar Projects, are intended to bring water for drinking and irrigation to 4.4 million acres in the drought-prone state of Gujarat. Project advocates claim that the dams will provide drinking water to forty million people, employ about one million people, and generate electricity, besides.

Designed to divert 9.5 million acre feet of water from the Narmada River, the Sardar Sarovar Projects would create a large reservoir on the Narmada and an extensive canal and irrigation system. The total cost of the projects was estimated to be more than $5 billion U.S., back in 1985. Estimates have since risen as high as $11 billion. Work was begun in 1985, after India and three of its state governments obtained a $450 million loan from the World Bank. Total funding has not yet been secured. In the past decade, India has more than tripled its external debt, to $72 billion, and last year it teetered on the edge of default.

The projects reflect the continuing legacy of Prime Minister Jawaharlal Nehru, who ordained high dams as India's "secular temples." Since independence, India has dedicated itself to this religion of construction and has become the world's greatest builder of dams.

Irrigation canals in the North have greatly expanded the practice of growing two and even three crops per year on fertile land. The irrigation projects, along with the use of chemical fertilizers, newly developed high-yielding seeds, and mechanized agriculture, allow India today to support more than double the population she had in 1950. Although most peasants live at a bare nutrition level, consuming mostly rough-grain calories, the increasing urban middle class and the wealthiest segments of India's population enjoy a richer, more varied diet than ever before.

From this point of view, it is surprising not that the Narmada River, the fifth-longest in India, is threatened with damming, but that it has not been dammed before. This is not an oversight—proposals for the project began in 1947—but rather a predicament. The river flows through three states, which could not, for thirty years, agree about the distribution of costs and benefits. Once those disputes were resolved, the brute work of resettling villagers began; two thousand people were removed from their homes to make land available for the project. But construction was held up, largely because of funding difficulties, and did not begin in earnest until 1987.

ॐ

THE FIRST VILLAGE that will be submerged by the waters of the first dam is named Manibeli. A typical home there is well lit and clean—simplicity itself. The people are healthy and, in their context, well educated. True, they may not understand much about technology, but then neither do most of us. They do understand the medicinal properties of woods, oils, barks, and leaves. They also know how to build their own homes, with posts and beams of teak. They know how to lay down layers of a mixture of cow dung and mud to make a floor. They weave bamboo to form walls, which they decorate with murals. The villagers make their own roof tiles. They fashion vessels of wood and mud, grow crops, make cloth, make wine, and make music.

As the water rises, one of the most spectacular gorges in the world will drown, and with it, one of Asia's largest forests. In addition, the Narmada Valley contains a wealth of antiquities in thousands of cultural centers, temples, and pilgrimage and holy sites. The earliest signs of human settlements on the Indian subcontinent were found in the Narmada Valley. According to some anthropologists, if properly excavated, the Narmada Valley could reveal a continuous thread of Indian civilization since time immemorial.

The Sardar Sarovar dam is the kind that makes environmentalists rage. Upon completion, it would submerge approximately ninety-two thousand acres of land, fertile fields as well as valuable forests. The dam is being built in a hilly region inhabited by tribal people who live off their land and surrounding forests. At least one hundred thousand people in 245 villages live in the area that would be submerged.

About thirteen thousand families would lose all or most of their land. Another 140,000 families would be affected by the canal and irrigation system, and thousands more downstream would be significantly affected. The government says it will relocate the displaced people. The World Bank agreement requires the government to provide "oustees" with at least the same standard of living they enjoyed previously as quickly as possible.

Those in favor of the project believe that the national interest requires people to resettle. In fact, they argue, if water for drinking and irrigation is not made available in these regions, thousands will be forced to migrate to escape the drought. Although securing supplies of food and drinking water, alleviating poverty, and providing energy are desirable goals, dam opponents say that the Sardar Sarovar Projects will not serve those goals. According to Patkar, the only areas that will actually benefit are the heavily industrialized and urban areas. The single greatest user of the precious water will be the chemical industry. Meanwhile, the "affected" tribal people would end up in urban slums or would become migrant laborers in sugar-cane fields; small landowners would become farm laborers. Moreover, the dam is not even necessary. Simply deepening the existing river channel or selective stretches of it could achieve the same result without massive engineering projects, expensive construction, or submergence, and without uprooting populations or damaging wildlife.

Seventy-five percent of India's population still lives in more than half a million rural villages, averaging from five hundred to five thousand inhabitants. Most villages are self-sufficient. They produce most of the basic goods and services they need, but each village also has extensive ties of marriage and trade to others in the region. These rural peoples are not the problem. In fact, they are living the solution: a simple, sustainable life-style that does no one harm.

Though the most remote villages remain isolated, without roads or paths to neighboring towns or cities, they can receive satellite-transmitted broadcasts from New Delhi. Tuning into the mainstream of national goals and aspirations, villagers are accelerating the process of modernization by generations—overnight. Rural values and ideals are being propelled from the bullock-cart ruts of antiquity to the fast lane of modernity.

Patkar first visited the Narmada Valley in 1985, when major funding from the World Bank was secured, and the development projects seemed viable. She visited as a social worker, a strong tradition in India. In the absence of state-funded welfare agencies in India, nongovernment organizations are involved in many areas of society, from social services to local economic development. These agencies have been immensely important in the struggle against the social damage caused by massive development projects.

Patkar came to work with the tribal people and to inform them of their rights. She gained their acceptance by living with them, learning their language (there are sixteen official languages in India and an estimated 1,652 dialects, many thriving in a single valley), and eating their food. She quickly learned that no adequate resettlement plan existed.

Patkar says, "Those few villagers who have shifted or are in the process, are being cheated to a large extent in the land dealings. They are shown one kind of land and given another kind. The tribals who are being shifted out of their forest surroundings find they really cannot survive there. Every resettlement site has problems." Problems include shortages of water, fuel, and fodder, and conflicts with host communities. Problems of land titles, inadequate land plots, disintegration of village units, and poor agricultural land have also been recorded by teams monitoring and evaluating the resettlement process.

No one who is still in Manibeli (ninety percent of the original population) has agreed to move. After a closer study of the whole project, Patkar concluded that there simply is not enough good land for all the displaced people. She questions the basic issue of justice in a developing society: "Who pays and who benefits?"

In an earlier era, involuntary resettlement was considered a necessary consequence of dam projects. Today, the algebra of suffering is more complex. It is not simply a question of dollars and homes; some human costs are impossible to quantify. The consequences of the development for the communities of the Narmada Valley in India were either ignored or evaluated too late.

In addition, Patkar discovered that a comprehensive environmental impact assessment has never been conducted. At about the same time, environmental groups around the country finally began to realize that most environmental battles were lost because environmentalists were too fragmented to operate effectively. They decided to pool resources to form a "collective will." It took very little time to zero in on the Narmada Project as an outstanding example of an environmental, social, and financial disaster—with its fudged cost/benefit analyses, its discriminatory wealth distribution, and its unsound environmental planning.

An umbrella organization called Narmada Bachao Andolan (Save the Narmada Movement) was formed in 1988 and included many nongovernment organizations. Patkar became one of the key leaders and soon raised within the environmental movement higher questions of social justice. The environmentalists resolved that "no one will move, the dam will not be built," come hell or high water.

Narmada Bachao Andolan began organizing demonstrations, marches, protests, and boycotts. In September 1989, sixty thousand people gathered in a national rally against "destructive development." It focused on the Sardar Sarovar Project, the first of the Narmada Valley Development dams. Throughout 1990, active opposition continued and culminated in a blockade in March 1990; some ten thousand demonstrators blocked a national highway from Agra to Bombay for forty-eight hours. In May 1990, more than two thousand activists and people who had been ousted from their homes held a sit-in outside the residence of the prime minister.

Regional governments responded to the protests with oppression, imposing laws to prohibit freedom of assembly, and increasing arrests and the use of the police force and tear gas. Meanwhile, dam building continued. Patkar and the demonstrators continued to respond with nonviolent tactics.

In January 1991, Patkar and others began an indefinite hunger strike, in a desperate attempt to gain public attention. "We thought it was necessary to pose this issue in such a way that it would affect the whole nation," she says. "Otherwise, we would never have been able to face the advertisement campaign, political tactics, and expensive strategies launched by the government against us." Patkar fasted for twenty-two days and nearly died.

As the monsoon season (May to September) of 1991 approached, the first huts were threatened with rising waters. In July 1991, Patkar led a sit-in from a hut. She and her supporters declared themselves a save-or-drown squad. The rains were so light that the water level rose only slightly; then police broke up the demonstration and arrested the demonstrators. Patkar, warned ahead of time, slipped into hiding.

Later in the year, though, she was caught, arrested, and charged with crimes she was alleged to have committed over the past eight to twenty months. If proven, the charges could lead to life in prison. She refused to post bail for crimes she never committed and remained in jail. Under international pressure from the press, the police quickly released her. All charges were dropped.

In March 1992, with another monsoon season approaching and villagers still vowing to drown rather than move, eight hundred policemen arrived in Manibeli with trucks and bulldozers. "Over the next few days, homes were demolished, and the agricultural fields of resisting villagers were ruined by bulldozers," says Patkar. "Officials used threats, offers of money, and other manipulations to coerce resisting Manibeli residents to move. People were beaten, and mass arrests were made. People were detained without food, drink, or medical care. Many were taken to jails more than thirty miles from Manibeli and released after midnight with no means of transportation home."

Fifty-five families remain in Manibeli, and the police force has been increased; at one point in 1991, estimates were as high as eleven hundred police. The harassment, violence, and arrests continued throughout 1992. A fire was set to terrorize the villagers, and about fifteen families have been forcibly resettled from Manibeli.

"I am committed to nonviolence," says Patkar, "and the people also are committed to nonviolence because they know it is not only a value, but it is the best practical strategy to win this battle. If we take to stones, then bullets will come from the other side, and we will be finished. We will be crushed within the moment. But the state is resorting to violence, and we cannot really forget our right to self-defense, either. The government seems to be intending to push the peaceful inhabitants of the valley towards violence."

While Patkar has centered her work in the village of Manibeli, she has been active on the larger, international stage as well. She has pressured and negotiated with government officials. She testified before the U.S. Congress and the World Bank on behalf of the "oustees." In a letter to a World Bank official, Patkar stated, "This fight will make all citizens increasingly aware of all of the distorted concepts and processes leading to such 'development actions' not only in India, but in the valleys and hills in almost every corner of the world." Because of the strong opposition, the World Bank dropped its plans to fund a second large dam, the Narmada Sagar.

The efforts of Patkar and her organization, along with an international campaign, have caused the Japanese government to withdraw its funding of the dam, and members of the European community have urged the World Bank to stop financing the project. Her efforts led to the World Bank ordering an unprecedented independent review of the project.

The World Bank, officially the International Bank for Reconstruction and Development, is a specialized agency of the United Nations. Founded in 1945 and headquartered in Washington, D.C., it was formed to reconstruct Europe after World War II. However, after the Marshall Plan took over that duty, the World Bank basically went around looking for business and gradually changed to serve Southern Hemisphere countries. With capital of $24 billion from taxpayers' money in major donor countries such as the United States and Japan, it makes loans for development projects, economic growth, and poverty alleviation. Exempt from the jurisdiction of any court of law, World Bank decision makers are the world's most powerful developers, all but unaccountable to the public they serve. In the eyes of many critics from developing countries, the World Bank is second only to the United States as a symbol of inequality and "progress gone mad." (In 1992, the United States contributed seventeen percent of the World Bank's capital.)

The establishment of the independent review seemed to indicate the bank was willing to admit that something might be wrong with the Sardar Sarovar Projects, or at least that the bank knew it was facing a public-relations fiasco. By the time the report was published in June 1992, it had cost the bank $945,000. The report was highly critical of the project's resettlement, rehabilitation, and environmental aspects. The review stated that while "no one wants to see this money wasted, we caution that it may be more wasteful to proceed without full knowledge of the human and environmental costs. We think the wisest course would be for the bank to step back from the projects and consider them afresh."

Nonetheless, the bank is proceeding with the Sardar Sarovar Dam. The Environmental Defense Fund, which has monitored the issue from the outset and has considerable influence in the U.S. Congress, has called for a permanent independent appeals mechanism to investigate World Bank projects and has called for funding to be cut off.

Tiny Medha Patkar has become a thorn in the paw of the mighty World Bank.

∾

IN MANIBELI, she is "Narmada mama," says one villager. "If she leaves, we would be motherless." At this writing, the monsoons of 1992 have been light. The water has risen to within inches of the first home in Manibeli, though, and the save-or-drown squad, including Patkar, continues to occupy the site.

"It is a popular movement, and the strength of the movement is the people's participation in it," says Patkar. "They are the ones who should lead the movement and are doing it, in a way. Certainly, we are there as catalysts. I reach out to them with the information about the errors in the laws, and they have come to know who the World Bank is, calling it a Big Bank in their own language. But they were already asking these questions: 'And how have they valued my tree and my forest?' 'How can they not ask us before starting to build a dam?' These are the questions the villagers were asking anyway. We just gave it an articulation and a form that would be understood by the ignorant, callous society outside the valley. So the people have always played a role in formulating the perspective and the priorities and the strategies of the movement. Today, the movement has reached a critical stage, and a real straight battle is to be fought between the repressive state on one hand and the so-called powerless tribal and indigenous communities in the valley on the other.

"The people of the United States must really look at this issue as not limited to the population that is to be affected by the projects there in the valley, but as issues which focus on the wrongs we have done up until now in the name of development—issues which talk not merely of immediate submergence but of land and water management and of international aid and exchanges. It's a wide range of issues that the Narmada Valley has raised. In order to address those effectively and understand, with the openness modern society boasts of, they must reach out straight to the people. It has to be a people-to-people dialogue and people-to-people exchange on what is happening, rather than depending on the benefit/cost ratios and the economic rates of return promulgated by the World Bank and their hired agencies.

"Because, first, the people of the United States have been to a large extent ignorant of what is happening with their tax dollars in terms of worldwide projects. Second, this part of the world should know what is happening to the resource base in countries like India. It matters to their own survival in the long run. Whenever there is a crisis situation—next monsoon when submergence is faced—let team after team come from the United States and join the tribals and say, 'This is not only your problem; this is our problem too. And if they are out not only to violate human rights but to submerge the forest and your life, then we will also form the fabled drum squads and join you to save your life and the lives of others.'"

∾

For more information about Narmada Bachao Andolan or Medha Patkar, contact the Environmental Defense Fund, 1875 Connecticut Avenue, NW, Washington, D.C. 20009.

Beto Ricardo

Harmonies in the Forest

BETO (CARLOS ALBERTO) RICARDO

Brazil

 BETO RICARDO HAS NEWS: "Everybody discusses the future of the rain forest, but people need to know that the Amazonian rain forest in Brazil is still there—around ninety percent. Sometimes I think people think everything is gone there. This is not true."

He should know. He has been keeping track of the Amazon and the people who live in it for more than twenty years. And it is good news because his country grows one-third of the world's rain forests. Only Canada contains more. (Yes, Canada contains the most rain forest in the world.) The region called Amazonia sprawls across the borders of Bolivia, Colombia, and Venezuela but lies principally in Brazil.

"Of course, in some parts, in just fifteen years, sixty percent of the forest came down, and if you project this to the whole Amazon, we're going to have a bad time in fifty years. But we still have a chance, and the indigenous people still have a chance."

Tall and handsome, Ricardo is one of the paler citizens of that country, where skin and hair color run across the entire human spectrum, as a result of immigration by everyone from the darkest African slaves to the blondest German farmers. The indigenous people are in-between in skin color, and they are caught in the middle politically. Descendants of Amazonia's original residents, they live almost without possessions in the great rain forests of Brazil. Today, they are the country's poorest people—and the victims of the worst discrimination.

Speaking with me, Ricardo struggles with broken English; his accent is thick and his vocabulary limited. A former university teacher of anthropology, he sees "a new paradigm in my country. The Indians [many Brazilian activists use the term "Indians" to refer to indigenous peoples] themselves are in a very strong struggle for their rights for the first time in our history. They have a lot of plans for their future." Though they still occasionally raid camps of settlers, ranchers, and miners, many of the indigenous people have sharpened the arrows of their political points to fight for the integrity of their lands and culture.

∾

GROWING UP IN BRAZIL, under a military dictatorship in a climate of terror, Beto Ricardo learned early and well to blend into the woodwork. Scion of a middle-class family—his father worked for a large, private company—Ricardo lived and studied in São Paulo, the most important industrial center in South America. In 1970, Ricardo was twenty years old, and São Paulo was a city of some six million mostly poor people; a study found sixty percent of the adults were undernourished. São Paulo is closer to eight million now—the largest city in South America.

Between secondary-school classes, Ricardo helped church groups working to provide information and support for democratic movements. "At that time," says Ricardo in hesitant English, "this was not a good cause. Nobody talk about this." The military dictatorship imprisoned and in some cases tortured and murdered people who spoke out for social justice and equity. Counterpoised against the terror were the churches, ninety percent of them Roman Catholic. They formed a humanitarian network throughout the country, including the Amazon, where missionaries had been working since the seventeenth century. (Brazil is the most populous Roman Catholic country in the world.)

In school, he studied business administration, economics, and anthropology. It was the anthropology that interested him most; it dealt with people and made him feel connected to them. He became particularly fascinated with the Brazilian indigenous people, but he soon discovered that no one knew much about them—how many they were, who they were, where they were, or what they did. Ricardo wanted to know all that.

He heard about an old Dominican who worked with the Indians in the Amazon and came to São Paulo once a year. Ricardo met the Dominican, who agreed to let him come along on a visit to an isolated village. From São Paulo, they took a plane to a small city unconnected by roads to any other city. From there, they traveled by boat and finally rode mules for two days until they reached a very small Indian community of about one hundred twenty people living a culture that was thousands of years old. Traditionally, the Indians of Brazil wear no clothes and only a few decorations—a little face or body painting, some beads, and a belt. In some tribes, women stick bamboo slivers into their faces like the whiskers of a jaguar; some men put disks into their lips to make them protrude. Their skin is brown, their hair thick, shiny, and black; their eyes are dark and expressive. Most tribes sleep in communal houses, each family slung in its hammock. They bathe in the river, play games and music, and live on a simple, healthy diet of maize and manioc, along with game and fish. They hunt (and fight) with bows and arrows. "They get their life from the river and the forest," says Ricardo.

"The forest of the Amazon is not merely trees and shrubs," says the British writer H. M. Tomlinson. "It is not land. It is another element. Its inhabitants are arboreal; they have been fashioned for life in that medium as fishes to the sea and birds to the air. Its green apparition is persistent as the sky is and the ocean."

In the Amazonian village, possibly for the first time in his life, Ricardo enjoyed himself fully, entering another world. He could remain in his familiar role as an observer and yet reach out. He felt a tremendous intimacy for an intense month, and then he left, taking with him precious memories that he has treasured forever. The nostalgia for what happened to him there still motivates his work more than twenty years later.

Back in São Paulo, he studied at the university, but at the time, "a lot of the good teachers were in exile outside Brazil. We could not even read their books; they were impossible to find." Ricardo learned that some of the old teachers were going to be attending a big scientific congress, so he went there. He found that the last update of information about the indigenous people had been in 1955. "I had just a small notebook with alphabetized sections, and I started collecting information—and I saw there was almost nothing. I was working with a puzzle, and a lot of people had just a little piece, but nobody could see the whole scene. I had to put this information together to see what was going to happen."

One of the obstacles to compiling the information was, of course, the sheer, colossal scale of Brazil. It is the world's fifth-largest country (after Canada, China, the Commonwealth of Independent States (formerly the Soviet Union), and the United States), covering nearly half of South America. Amazonia itself comprises a wilderness the size of Europe, dense with thickly forested lowland surrounding the largest river in the world—so much larger than any other, it reduces the rest to the category of storm drains. No one has ever identified a single source of the Amazon, but it begins in glaciers some sixteen thousand feet up in the Peruvian Andes. The snow-melt water tumbles in streams and through lakes, joining seventeen major tributaries from four countries. Then it breaks out into a steaming tropical delta (ninety percent humidity in the air most of the year) that merges into the Amazon River and flows east along the line of the equator through Brazil to the Atlantic.

Until fairly recently, the river and its tributaries provided the only highways through the region. Most travelers today experience the Amazon much the way the first Indians did twenty or forty thousand years ago after they had walked across the Bering Strait frozen to a causeway by the last ice age, and walked thousands of miles to the river rain forest. The modern traveler passes through the brush and corridors of trees hanging with vines where a tall canopy of green cools the blazing sunlight and carves it into shafts, while the macaws squawk, monkeys crack Brazil nuts against the tree trunks, boa constrictors slither around the limbs, and bright-colored butterflies fly up in swarms.

∾

WHEN THE MILITARY DICTATORSHIP started a massive road-build-ing program between 1970 and 1976 to open up the undeveloped territories, the roads in the Amazon expanded tenfold. The Trans-Amazonian Highway comprises one-third of the total. It slashes open the forest from the Atlantic coast to the western frontier bordering Peru. Most of the roads remain unpaved; they are expensive to maintain, and they are often impassable during the long rainy seasons. (The moisture of the leaves in this two-million-square-mile forest accounts for more than half the rainfall in Amazonia, where the ninety-three inches of rain per year produce twenty percent of the world's fresh water.)

Despite this new access, "it was impossible to know what was going on in the whole country," Ricardo says. Nonetheless, in 1978, he was able to put together a report, which he sent to colleagues in Europe. By then, Ricardo and a group of friends had founded an orga-nization, the Centro Ecumênico de Documentacão y Informacão (Ecu-menical Center for Documentation and Information), or CEDI. Innocent sounding, it was in fact researching human rights cases, including those involving political prisoners. Ricardo believes in free and open information; no matter what your political opinion, you should have the right to express it. The Europeans who read his report gave CEDI enough financial support to pay six months' salary of a full-time activist who would work for the rights of indigenous peoples. At the time, Ricardo was a university teacher and had his career in front of him; he was married, with a small daughter; but he wanted to work for CEDI full time. "It was not an easy decision. All the colleagues are telling me, 'You're crazy. You're going to do something that you don't know what's going to happen six months after that? You have just a bite of this money and nobody knows if you can get some money for the next six months.'"

Ricardo can remain cool when others get heated; he can detach from emotional issues and move toward planning. To him, money is only good for the independence it brings. He was willing to start this impor-tant but obscure project and to work behind the scenes to develop his broad-based view of human rights. "I decided I would go and see what was happening. If it was impossible, I'd find another job. So I start to work for CEDI. We put together a little team of people—four or five persons—to organize the information and send it back out to the people. I had to gather information from people in the field—missionaries, anthropologists, journalists, photographers, health workers— good people. But, of course, you have a lot of people who have contact with the Indians who are not supporting their rights. You have to know exactly what kind of people are inside your network. This is a very important point. Information is not a data base; information is social relations."

He and his team developed a questionnaire that they sent out, as well as many letters. They gave speeches at conferences. They collected thousands of letters, many maps of the indigenous lands, and lots of photos of the Indians. They started to learn their languages and understand their names. "You had this process in the United States in the nineteenth century, but we didn't.

"In Brazil, five hundred years ago, when the Europeans first arrived, there were between two and five million indigenous people. By the 1950s, there were only one hundred fifty thousand. One anthropologist who did his research in the 1950s estimated that in fifty years, eighty-three tribes disappeared." Today there are an estimated one hundred eighty Amazonian tribes, who speak nearly as many languages and dialects and live in groups seldom larger than two hundred people. Undiscovered tribes, such as the group of ninety-five Arara Indians first documented in 1984, undoubtedly exist. In fact, we know of about fifty, though modern society has had no contact with them.

"So we started to organize an archive and a data base, without a computer, without anything. When you see it today—books, reports, data bases in the computer—everything seems so professional. The numbers are there, the names are there, and so on. And it was just social relations to put this together. So this is what I mean: Information is social relations. A social process between people. Many people behind the numbers."

Ricardo's little notebook of information expanded so much that he planned to publish a set of books, with one chapter for each tribe. He originally thought his team could do this in two years. That was many years ago, and it still has not been completed.

"We had a network of people who sent information to us, around a thousand people. And then we have a little team inside that can organize this and put this out in books, reports, or technical papers for specific cases. And we sent out information to around five thousand key people. So it's a system: A way in and a way out, and we are in the middle.

"It's a lot of work, and we are going to keep doing this to support the indigenous struggles and to monitor the activities of the Brazilian government. We are doing this for all the indigenous people in the whole of Brazil, not just Amazonia. Right now, there are one hundred fifty thousand indigenous people in Amazonia, and another one hundred thousand indigenous people in other parts of the country. The big difference is that in the Amazon, they still have a chance to keep the traditional lands in their hands. In the other parts of the country, the indigenous have just a piece of this land.

"So we were working to support indigenous rights, indigenous struggles, to put this indigenous question together with democracy and the national question, as well as with our land problem in Brazil."

"Democracy and the national question," of course, have to do with the end of the military dictatorship in 1985, which led to the overhaul of Brazil's constitution. Powerful agricultural and mining interests lobbied heavily to reduce the already-limited rights of indigenous peoples. Ricardo worked with socially concerned Brazilian geologists to prepare a report, complete with satellite map overlays, that made it clear which groups had an interest in denying land rights and opening up mining operations in the Amazon. Though the civilian government relaxed the stranglehold of terror in Brazil, extremely powerful vested interests were lobbying against Ricardo and CEDI. Newspapers front pages frequently accused CEDI of being unpatriotic and of working with foreign companies against Brazil's best interests. "Every two or three months they put this out again," says Beto. Nevertheless, in 1988, Ricardo successfully mobilized national concern to grant Brazil's indigenous tribes stronger guarantees in the new constitution. However, in a classic example of the fact that environmental battles are never really won, the constitution comes up for review in 1993. "So this year in Brazil, everything is going to happen again," Ricardo says.

The land problem he refers to is the fact that one percent of the people own fifty percent of the land, while fifty percent of the people own three percent. Very few people live in some parts of the country, and far too many live in other parts. Most Brazilians today—ninety percent of the country's population—live in cities, and most of the cities are near the beach, more than three thousand miles of palm-fringed, white sand along the Atlantic Ocean, with temperatures that rarely fall below 20°C. Many Brazilians are migrating toward the southern coast, where average incomes are three times higher than in the Northeast. In 1980, the South had a population fifty times denser than in Amazonia. Though larger than India, Amazonia is as sparsely settled as the Sahara. Looking at the numbers alone makes many people think the Amazon could siphon off the country's starving peasants and slum dwellers, who might be given a new start on little farms. And this quick fix is exactly what has been tried recently.

In the 1980s, promises of free land and prosperity in the Amazonian state of Rondonia lured more than a million immigrants, who cleared the frontier of twenty-five percent of its rain forest. Unfortunately, the Amazon subsoil is actually quite poor and unsuitable for farming. Once cleared, the land quickly loses its nutrients, which are washed away by tropical rains. Rondonia soon became dotted with barren, dusty towns of peasants scraping to keep body and soul together as they battle poor soil, malaria, and bank payments. Many of them sell or abandon the land and push on farther west or back east to the large cities. Funded by hundreds of millions of dollars from the World Bank, the resettlement project in Rondonia has resulted in chaos, misery, and the loss of an area of wilderness three-fourths the size of France. Despite growing international criticism of the project, the World Bank continues to fund it. Meanwhile, there is enough cultivable land outside Amazonia to give each Brazilian nearly two and a half acres. And, despite the money poured into the settlement of Amazonia—estimated at $12,000 per settler—the region still has only ten percent of the population and produces only two percent of the country's gross national product.

The lushness of the Amazon depends not on fertile soil, but upon the intricate interdependency of its life-forms; it is luxuriant because nothing is wasted. The highest trees get full sunlight, and their fruits and leaves are home to colonies of monkeys, snakes, and birds that rarely leave their treehouses. Lower down, a second layer of trees, shade lovers, house other animals. Tangled through and over these layers are climbing plants, ferns, orchids, algae, and mosses, feeding on each other. Only the shadowy forest floor, which receives a mere ten percent of the equatorial sun, remains uncluttered, because even falling leaves become food for someone or something before they reach the ground. The roots of the trees do not dig down any more than two feet into the ground; there are no nutrients there. What keeps the tall trees standing, mostly, are the woody vines, thin as spider webs or thick as pythons, roping trunk to trunk.

∾

A POPULAR FABLE of the Amazon was El Dorado, a legendary lake that was a source of endless gold. Thousands of Spanish conquerers sailed up the muddy river looking for it; most found only misery and death. (The name of the river comes from an account by a friar who sailed with the first party of Spaniards to navigate the length of the waterway in 1541. According to his diary, they were met by fierce women warriors. The royal court in Spain recalled the Greek myth of the Amazons and named the river for them.)

When the military dictatorship of Brazil was finally forced to turn power over to civilians in 1985, the administration left the military in charge of the occupation of the Amazon. Almost immediately, the military opened up the entire northern region to dozens of military installations and mining projects. Airstrips, roads, and some two dozen military bases were constructed; thousands of gold miners used the landing strips to penetrate the region. Most of the gold mines produced more misery than gold, which is found primarily in small, isolated deposits. In any case, the difficulties of the terrain often make large-scale mining impossible. As a result, the gold miners are an independent army of perhaps half a million people who pan the mud and sand of hundreds of hillsides and rivers. Many die from tropical diseases, in accidents, or in fights with other miners. Some die in fights with tribal peoples, who do not care about the gold. They wear feathers, leaves, or beads for decorations, not gold; what they want is only their land.

Yet, despite the gold mining and the discovery and mining of the world's largest iron mountain, Brazil's economy and debts are in terrible shape. In 1992, inflation galloped at twenty-five percent monthly, and foreign debt climbed to more than $120 billion. The debt was the highest in the Third World and was so great that if Brazil were to default, the entire Western world's economy would be threatened. With all her riches, Brazil's problems can be solved, and most of the world's most brilliant economists have suggestions how to do so. Some suggestions (and some economists) are more sensitive to the wilderness, the indigenous people, and reality than others.

Most mining projects have proved uneconomical because of the impenetrable forest, the lack of infrastructure, the expense of importing skilled manpower, and the mines' distance from the markets. Yet many other people see the Amazon as a different kind of treasure chest, one that can be exploited only by leaving it alone.

Within this three-million-square-mile greenhouse, a few acres can contain as many as three thousand species of animals, half of which may not be found in a similar area half a mile away. The awesome range of biological diversity has been explained as a result of geological periods when rainfall decreased, causing the forest to shrink into relatively small and separate pockets in which speciation could occur. With subsequent changes in climatic conditions, regrowth entwined the forest.

The result is an unrivaled diversity of life-forms; the Amazon contains about half the world's gene pool—and fifty percent of its species are still unidentified. In October 1992, a biologist reported the discovery of a completely new species of monkey: a pocket-sized, koala-faced, zebra-striped marmoset christened the Maues, after the tributary near which it lives. The Maues marmoset is the third new monkey to be discovered in Brazil since 1990. Brazil now has sixty-eight known species of primates, more than twenty-five percent of all the primate species in the world.

There is evidence that the destruction of tropical habitats is resulting in the emergence of lethal viruses, such as human immunodeficiency virus (HIV), which came out of the rain forest of Central Africa. In the natural order, viruses serve to keep populations from growing out of control. They actually benefit the host species by thinning it out. However, destruction of an ecosystem, such as the rain forest, kills off many species and causes population explosions among others. The survivor species, usually hardy creatures such as rodents, insects, and soft ticks, carry viruses capable of infecting humans, rapidly mutating and causing epidemics. As lethal viruses go, HIV is not very infectious because it is not airborne. Many people suspect that this virus is just an early warning. And it is undoubtedly just one of millions of strains of viruses that are part of the rain forest's awesome reservoir of species.

This greenhouse also grows the raw materials for about one-third of the world's medicines, such as mushrooms that cure diphtheria, earache, and diarrhea, and fifteen different plants that can be used as female oral contraceptives. Of the three thousand plants identified as having anticancer properties, seventy percent are rain forest species. For example, the drugs vincristine and vinblastine come from a tiny rosy periwinkle and are effective in causing remission of children's leukemia. Scientists need decades to evaluate the potential uses of the Amazon's eighty thousand plant species, but the native peoples who already use more than one thousand native plants for medicinal and other purposes may be the key to unlocking the forest's secrets. Indian wisdom has given us curare, a muscle relaxant for heart disease victims, and rotenone, a safe, biodegradable insecticide. Every time one of the Indian tribes dies, its knowledge dies with it.

Learning indigenous peoples' wisdom about plant properties may lead us to other wisdoms as well. The plants used by the Indians as hallucinogens, such as *daime,* the "plant of wisdom and self-revelation," may be valuable in treating psychological disorders. Another natural hallucinogen, *icacuana,* is used by shamans of the Yanomami to communicate with the spirits. One shaman reported seeing the future: "The sky can burn, it is like plastic. The factory is very strong, and there the smoke goes into the sky, the winds carry it, and it arrives in the sky and melts it, like plastic. I know this is beginning. I know it is no good. It's bad, not just for me, but for you, too. Families, sons, not just the Indians." Sounds like a pretty good description of the ozone hole.

Exploitation of the northern basin of the Amazon brought the case of the twenty thousand Yanomami to a crisis. The largest traditional indigenous group in the Americas, the Yanonami have avoided modern people and materials. They wander the forest in small groups, moving every five years or so, when the fertility of their gardens is depleted and game is getting scarce. Their life is in a flow with the river that they recognize as being so much more powerful than they. Just as riverbanks crumble and vanish under floods, and new islands emerge and old ones disappear, constant movement is expected in life. After they leave an area, the forest reclaims it.

To help them preserve their land, their identity, and their way of life, Ricardo and others formed the Committee for the Creation of the Yanomami Park (CCPY). Though the constitution of Brazil specifies that all lands used by the Indians for hunting, fishing, and agriculture are for the Indians' use alone, the government devised a plan that designated only the areas around the actual villages to be exclusively for indigenous use. The larger surrounding territory, which the Yanomami had wandered for thousands of years, was designated forest reserves, national parks, or biological reserves, any of which could be invaded by miners, loggers, or anyone else. The Yanomami's legally recognized territory shrank from twenty million acres to less than six million acres in separate parcels surrounded by areas open to development. More than seventy percent of their land was opened to invasion and theft. CCPY was expelled from the area, along with church workers and other support groups.

While that was creating an enormous issue for government procedures to address, the gold rush was ruining the purity of the rivers, as well. The gold miners use a process with mercury, one of the deadliest toxins on earth; as much as one thousand tons of mercury are dumped or burned in the Amazon each year. The miners suffer the greatest risk, but they are also polluting the entire river system that carries twenty percent of the world's fresh-water supply. If Brazil goes ahead with its plans to build seventy dams in the Amazon, the reservoirs will create giant lakes throughout the region contaminated by mercury-laden sediments.

Dams being built in the Brazilian Amazon are destroying more rain forest than anywhere else in the world. If all of the dams the government plans to build go up, we can all say good-bye to indigenous peoples, their cultures, animals, plants, medicines, and pure water. Say hello to an impoverished way of life for us all. That is what the people coming out of the Amazon are telling us.

"In the old days, my people were great warriors," says Paiakan, chief of the Kayapo. "We were afraid of nothing. We are still not afraid of anything. But now, instead of war clubs, we are using words. And I had to come out to tell you that by destroying our environment, you're destroying your own. If I didn't come out, you wouldn't know what you're doing."

In 1992, the Nobel Peace Prize was awarded to Rigoberta Menchu, an Indian of Guatemala. Her message on behalf of her hemisphere's thirty million Indians was simple: "We're not myths from the past . . . nor do we belong in zoos. We are peoples, and we want to be respected."

ॐ

THE KAYAPO TRIBE in the Amazon was first recorded in 1965. Their chief, Paiakan, was a young boy then, but the tribe had known since his birth that he had a special destiny. "I knew that one day I would go out into the world to learn what was coming to us," he said. Soon after the first contact with the modern world, the young boy was sent to missionary school. Gradually, he learned to live, dress, and act like modern men, and to speak Portuguese, the official language of Brazil. He saw the invasion of ranchers, miners, and loggers tearing down vast tracts of forest and polluting the rivers closer to his homeland.

When he learned about a government proposal for a series of dams that would inundate an important part of the Kayapo homeland, Paiakan asked Ricardo and the CEDI team to help organize a large demonstration in 1989. Hundreds of indigenous people, environmentalists, and journalists were invited from all over the world. As a result, CEDI, the largest human rights organization in Brazil, came together with the environmental community for the first time. "We didn't know too much about this environmental movement," says Ricardo. "We just supported the very big meeting of the indigenous people to protest the hydroelectric dam."

CEDI's detailed information on the impacts of the dams to the Kayapo lands was extremely useful to the Environmental Defense Fund and to others. This information helped them present the key funder, the World Bank, with incontrovertible evidence of violations of loan conditions and enabled them to provide objective information to the bank's Executive Board about the actual status of Indian and forest lands that lie within the boundaries of proposed projects. "Without that element," says Steve Schwartzman, the Environmental Defense Fund's Brazil expert, "we no doubt would have never been able to make a case in the United States that World Bank projects were flagrantly in violation." As a result, the $500 million World Bank loan was withdrawn, and the dams have been delayed.

Paiakan and indigenous leaders like him are part of the new paradigm that Ricardo sees emerging and that he believes is essential to the Indians' future. "If the Indians are to have a chance to keep their lands, they have to fight. If they don't fight, even if we do everything we can—we can spend the next fifty or one hundred years making philanthropic work—and they're going to disappear, or they're going to stay on just a small piece of land. One of the indigenous groups in Brazil now lives on a really small piece of land in the South, and they have a lot of cases of suicide—it happens every week. Indigenous peoples are going to have to keep their lands if they want to keep their identity and their way of life. We're trying to give them information, but this is not enough."

The indigenous people live in equilibrium with the land, using the rain forest as a place where they have sacred sites, where materials abound for building houses, and for making baskets, bows and arrows, and everything else they need. They respect the rain forest and live together with it. Ricardo says, "Traditionally, the indigenous groups respect the land. Not preserve—respect. Society has to preserve what is left. This kind of preservation is typical of a society that doesn't perceive an equilibrium between man and nature. So now, the indigenous groups might want to sell five hundred trees to get money—they need the money for their own reasons. And if the environmentalists want them to preserve this, then they have to pay for it. The environmentalists elected the indigenous people in Brazil as a kind of heroes of the earth. And sometimes this is true, and sometimes this is an overly generous view of the indigenous people.

"So there are many different perspectives going on. But if we can work very fast and build alternatives at the local level for them, maybe we have a chance for them to have new conditions in the future.

"And the point is, really, do we think it is important to support indigenous groups and their lands for the future? We're not doing this mainly for ecological reasons. We're doing this because we feel this is a kind of basic people's right. Even if the Indians want to sell every tree, we still are going to support their right to do that. This is peoples' rights. Not human rights—those are individual rights, rights of the person. But we're talking about the indigenous people. As the Jewish people, the Marshall Islands people—as a society." We are talking about whether or not we want to allow genocide.

Ricardo translates a quote from a popular Brazilian poet:

I'm not waiting for the day when all men agree with each other
I'm only aware of various beautiful harmonies that are possible
without a final judgment
something is out of order
out of the new world order.

∾

THE NATIVE PEOPLE of the Amazon have begun uniting on regional, national, and international levels to fight for their legal rights. In doing so, they have emerged as one of the most vital components of the international movement to save the rain forests. But the first step is for them to get title to their traditional lands. Not until then can the indigenous community itself decide what form of development—if any—it wants.

In the late 1980s, Ricardo developed a computer data base on the status of all the Indian lands in Brazil. By regularly incorporating data from scanned satellite photos, this unique data base can create a powerful tool to protect Indian lands from invasions by miners, ranchers, and peasants. (However, each satellite image costs about a thousand dollars, and CEDI has limited resources.) If an invasion is noticed, the CEDI computer can identify who owns the lands surrounding each Indian area, to help identify who is responsible for the invasion. The information is transmitted to the Nucleus for Indigenous Rights, a legal defense organization that Ricardo cofounded. The nucleus can then start legal prosecution within weeks. In the past, it might have taken years to start legal action, and by then, an invasion would have been accomplished, and it would have been too late to reverse it.

Nucleus for Indigenous Rights is located in Brasília, the country's capital. Ricardo is a director, as well as associate secretary general of CEDI. One of the first cases the nucleus brought was against the

Brazilian federal government, forcing the government to remove tens of thousands of gold miners who had illegally invaded Yanomami land. In July 1991, after more than fifteen years of struggle, Brazil's President Collor finally issued a decree creating a continuous reserve for the Yanomami people.

Meanwhile, the CEDI office in São Paulo now has an archive of fifty thousand paper documents, twelve thousand photos, four hundred hours of video, as well as computer mapping systems, and five or six full-time staff in the office—all at a cost of $150,000 per year. An ambitious institution, it supports programs for peasants, urban workers, children's and women's organizations, as well as indigenous people.

Ricardo continues to apply his creative approach to public education. "Information is social relations." When Brazilian pop singer Milton Nascimento demonstrated an interest in the Amazon and its indigenous people, Ricardo escorted him on a river trip for eighteen days in 1989. Ricardo wrote about it: "Nights spent on the beaches, in the homes of river people, learning the latest news in an everyday life marked by the abundance of the cultivated wetlands and plentiful rivers and the happiness of the Kampa families enjoying the sun in their *tapiris* along the riverbanks, drinking *caissuma*, weaving their cotton *cusmas,* and singing their songs. The pink dolphins playing in the morning mist of the tepid waters."

On the trip, Nascimento sang and played music with improvised groups of local musicians. Back in Rio, he began composing songs and working with lyricists on his impressions and the vibrations of the journey. Meanwhile, a team from CEDI recorded music in the villages. Many hours of studio time later, the album *Txai,* benefiting the Alliance of the Peoples of the Forest, was born. The word *txai* is used by indigenous peoples as a form of respect and caring for all those who are allies of the forest. It means companion, and it means "the other half of me." The album contains cuts of Kayapo, Yanomami, and other Amazon tribes singing and playing traditional instruments (their musical patterns sound so oriental, you have no doubt these people came from Asia), as well as cuts of Nascimento singing. In one haunting song, Nascimento and modern instruments are joined by tribal bamboo flutes, drums, and a children's chorus.

From the samba to the lambada, Brazil's catchy popular music is the country's best-known art form internationally. The album has sold well all over the world. Nascimento also gave two benefit concerts in São Paulo that drew one hundred thousand people each. *Txai* is available in the United States from Columbia Records.

CEDI uses other cultural events as an inroad to public consciousness. In October 1992, it mounted a two-month multimedia exhibition in São Paulo using photos, video, text, paintings, and books for children.

That little notebook Ricardo started with? It is still in progress as an eighteen-volume series of books documenting the state of Brazil's native population. Many numbers, many people behind the numbers.

∾

Beto (Carlos Alberto) Ricardo, Centro Ecumênico de Documentação y Informação, Avenida Higienopolis 983, São Paulo, SP 02138, Brazil.

About Sources

THE VAST SCOPE OF THE WORK OF THESE INDIVIDUALS and the enormous reliance I had to place on outside references created a situation where small mistakes could be made or perpetuated. When possible, I sent each chapter to the appropriate individual to check for accuracy. Some individuals were able to reply speedily, others not at all. I apologize for any errors and hope they do not cause readers or activists any inconvenience.

Bibliography

I HAVE MADE NO ATTEMPT to list all the books, articles, clippings, reports, interviews, and letters I consulted in preparing this book. But for the benefit of readers interested in learning more, I have listed books and articles I found most useful.

BOOKS

Ackerman, Diane. *A Natural History of the Senses*. Random House, New York, 1991.

———. *The Moon by Whale Light*. Random House, New York, 1991.

Barnes, James N. *Let's Save Antarctica*. Greenhouse Publications, Sydney, Australia, 1982.

Beard, Peter. *End of the Game*. Doubleday, Garden City, N.Y., 1977.

Blixen, Karen. *Out of Africa*. Harcourt, Brace, Jovanovich, New York, 1975.

Brewster, Barney. *Antarctica: Wilderness at Risk*. Friends of the Earth, San Francisco, 1982.

Campbell, Joseph, with Moyers, Bill. *The Power of Myth*. Doubleday, New York, 1988.

Caufield, Catherine. *In the Rainforest*. University of Chicago Press, Chicago, 1986.

Chatwin, Bruce. *The Songlines*. Viking, New York, 1987.

Davis, Shelton. *Victims of the Miracle*. Cambridge University Press, Cambridge, 1977.

Dibblin, Jane. *Day of Two Suns: US Nuclear Testing and the Pacific Islanders.* New Amsterdam Books, New York, 1990.

Dobson, Andrew, ed. *The Green Reader, Essays Toward a Sustainable Society.* Mercury House, San Francisco, 1991.

Dwyer, August. *Into the Amazon, The Struggle for the Rain Forest.* Sierra Club Books, San Francisco, 1990.

Fossey, Dian, *Gorillas in the Mist.* Houghton Mifflin, Boston, 1983.

Gennino, Angela, ed. *Amazonia, Voices from the Rainforest.* Rainforest Action Network, San Francisco, 1990.

Gibbs, Lois Marie as told to Murray Levine. *Love Canal: My Story,* State University of New York Press, Albany, 1982.

Goldsmith, Edward, and Hildyard, Nicholas. *The Social and Environmental Impacts of Large-Scale Hydroelectric Dams.* Sierra Club Books, San Francisco, 1984.

Hamilton, Lawrence S., and Snedaker, Samuel C., ed. *Handbook for Mangrove Area Management.* East-West Center, Honolulu, 1984.

Harrington, Richard. *Richard Harrington's Antarctic.* Northwest Publishing, Anchorage, 1976.

Leatherwood, Stephen, and Reeves, Randall R. *The Sierra Club Handbook of Whales and Dolphins.* Sierra Club Books, San Francisco, 1983.

Maathai, Wangari. *The Green Belt Movement.* Environment Liaison Center International, Nairobi, 1988.

Matthiessen, Peter. *The Tree Where Man Was Born.* Collins, London, 1972.

May, John. *The Greenpeace Book of Antarctica.* Doubleday, New York, 1988.

McPhee, John. *Encounters with the Archdruid.* Farrar, Straus and Giroux, New York, 1971.

Minasian, S., Balcomb, K. C., and Foster, L. *The World's Whales.* Smithsonian Books, Washington, D.C., 1984.

Morse, Bradford, and Berger, Thomas. *Sardar Sarovar: Report of the Independent Review.* Resources Futures International, Ottawa, 1992.

Muir, John. *The Mountains of California.* Doubleday, Garden City, N.Y., 1962.

Naipaul, V. S. *Finding the Center: two narratives*. Knopf, New York, 1984.

——. *India: A Million Mutinies Now*. Viking, New York, 1991.

Norris, Kenneth S. *Whales, Dolphins and Porpoises*. University of California Press, Berkeley, 1966.

Padoch, Christine, and Denslow, Julie Sloan, ed. *Peoples of the Tropical Rainforest*. University of California Press, Berkeley, 1988.

Palmer, Helen. *The Enneagram*. Harper & Row, San Francisco, 1988.

Penny, Malcolm. *Rhinos: Endangered Species*. Christopher Helm, London, 1988.

Quigg, Philip W. *A Pole Apart, The Emerging Issue of Antarctica*. Twentieth Century Fund Report. New Press, New York, 1983.

Robie, David, *Eyes of Fire, The Last Voyage of the Rainbow Warrior*. New Society Publishers, Philadelphia, 1987.

The Audubon Society Pocket Guides. *Familiar Marine Mammals, North America*. Alfred A. Knopf, New York, 1990.

Toyosaki, Hiromitsu. *Goodbye Rongelap*. Tsukiji Shokan, Tokyo, 1986.

Wallace, David Rains. *The Quetzal and the Macaw, The Story of Costa Rica's National Parks*. Sierra Club Books, San Francisco, 1992.

PERIODICALS

Ackerman, Diane, "Insect Love," *The New Yorker*, August 17, 1992.

Asia Watch, "Before the Deluge: Human Rights Abuses at India's Narmada Dam," June 17, 1992.

Brower, Kenneth, "The Destruction of Dolphins," *The Atlantic*, July 1989.

Caufield, Catherine, "The Ancient Forest," *The New Yorker*, May 14, 1990.

Morrow, Lance, "Africa: The Scramble for Existence," *Time*, September 7, 1992.

Norris, Kenneth S., "Dolphins in Crisis," *National Geographic*, September, 1992.

Preston, Richard, "Crisis in the Hot Zone," *The New Yorker*, October 26, 1992.

Williams, Philip. "The Debate Over Large Dams: The Case Against," *Civil Engineering,* August 1991.

World Rivers Review, Third Quarter, 1992, International Rivers Network.

STATEMENTS

Anjain, Senator Jeton, "Statement on Behalf of The Rongelap Atoll Local Government and The Rongelap People Presently Living in Exile Presented to the House Committee on Appropriations Subcommittee on Interior and Related Agencies, May 9, 1991"

Patkar, Medha, "Statement on Behalf of Narmada Bachao Andolan Concerning a Critique of the World Bank Financed Sardar Sarovar Dam with Special Reference to Environmental and Social Problems Before the Subcommittee on Natural Resources, Agricultural Research & Environment Committee on Science, Space & Technology, October 24, 1989"

PAMPHLETS

The Ecologist. *Briefing Document: The Social and Environmental Effects of Large Dams,* Camelford, Cornwall, U.K. (no date available).

Acknowledgments

I AM DEEPLY GRATEFUL to the twelve individuals profiled in this book for their willingness to share with me and with the readers their stories and some insight into the forces in their lives that keep them active and effective. Knowing them has been moving and inspiring to me, and I hope to have done some justice to their heroism in my writing.

My deep gratitude also to my editor, David Gancher, who first had the idea for this book, and who has helped shape it in large and small ways throughout the writing, editing, and publishing process. His assistance has been invaluable and unflagging.

Mercury House executive editor Tom Christensen has lent his strong support and belief in the project, even when my deadlines were slipping like lines drawn in quicksand.

Special tribute goes to Helena Brykarz and Diana Donlon at The Goldman Environmental Foundation who assisted with introductions, access to their files, suggestions, and leads as well as in many other ways.

A salute to Gail Kurtz who provided strong backup in her speedy and accurate transcriptions of interviews that were frequently recorded under nearly the worst situations: in sidewalk cafés, airplanes in flight, and lecture halls.

Special thanks to my friends, especially Daniel Carter, who encouraged me with warmth and respect.

About the Author

Aubrey Wallace has been writing about environmental issues for many years. She was literary editor of *The New Environmental Handbook*, published by Friends of the Earth, and later served as development associate for Friends of the Earth. She has published widely in magazines and newspapers. She lives in Tiburon, California, where she enjoys the blend of urban culture and country charm.

About the Editor

David Gancher served as Assistant Director of Public Affairs for the Sierra Club, as senior editor of *Sierra*, editor of *Not Man Apart*, and contributor to *Ascent*. He is the author of the foreword to the U.S. edition of *The Green Reader* by Andrew Dobson, published by Mercury House in 1991. He lives in Oakland, California, with his wife and two daughters.

About the Foreword

Oscar Arias, former president of Costa Rica and recipient of the Nobel Peace Prize, is currently president of the Arias Foundation.

❧

This book was designed by Amaryllis in San Francisco, and set in Sabon. It was edited by David Gancher, copyedited by Karen Sharpe, and proofed by David Sweet. R.R. Donnelley did the printing and the binding.